MW01114569

Using the Power of Purpose

How to Overcome Bureaucracy and
Achieve Extraordinary Business Success!

Dean E. Tucker

authorHOUSE®

AuthorHouse™
1663 Liberty Drive, Suite 200
Bloomington, IN 47403
www.authorhouse.com
Phone: 1-800-839-8640

First published by AuthorHouse 4/2/2008

ISBN: 978-1-4343-6492-0 (sc)
ISBN: 978-1-4343-6493-7 (hc)

Library of Congress Control Number: 2008901389

Printed in the United States of America
Bloomington, Indiana

This book is printed on acid-free paper.

Dedication

I dedicate this book to my wife, Karen, who has shared over three decades with me and without whom my life would not be complete, and also to my son, Michael, and my daughter, Kristen, whose successes continually amaze me. For me, children give meaning to life and a hope for the future. It is for a better future for all children that I have written this book.

This book is also dedicated in memoriam to my parents, Carl and Lula Tucker, who raised eight children of whom I was number seven. Any success that I have had in life is directly attributable to their influences on me.

Acknowledgments

First, I would like to thank all the people who, when we had the opportunity to discuss the concepts in this book, would say, "You need to write a book." Without their continual urging to do so, this book would not have been written. Also, thanks to Ginger Eddy for her untiring and patient efforts in reviewing the many drafts of this book. Thanks to Chris Sakurada for her insights and contributions, especially regarding Generations X and Y. Thanks to Dr. Pat Traynor for her guidance and feedback most specifically in the area of leadership, and finally, to Toni Portmann for her guidance regarding purpose and the individual.

Table of Contents

Preface

This book is about the three major obstacles facing every company in the 21st century and a solution for overcoming each of these obstacles. These obstacles or issues will have a dramatic impact on the success of all companies and the future economic security of every employee.

The first major issue is the massive labor shortage that will be created by the retirement of the Baby Boomer generation. The birth rate of the replacement Generations X & Y is 800,000 or 18% less than the Boomer generation. For organizational leaders, this means that for every 5 Boomers who retire, there will only be 4 Generation X or Y employees available to replace them. These compounded shortages will last for 17 years and a deficit of 3.5 million employees is expected by 2012.

The second major issue facing business is the fact that the new labor force will be sourced primarily from Generations X and Y. This will be a problem for business because Generations X and Y have the following characteristics:

1. A lack of trust in business and government.
2. Independence with a "get off my back" attitude.
3. Knowledge of how they want to be managed and what they will and won't accept.
4. No fear of quitting and finding another job.

Because of these and other characteristics, Generations X and Y will demand a balance between their work and personal life. Also, they will not tolerate the bureaucratic management-by-intimidation approach that is used in most companies today. They will simply quit and go find another job. This will create high turnover rates and increased expense levels for recruitment and employee training, resulting in low levels of productivity, customer service and sales.

For those companies that continue to utilize the old "top-down" management structure, it will be difficult if not impossible to attract and retain the Generations X and Y employees necessary to sustain success in the future. This is critically important as these two generations are approximately 140 million strong and will soon comprise the majority of the workforce.

The third issue facing companies today is the arrival of the information age and the changes that rapid technological advances have had on the business environment. When compared to the business environment of the industrial age (1850 to 1920), there has been a 180-degree shift between then and now. For example, in the industrial age, the producer held the marketplace power because the customer of that time had virtually no marketplace choice. Customers traveled by foot or horse to the nearest general store, and once there, they had to buy what the store had or do without. Today, however, the customer has numerous choices and will evaluate criteria such as quality, service, and price when making a purchase decision. Therefore, in today's business environment, the customer holds the marketplace power, not the producer. This is just one of many 180-degree shifts that have occurred since the days of the industrial age. As a result of these shifts, businesses are being managed with an obsolete, inefficient business model that was designed for the industrial age and that cannot meet the needs of companies or customers in today's radically different information-age business environment!

Further, the coming labor shortage will create tremendous pressure on business to increase productivity as a way to produce more output with fewer workers. The question is, how can a company address all of these issues? How can a company dramatically increase productivity while attracting and retaining Generations X and Y? What will it take to unleash the human potential that these generations possess and to create a work environment that empowers these generations to fully utilize all of their knowledge and creativity? Is there a solution that can address all of these issues?

The answer to these challenging questions is a resounding YES! The solution is to transition to the new information-age purpose-driven business model that is designed for the new business environment of the 21st century. The new model utilizes the power of purpose and empowers self-directed teams to do the work. It operates on the basis of trust, which has the capability of unleashing the human potential of Generations X and Y while dramatically increasing productivity. The purpose-based business model provides new methods of management and organizational structures that are designed for the new information-age business environment. It not only provides a framework for company success, but it also provides meaningful, fulfilling and financially rewarding work for the employees today and far into the future.

Highlighted in this book are 71 companies whose financial results exceed that of their peers by a factor of 6 to 1! One secret to this superior performance is how these companies utilize the power of purpose. Research shows that young employees rate finding meaning and purpose to their lives as being more important than making a lot of money by a factor of 5 to 1. Therefore, a noble and shared company purpose, not money, is the best vehicle for the creation of a strong company focus, teamwork, great financial performance, incredible productivity and superior levels of employee and customer satisfaction! Every manager and employee must understand both the impact that the information age has had on the business environment and how the power of purpose can be used to achieve extraordinary business success in the future. Only by working together in transitioning to the new business model and jointly pursuing a shared company purpose can companies be successful in addressing the three issues facing them. The company's survival, the employee's economic security and the country's economic future are at stake. The labor shortage is coming and the information age is here, so there is no time to waste!

Chapter 1
The Challenges Facing Business Today

The challenges facing companies today are greater than any challenges they have faced since the great depression of the 1930s. The source of these challenges other than the normal competition between companies fighting for the same market is the changing dynamics of the business environment brought on by three forces. Those forces are: (1) the coming labor shortage as the Baby Boomer generation retires, (2) the issues with hiring and retaining Generations X and Y to replace the Boomer generation, and (3) the arrival of the information age.

Challenge 1: The Coming Labor Shortage

The birth rate of Generations X and Y was less than the birth rate of the Baby Boomer generation by approximately 800,000 births per year, which represents a decrease in births of 18 percent. This means that for every five Baby Boomers that leave the work force, there will only be four Generation X or Y employees to replace them. This trend will go on for about seventeen years resulting in critical labor shortages during the next two decades. As the Baby Boomer generation leaves the work force at rates faster than they can be replaced by Generation X and Y, the labor force in the United States and indeed, around the world, will begin to shrink. This will be especially true in the higher skilled segments of the labor force. Shortages are already being seen in areas such as teaching, policing, nursing and information technology. These shortages will only get worse as time goes on.

As the labor shortage increases, a shift will occur. Rather than companies selecting the employees that they want to hire from a pool of applicants, it will be the applicants that will be selecting the company they want to go to work for from the list of offers that they have received. In this environment, companies will be attempting to portray themselves as the employer of choice. To be successful in attracting the needed employees without just paying an exorbitant amount in the form of salaries, companies must understand and offer the things that are important to Generation X and Y. These are such things as an attractive work environment, work life balance, involvement with the environment and so on. In addition, companies must find ways to dramatically increase productivity as a method to compensate for the declining work force. This increase in productivity will be required if companies want to maintain or grow their current level of sales as the workforce decreases.

Challenge 2: Hiring and Retaining Generations X and Y

The competition for employees will be further complicated by the unique characteristics of Generations X and Y, which are different from the prior generations in a number of important areas. For example, X and Y combined possess the following characteristics:

- They do not trust business or government.
- They do not fear losing a job.
- They know how they want to be managed and will not have it any other way.
- They rebel against rigid, bureaucratic rules, formality and micromanagement.
- They demand to be treated as equals and with respect.
- They are independent with a "get off my back" attitude.

If these generations feel that the management or workplace environment is not to their liking, they will just up and leave. On the flip side however, these generations also have the potential to be the most productive generations ever while being very innovative and creative in developing new ways to accomplish work. These two generations are the first generations to be influenced by the information age and, as a result, these generations view the world differently, think differently and have a great deal to offer. These generations:

- Can parallel process data and multitask
- Function extremely well on teams
- Are lightning quick learners
- Are open-minded and socially conscious
- Are self-confident, optimistic and goal-oriented
- Are talented and techno-savvy
- Are hard workers
- Are eager for responsibility

As the prior characteristics of Generations X and Y point out, hiring and retaining these employees will be a challenge for companies that utilize the rigid, bureaucratic command-and-control style of management. When the labor shortage intensifies and the competition for these highly sought after Generation X and Y employees becomes more competitive, companies must find a way to create management styles and work environments that are attractive to Generations X and Y, or they will find themselves in very bad situations or out of business.

Challenge 3: The Arrival of the Information Age

While there is no exact date, the information age as commonly understood began to manifest itself in the 1985-to-1990 timeframe. Some people are more precise and mark 1989 as the beginning of the information age, but picking a specific year is not important. What is important is to recognize and deal with the changes that the information age is making on the business environment.

The information age is being driven by new technologies and an explosion of information that is flooding into an ever-increasing number of new products with increasing levels of knowledge content and complexity. Every day, it seems that there is something new on the market that we know nothing about. There are new products such as Apple's iPods, iPhones, digital recorders to replace the VCR, 4G cell phones, digital cameras with software for editing pictures, cars with multiple computers and navigation devices, video games, etc, etc. All of these new and functionally rich products with imbedded computer chips and the associated software require a great deal of additional information before the purchaser of these new products can use the functions provided. While these are examples of personal-use items, the same phenomenon is also true of industrial products. Today's employees are continually faced with new computer software and devices that have much higher functionality and require much more information and education before they can be properly used.

There is so much new information required to properly utilize all the new technologies that it is almost impossible to absorb it all. To gain some understanding of the amount of information being generated today, we must have some way to put it in perspective. While different experts have different estimates, the following statement is generally accepted as being quite accurate:

"Ninety percent of all the information that we have today, in the history of mankind, has been created in the last fifteen years."

Now, just reflect on that for a minute. Ninety percent of all the information that we have today, in the recorded history of mankind, has been created in just the last fifteen years! If that were not bad enough, that information is expected to more than double again in the next five years. No wonder we feel like we are in information overload!

As this information explosion makes its way into the business environment, it dramatically increases the information content and complexity of today's jobs. To reflect this change, employees are now referred to as "knowledge workers." Because of the ever-increasing amount of information that must be absorbed by the knowledge workers to perform their jobs in the information age, it is difficult for them to keep current with all that they need to know. Not only is it difficult for the knowledge worker, but it is now impossible for a manager of ten or fifteen people to have a current understanding of how to perform the jobs of their employees. Because of this, managers are not really in a position to "manage" the employees like they once were.

In contrast, in the early part of the industrial age, from 1850 to 1900, the jobs in industry were relatively simple and, as a result, required little or no education on the part of the employees. In fact, as late as 1903, only 6 percent of the labor force could even read. In that timeframe, managers knew how to do the jobs of their employees and were therefore able to "manage" them. The situations then and now are quite different and have become much more challenging for today's managers. Today is the age of the knowledge worker. Today's employees must not only be able to read, but they must have at least a high school education, if not a college degree. To get the most out of this educated workforce, they must be treated like the responsible, educated adults that they are. That is a far cry from the day when only 6 percent of the workforce could read, and laborers were only hired for their backs and not their brains.

Another phenomenon that is occurring along with the information age is a rapid rate of change, which continues to accelerate at massive rates around the world. Unless a person stops and reflects on this phenomenon, it could go virtually unnoticed. If we compare the changes since 1900 to all the changes prior to 1900, the rate of change will begin to stand out. For example, for thousands of years prior to 1900, the primary mode of transportation was either by foot or animal. Since 1900, transportation has gone from foot and animal to the automobile to propeller-driven airplanes to jet-powered airplanes to rocket-powered spacecraft. Even more astounding is the fact that transportation advanced from the early days of the automobile in 1903 to landing a man on the moon in 1969. A span of only sixty-six years! Think about that! In the history of mankind prior to 1900, the primary mode of transportation was by foot or animal. Then, in a span of only sixty-six years, we went from the automobile to landing on the moon. This is just one example.

Similar advances have occurred in communications, medicine, education, electronics, and the list goes on and on. In the forty years from 1920 to 1960, computers, television, plastic, and vaccines were invented and the first satellite was put in space. Since 1960, advances such as the discovery of DNA, CAT scans, the Internet, personal computers, cellular phones, fiber optics, and satellite communications have brought dramatic changes.

As another example of the dramatic changes of the information age, in 1971, the Intel pc processor could execute 60,000 instructions per second. Today's Intel processors have a theoretical maximum of 10.8 billion instructions per second, an increase of 180,000 times. The Intel chip in 1971 could hold 2,300 transistors. Today's Itanium chip holds 410 million transistors for an increase of 178,260 times.[1] That is an average increase of over 11.3 million transistors per year!

Four additional technologies are bringing dramatic and fundamental changes to both the business environment and the way we do business today. Those technologies are the Internet, fiber optics, satellite, and wireless communications. In 1995, when Netscape went public and brought their Internet browser to the marketplace, web browsing and email were enabled for the masses. The creation of a fiber-optic network in the late nineties that spanned North America and many parts of the world including Europe and Asia enabled high-speed broadband communications around the world for billions of people. Communication satellites have enabled live video and teleconferencing around the world. Wireless communications have enabled people to do everything from anywhere at anytime. These technologies are bringing a profound change in the way work is accomplished, how business is conducted, and how different groups can collaborate to accomplish a task. The groups involved in accomplishing a task are no longer limited to a company or a country. These technologies have enabled companies and groups to collaborate on a worldwide basis twenty-four/seven. These technologies have also dramatically changed the speed at which things happen, and all of these elements are flattening the old industrial age business hierarchies and speeding up the rate of business.

Thomas L. Friedman, in his book *The World is Flat*, describes ten forces that have flattened the old hierarchies and leveled the business playing field for billions of people. One example of this is from the military; if there was ever a rigid hierarchy, the military has it! This example comes from a battle in Iraq.

Mr. Friedman, while traveling with General Richard Myers (Chairman of the Joint Chiefs of Staff), was in a military control center in Iraq and noticed a large display screen on the control center wall that seemed to be displaying live video of a military operations site. "What is that?" he asked. It was explained to him that the video that he was seeing was coming from a drone (a small, pilotless aircraft with high-power cameras) that was flying over the operations site. The high-resolution, live video showed our troops, some buildings, and some people behind the buildings. The drone was being controlled by an expert sitting in Nevada. The video image was being sent live via satellite communications to the United States Central Command in Tampa, CentCom headquarters in Qatar, the Pentagon, and the military headquarters in Fallujah. On the side of the screen was an active instant message chat room. All of the different centers were collaborating in real time on the events being seen on the live video feed from the operations site. Mr. Friedman says, "Before I could even express my amazement, another officer traveling with us took me aback by saying that this technology had 'flattened' the military hierarchy—by giving so much information to the low-level officer, or even enlisted man, who was operating the computer, and empowering him to make decisions about the information he was gathering." This speed of information flow is leveling the military playing field.[2]

The speed of information flow is also flattening or eliminating the hierarchy in the business environment. One example of this comes from Wal-Mart. When a customer checks out and the items' barcodes are scanned, the information goes via satellite from the Wal-Mart store to the Wal-Mart headquarters and then to the Wal-Mart supplier wherever that supplier is. The supplier could be in the United States, Mexico, China, or anywhere in the world. Within minutes of a customer purchasing an item, the supplier knows that it has been sold and can start the replenishment process. Twenty-four/seven, 365 days/year, the story plays over and over again.[3] No longer does the information pass through the hierarchy at Wal-Mart or the hierarchy of the supplier; those hierarchies have been flattened. In both prior examples, decisions that were previously made by the managers in the hierarchy must now be made by the first-line personnel who are receiving the information directly. The hierarchy has been eliminated from the information flow and therefore, from the decision-making process. To insert the hierarchy back into the information flow would introduce a time delay that would be unacceptable. To address these changes that the information age is forcing on the business environment, companies must find and implement new management methods and organizational structures that are compatible with the new information age environment.

One challenge of these new methods of management is for management to find a way to "manage" these front-line employees who must now make decisions that were only made by management in the past. The speed and volume of the information flow enabled by the new technologies of today make it impossible for the manager to absorb and process those volumes of information. Only the employees have any chance of doing that. Therefore, even if management was inserted into the line of information flow, the manager could not handle the volume of information. So, there is no choice. The first-line employees must be empowered to make many decisions that in the past were made by management alone. The Wal-Mart and military examples show clearly the impact that the information age and its new technologies have had on the business environment and they give some insight as to how employees will be managed in the future. They also highlight that the fact that the old command-and-control structure of the bureaucratic management system must be changed when attempting to deal with the requirements of the information-age business environment.

One challenge that is annually given to management and employees is to "Do more with less!" To accomplish the objective of "Doing more with less," management will try many things, but the one thing they *must* do, is to increase productivity. In their attempt to increase productivity, management will buy more productive tools, hire consultants, invest in new computers and software, raise the objectives such as sales quotas, and give strong marching orders to the employees to reach the new objectives. If the objectives are not being achieved, then management may bring in motivational speakers to help boost morale, teamwork, and output. To achieve the company's strategic goals will require management and employees to focus on the goals and to work as a team to achieve them. *However, despite management's best efforts, the employees do not seem to be focused on the company's strategic goals, and real teamwork is difficult, if not impossible, to achieve.* Throughout the organization, there appears to be a lot of departmental conflict, and within the departments, there is more competition than teamwork. While management and the employees realize that there is a disconnect between the company's goals and the employees' goals, they are not aware of the magnitude of the disconnect. They are also not aware of the magnitude of the lack of teamwork within the organization.

A recent survey by Harris Interactive of 23,000 U.S. residents employed full-time in key functional areas of their companies found the following:

1. Only 37% said they have a clear understanding of what their organization is trying to achieve and why.
2. Only one in five was enthusiastic about their team's and organization's goals.
3. Only one in five said they have a clear "line of sight" between their tasks and their team's and organization's goals.
4. Only 15% felt that their organization fully enabled them to execute key goals.
5. Only 20% fully trusted the organization they worked for.[4]

The results of the Harris Interactive survey are a little difficult to understand and to make sense of. However, if we take the Harris Interactive data and apply it to a football team, then the survey data will become much clearer and easier to understand. In this case, it shows that, out of the eleven football players on the field:

1. Only four of the eleven players would know which goal was theirs.
2. Only two of the eleven would care.

3. Only two of the eleven would know what position they play and know exactly what they are supposed to do.
4. All but two players would, in some way, be competing against their own team members rather than the opponent.[5]

The example of the football team relative to the Harris data clarifies the degree to which the employees do not understand what the strategic direction of the company is or why it is important. It also makes quite clear the lack of any meaningful teamwork in companies today. The survey data clearly shows the degree to which the current industrial-age business-management model has been rendered ineffective by the changes in the work environment since the inception of the information age. The data also points out the fact that if management could find a way to get all the employees and managers headed in the same direction and working as effective teams striving to achieve the same goals, that there is a huge potential for increased productivity and bottom-line results. Can you believe it? Only four of eleven players know which goal is theirs! If that is not bad enough, only two of the players would even care!

Another challenge facing management today is to be adaptive to the needs of their customers and responsive to their requests. In the past, the customer had little choice when it came to buying a product, and they were at the mercy of the producers. When the customer had little choice, the producers could get away with ignoring the customers' wants and needs. As Henry Ford is reported to have said, "They can have any color they want as long as it is black." That type of mentality is no longer viable in today's market. Today, the customer has a choice of whose product they purchase, and the producers must now be adaptive and responsive like never before if they want to be successful. If management cannot ensure that their organization and employees are adaptable to customers' needs and responsive to customers' requests, the company will not survive long in today's market.

The Wal-Mart example shows how one company can adapt to the customers' buying patterns in near real time. The vendor for the product knows immediately which size, color, and flavor the customers are buying. In near real time, the supplier can adapt and respond to the customers' buying preferences. However, to make a Wal-Mart-style supply system work efficiently requires several things. It requires changes in the level of trust between companies, a high degree of collaboration/partnership between companies, and empowered cross-functional teams to receive and act on the information flow without delay. This, in turn, demands a change in the structure of the management system that is used.

The prevailing methods of management in the United States and also around the world are commonly known as the Autocratic Management System and the Bureaucratic Management System. One focus of this book is on the Bureaucratic Management System and how to overcome its limitations. This system as we know it today evolved during the industrial age between the years 1850 and 1920, reaching its final form in the early 1920s. Since that time, it has changed very little, and with the arrival of the information age it has become a very inefficient method of managing a company. That is why business book after business book, magazine article after magazine article, and person after person say things like "get rid of the bureaucracy" and "flatten the hierarchy" and "empower the employees." The problem is that, up to this point, no one has offered any new management methods to replace the currently used, outdated, obsolete, and inefficient Bureaucratic Management System. That is, until now.

The first step in fixing a problem is to understand the root cause of the problem. This book will explain the source of the dissatisfaction with and inefficiencies of the Bureaucratic Management System and then it will describe the new information-age management methodologies that can be used to replace the old methodologies. These new methodologies have been used by a small number of companies who have proven beyond any question that the techniques described later in this book will allow any company to achieve the following:

1. Overcome bureaucracy

2. Attract AND retain Generations X and Y
3. Dramatically improve productivity and financial performance
4. Transition to new, highly effective, efficient and productive methods of management

By transitioning from what will be described as the Industrial-Age Profit-Driven Business Model to the new Information-Age Purpose-Driven Business Model, companies can successfully address the challenges they are facing today as well as achieve dramatic increases in productivity and financial performance. Not only can companies dramatically improve their productivity and financial performance, but they can also create a work environment that is rewarding and fulfilling for management and all of the employees. This has been proven by the seventy-one companies that are highlighted in the later chapters.

Chapter 2
The Generational Challenge

One of the three major challenges facing every business today is the coming labor shortage that will be created as the Baby Boomer generation leaves the work force in numbers greater than the following generations can supply. As the Baby Boomer generation retires, their replacements will come from the generations known as X and Y. Because Generations X and Y have some unique characteristics that are not well suited for the work environment of a bureaucratic command-and-control organization, it will be a challenge for many businesses to attract and retain these generations.

The Coming Labor Shortage

In the not-too-distant future, human capital management will be at or near the top of the list of critical items for all businesses in America. The reasons for this are due to the following projections:

- Two workers will leave the workforce for every one worker entering starting in 2008.

- The twenty-five to forty-four-year-old age group will decline by 15% during the next fifteen years.

- Soon there will be a shortage of 10 million workers as compared to the jobs available.[6]

There is much discussion today about exactly how large the labor shortage will be or if it will exist at all. However, an examination of the birth rates for each of the four generations shows the following:

Veterans   1922 – 1943   21 years   2.47 million annual average births

Boomers   1943 – 1960   17 years   4.30 million annual average births

Generation X 1960 – 1980   20 years   3.50 million annual average births

Generation Y 1980 – 2000   20 years   3.48 million annual average births[7]

This data clearly shows that the Boomer generation averaged 4.3 million births per year while the following generations X and Y averaged only 3.49 million births per year. That is a drop of 800,000 per year or 18 percent. The Bureau of Labor Statistics projects that the growth in the labor force will shrink from the 1.6% average growth between 1950 and 2000, to only 0.6% between 2000 and 2050. That is a full one-percentage-point difference. By 2012, the Bureau projects the labor force to be at 162.3 million. By applying the difference of one percent to the projected labor force, that would mean that in 2012, there would be 1.62 million fewer people entering the workforce than in the past.

The projected shortage of workers and declining pool of new workers becomes even more alarming when the projections are broken down by industry and skill level. Of particular concern is the projected shortage of highly skilled workers. As an example, the National Center for Education Statistics shows that 77,066 students earned bachelor's degrees in engineering in 1984-1985. But fifteen years later, only 63,635 students received bachelor's degrees in engineering in 2000, a drop of 18 percent. It is interesting to note that this is the same percentage difference as was shown in the birth rates of the Boomers versus the Generations X and Y. As further evidence, the average age of nurses is almost fifty, and half of all certified teachers are expected to retire in the next five years. These examples of the coming labor shortage clearly show that most companies will not be able to attract enough young skilled workers to replace the boomers who will be retiring in large numbers very soon. We are already seeing shortages in some industries such as elementary school teachers, truck drivers, registered nurses, police and accounting. Every industry will be affected by the labor shortage, with the education, transportation and health industries being projected to experience more severe difficulties than other industries. It is clear that as the labor shortage makes its way into the workforce, the only way business can maintain the same or greater level of economic output will be to dramatically increase productivity. A new business model for achieving the needed increase in productivity will be described later.

Sourcing New Employees

In the environment of a projected labor shortage, all companies will be attempting to portray themselves as "the employer of choice." That is because companies will be competing vigorously for new employees to meet their workforce needs. When the labor shortage hits the employment scene, no longer will companies be picking from a pool of qualified candidates; it will be the candidates choosing from a pool of prospective employers.

This competition by companies to fill their job vacancies will without doubt cause labor cost to go up. The challenge for industry will be to find a way to counterbalance the increased labor cost with an equal or greater amount of productivity improvement so that a higher labor cost becomes a non-issue. This is a critical point, and the issue of productivity will be discussed throughout this book, both directly and indirectly. The point is this. If labor cost increases twenty percent, and productivity increases only five percent in the same timeframe, then that will cause prices to rise to cover the increased labor cost. The price increases will then lead to inflation and a lower standard of living. If however, productivity should increase thirty percent over the same time period as the labor cost increased twenty percent, then the relative labor cost would decline by ten percent. That would then lead to lower prices, no inflation, and a higher standard of living. Therefore, the challenge for business today is to find a way to in effect absorb the labor cost increase by increasing productivity at a faster rate so that inflation does not become an economic problem.

To understand the challenges industry will face when attempting to hire new employees, it is necessary to understand the various generations in the workforce and their individual characteristics. As it turns out, each generation has its own unique view of the world and, more specifically, view of what workplace characteristics they find to be acceptable or unacceptable. An understanding of what the different generations find to be acceptable or not acceptable will be critically important to businesses as they attempt to hire and retain new employees in the future.

For purposes of discussion and analysis of these issues, the workforce is divided by year of birth as follows:

- The Veterans   — 1922–1943 (52 Million)

- The Baby Boomers — 1943–1960 (73 Million)

- Generation X — 1960–1980 (70 Million)

- Generation Y — 1980–2000 (70 Million)[8]

The years of birth for each group may be different by a few years depending on who is doing the grouping and research, but the premise of the differences for each group still holds true despite the differences of years used. Each of these groups experienced significantly different events during their formative years from five to twenty-two years old. These significant events that occurred during the formative years of each group became a "significant emotional event" for each group. It is these "significant emotional events" that have helped to form the characteristics of each group, and these characteristics will last for a lifetime.

The Veterans

The characteristics of the veterans (1922–1943) were formed primarily by the following list of significant emotional events:

- 1927 Lindbergh completes the first transatlantic flight
- 1929 Stock market crashes

- 1930 U.S. Depression deepens
- 1931 Star-Spangled Banner becomes national anthem
- 1932 FDR elected
- 1933 The Dust Bowl
- 1933 The New Deal
- 1934 Social Security system established
- 1941 Pearl Harbor
- 1944 D-Day in Normandy
- 1945 Victory in Europe and Japan
- 1950 Korean War[9]

It is the veteran generation that is responsible for the world as we know it today. They created it with their hard work, dedication, sacrifice and their vision of what the world should be. This generation defined the "great American value system" as we understand it. They gave us leaders such as Kennedy, Carter and Bush number forty-one. In the business world there are leaders such as Lee Iacocca, Jack Welch, Mary Kay Ash, Lou Gerstner and Warren Buffett that carry on the values of this generation.

These children of the 1920s and 1930s grew up in hard times.[10] "In 1929, the Stock Market crashed and the bottom fell out of the American economy. The early 1930s ushered in the Great Depression. Nine million Americans lost their life savings. Eighty-six thousand businesses closed their doors for good. More than two-thousand banks failed. Millions of workers lost their jobs, and, by 1932, about fourteen million people were unemployed—nearly one of every four workers."[11] The veterans experienced uncertainty and insecurity during the Great Depression and watched as many lost their jobs. As a result, veterans don't take a job for granted: instead, they are grateful for it. They view work as noble and ennobling.[12]

Then things got worse. The drought in the thirties created the dust bowl and then in 1941 came the most significant event in the lives of the veterans. On December 7, 1941, the Japanese attacked Pearl Harbor and World War II began. During WWII, this generation lived on rations and learned to use it up, wear it out, make do or do without.[13] This generation grew up with the value of obedience over individualism in the work environment and was taught to respect the leaders of their institutions.[14]

The combination of the Great Depression of the 1930s and World War II were unique and dominant factors in the formation of the core values of the veteran group which are as follows:

- Dedication/Sacrifice
- Hard work
- Conformity
- Law and order
- Respect for authority
- Patience
- Delayed reward
- Duty before pleasure
- Adherence to rules
- Honor[15]

The veterans' core values make perfect sense when viewed in the context of the significant events they experienced. This group experienced two wars and the Great Depression of the 1930s. Because of the values of conformity, respect for authority, and adherence to rules, this group works well within the structure of the industrial age bureaucratic management system.

The veterans grew up in a hierarchical world. The hierarchical structure worked very well for the military and business during the years of their work experience. They understand it, know how to work with it, and are comfortable with it. Veterans have no issues with top management making the decisions. For this generation, "it worked best to have the brains at the top, in the executive ranks, and the brawn at the bottom, on the front lines. Top management, the generals, made the important decisions and passed them down the chain of command, where they were carried out without comment, respectfully and thoroughly."[16]

For the bureaucratic manager, the veteran employee is a dream. This group is conformist, they believe in logic, not magic, and they are disciplined.[17] The veterans are not terribly unhappy with the bureaucratic management system as it is used today. It is all they have known for their entire working lives, and they have resolved their issues with its shortcomings.

On the job, the veterans display the following characteristics:

On the Job — Assets

- Stable
- Detail-oriented
- Thorough
- Loyal
- Hard working

On the Job — Liabilities

- Inept with ambiguity and change
- Reluctant to buck the system
- Uncomfortable with conflict
- Reticent when they disagree[18]

The veterans, because of their core values and on-the-job characteristics, are loved by their bureaucratic managers. This group toes the line and does not complain or challenge the status quo. They are everything the bureaucratic manager wants in an employee except for their age. The changes brought on by the information age, however, can be challenging for many veterans. While they have access to personal computers and the Internet, their usage of the new Internet-based capabilities is usually limited.

Summary

The Veteran generation is very comfortable with the command-and-control structure of the Bureaucratic management system.

They expect decisions to be made at the top and passed down to be executed. It was this command-and-control structure that served them so well during WWII. That is exactly the way they would have designed the management system if they had done it themselves.

The Baby Boomers

The personality and characteristics of this generation, like every other generation, would be influenced by their own set of "significant emotional events" which were as follows:

- 1954 McCarthy HCUAA hearings begin
- 1955 Rosa Parks refuses to move to the back of the bus in Alabama
- 1957 First nuclear power plant
- 1957 Congress passes the Civil Rights Act
- 1960 Birth control pills introduced
- 1962 Cuban Missile Crisis
- 1962 John Glenn circles the earth (in space)
- 1963 Martin Luther King Jr. leads march on Washington D.C.
- 1963 President John Kennedy assassinated
- 1965 United States sends ground combat troops to Vietnam
- 1966 Cultural revolution in China
- 1968 Martin Luther King Jr. and Robert F. Kennedy assassinated
- 1969 First lunar landing
- 1970 Kent State University shootings[19]

The single biggest "significant emotion event" for the Boomers however, was the Vietnam war. The effect on the Boomers was profound and divisive.[20] "The U.S. intervention in Southeast Asia caused many young Americans to question the integrity of our leaders as never before. Feelings about the war divided many a family, even close siblings." The Boomers "fought, died, were wounded, and returned home without ever understanding how their actions contributed to the long-term goal or even what the goal was. Many returned and turned bitter and skeptical of authority, particularly governmental authority."[21] The distrust of the country's leadership that began with the Vietnam war not only affected the Boomers, but it has also carried through to the following generations.

The Boomers were the generation that reversed the population trend in the U.S. "For nearly two hundred years the American population had been declining in size. The rigors of settling a raw wilderness, a tumultuous civil war, and a decade of economic depression had eroded the population of America faster than immigration and birth rate combined could replace the fallen. Then, in 1946, almost precisely nine months after VJ day [victory in World War II], a tsunami of babies broke across the fruited plain and changed its physical and psychological geography forever."[22] The data shows that the birth rate of the Boomer generation averaged 74% more than the prior Veteran generation.

The baby boomers of the late forties and fifties also grew up in the greatest economic expansion this country has ever known, and for the most part are an optimistic group.[23] Their group personality and core values were heavily influenced by the good economic times, the civil rights movement, the Vietnam war and their large numbers. "In school and at home, the Boomers learned about teamwork. There were so many of them, like puppies in a pile, that they had to collaborate and cooperate, sharing texts and sometime desks. They were the first generation to be graded on 'shares materials with classmates' and 'works with others.'"[24] The Boomers believe in growth and expansion, think of themselves as stars, and "have pursued their own personal gratification, uncompromisingly, and often at a high price to themselves and others. If the marriage wasn't working out, they dumped it and looked for another. If they didn't like the job, they moved on. Caught in a shady deal? Apologize, shed a few tears, blame some circumstance and move on. They turned resurrection – and self-forgiveness – into a high public art. William Jefferson Clinton, the first Boomer President of the United States, has turned public apology and the expectation of instant, soap-opera-like forgiveness into a political norm."[25]

With this as their background, the Boomers developed the following core values:

- Optimism
- Team-orientation
- Personal gratification
- Health and wellness
- Personal growth
- Youth
- Work
- Involvement[26]

The Baby Boomers, while they did not rebel against the bureaucratic management system, were not as well suited to it as the veterans were. The boomers' core value of team-orientation could not be easily satisfied within the bureaucratic management system. Their value of involvement led them to advocate teams, team-building, consensus, quality circles, and participative management (The boomers think they invented participative management.) in the workplace.[27] While the boomers adapted relatively well to the bureaucratic management system work environment, their desires for teams, personal gratification, growth, and involvement began to put them in conflict with the rigid structure and top-down authority of the bureaucratic system. The boomers are desired employees, but they are not coveted employees by the command-and-control manager like the veterans are.

On the job, the Boomers display the following characteristics:

On the job – Assets

- Service-oriented
- Driven
- Willing to "go the extra mile"
- Want to please
- Good team players

On the job – Liabilities

- Not naturally "budget minded"
- Uncomfortable with conflict
- Reluctant to go against peers
- Overly sensitive to feedback
- Judgmental of those who see things differently
- Self-centered[28]

On the job, Boomers are usually good team members, but not always. "Boomers can be very political animals, especially when their turf is threatened. At times like these, those well-honed rapport skills are used to sell a plan for self-protection, territorial improvement, or self-betterment masked as concern, the best interest of the common good, or helping someone overburdened or with too much to do already. The net result is frequently confusion, frustration, and misunderstanding on the team."[29] When it comes to leadership, the Boomers "are the ones who advocated turning the traditional corporate hierarchy upside-down. They are genuinely passionate and concerned about participation and spirit in the workplace, about bringing heart and humanity to the office, and about creating a fair and level playing field for all. The Civil Rights movement of the 1960s had a profound impact on their generational personality."[30]

It is in the execution of their beliefs where the Boomers have some difficulty. "Boomers grew up, for the most part, with conservative parents and worked in their early careers for command-and-control-style supervisors. Boomer managers sometimes have a hard time actually practicing, day in and day out, the management style they profess. Many, for instance, truly believe they are managing participatively, when, in fact, they're just giving it lip service. Participative management requires great skill in understanding, communicating, motivating, and delegating."[31]

Summary

The Boomers learned to work together as youngsters and then were moved by the Civil Rights movement of the 1960s. The Boomers learned to work in groups and teams at a very early age because there were so many of them. As a result, they challenged the command-and-control Bureaucratic management-style system and attempted to implement participative management, teams and a more level playing field for everyone. Even though they many times fell short of their goals in these areas, they were trying their best to make significant changes to the way companies were managed.

Generation X — 1960–1980

Generation X had the misfortune to come behind the Boomer generation. That in and of itself would be a lot to live up to, but this generation also got off to a poor start. Many of the significant emotional events that occurred during their formative years were not positive. Those events were as follows:

1970   Women's Liberation protests and demonstrations
1972   Arab terrorists at Munich Olympics
1973   Watergate scandal
1973   Energy crisis begins
1976   Tandy and Apple market PCs
1979   Iran holds sixty-six Americans hostage
1979   U.S. corporations begin massive layoffs
1980   John Lennon shot and killed
1980   Ronald Reagan inaugurated
1986   Challenger disaster
1987   Stock market plummets
1988   Terrorist bomb blows up Flight 103 over Lockerbie
1989   Exxon Valdez oil tanker spill
1989   Fall of Berlin Wall
1991   Operation Desert Storm[32]

Because of the many negative events that occurred during the impressionable years of Generation X, they became preoccupied with their own survival on two levels; the economic and psychological levels. Their view of the future is that things are *not* going to be okay. A quick review of these negative events of their time will make this easy to understand. The young Generation Xers watched as:

1. The United States lost its first war in Vietnam.
2. The vice president of the United States, Spiro Agnew, resigns because of alleged tax evasion charges, and then Richard M. Nixon becomes the first president to resign, because of the Watergate scandal.
3. The 1973 oil embargo caused surging gas prices and gas shortages with long lines at the gas pump, if there was any gas to be bought.
4. In the 1970's and 1980's, the Japanese attack the US economy with cheap cars and steel creating the term "rustbelt".
5. The 1980's bring massive layoffs called "down sizing" or "right sizing"and their parents are laid off.[33]

When the Generation Xers finished college and went looking for a professional job, there were not enough jobs to go around. The U.S. economy was in a mess and interest rates were sky high. With the scarcity of jobs, many ended up with either one or two low-paying jobs. Soon, they came to the realization that they could not afford their own place to live and had to move back in with their parent(s). Then, to make things worse, there is the Social Security issue. The media had blasted the Generation Xers with dire predictions of Social Security going bankrupt and Medicare expenses going through the roof as the Boomers retire in record numbers. As a result, the Xers anticipate inheriting a country that is flat broke and ecologically bankrupt, with millions of old people to take care of.[34] Things were not getting off to a good start. This bad start was then compounded by the conditions under which many of the Generation Xers were raised.

First, almost half of their parents' marriages ended in divorce. Generation Xers were the first generation to be exposed to joint custody, visitation rights and weekend fathers in large numbers. Second, for those whose parents did not divorce, there was the two-income family. Even though their parents were married, they were still not around; they were at work. These changes in society meant that the Generation Xers came home to an empty house. These were the "latchkey" kids. For several hours a day, they were on their own. They had to learn by themselves, solve problems by themselves, be independent and grow up fast.[35]   From the viewpoint of the young Generation Xers, the future did not look bright. This generation learned at an early age that they could not rely on the government, business or even their own parents to look out for them. They must learn to rely on only themselves and their friends. Everyone else had deserted them. The government was corrupt, business had no good-paying jobs, and their parents were nowhere to be seen.

It was against this background that the Generation Xers formed the following core values and characteristics:

Generation X Core Values

- Diversity
- Thinking globally
- Balance
- Technoliteracy
- Fun
- Informality
- Self-reliance
- Pragmatism[36]

Generation X Characteristics

- Lack trust in business and government
- Judge on merit rather than on status
- Independent

- Function extremely well on teams
- Transient
- Lightning-quick learners
- Receptive to women in management
- Multi-task oriented
- Computer literate
- Involved in the community[37]

The above list of characteristics provides some insights into the type of employees that Gen Xers will be, but there are eight characteristics that deserve special inspection and understanding because each one will have a large influence on Generation Xers in the workplace.

1. Generation Xers are seeking a sense of family.

The Veteran and Boomer generations came home to a doting mother every day after school. When dad got home from work, the family would sit down at the dinner table together and eat the meal that mom had prepared. The family was together. For the Generation Xers, the latchkey kids, a "family life" was something they only read about or heard about and they are still looking for it. To compensate for the family life they did not have because of the absentee parents, they will create a surrogate family by assembling a close circle of friends or, if they haven't found it elsewhere, they will look for it on the job.[38]

2. Generation Xers demand balance in their lives.

Generation Xers watched as their parents devoted their lives to the companies they worked for, spending evenings and weekends at the office. They also observed that their parents and most adults seemed to decide their self-worth based on their success on the job. It was also very obvious to the Generation Xers that the companies did not appreciate the time, energy and loyalty that their parents had given to the company. Their reward for all this dedication and loyalty was to be laid off in the down-sizing of the 1980s. As a result, Generation Xers are committed to, and will demand a balance between, their personal and professional lives. As they see it, their parents lived to work, but their plan is to work so they can live.[39]

3. Generation X has a nontraditional orientation about time and space.

The formative years of Generation Xers were greatly impacted by divorced parents, working parents, day care, and coming home to empty houses. Because of these elements, Generation Xers learned early in life that they must be independent and rely on themselves and their friends to get things done. It was left up to them to get their homework done and they could do it more or less on their own schedule. If they ran into problems, it was up to them to find a solution. As a result of these early learning experiences, Generation Xers see and do work differently than the prior generations. "'As long as I get my work done, what does it matter how and when I get it done?' They show up late, leave early, and appear to be 'slackers' because they are keeping their eye on what they think is the ball – getting the work done. If they do it at home, at odd hours, in the car, on the cell phone, or while telecommuting, they think that's their business, not their supervisor's. They don't come close to understanding 'line of sight' managing. Nor do they understand the idea of being carefully hired and matched to a job, then being policed like a jailed felon."[40] Generation Xers will rebel when they feel they are being micromanaged. That is in direct conflict with their independence and self-reliance. What the Generation Xers need, is to be given the objective and then left alone to figure out how to achieve the objective by themselves or with the help other employees. The following analogy will make the point.

"There is the old saying, 'You can lead a horse to water, but you can't make him drink.' In this case, you do not have to lead the employees to water. Just explain why the water is important, and they will find it, drink it, figure out a way to make it easier so that you do not have to bend over to drink, and take care of the rest."[41]

As the prior analogy shows, Generation Xers require far less direction and "supervision" than prior generations. In fact, what many managers consider just normal supervisory oversight, Generation Xers consider to be micromanagement. These characteristics often leave their Veteran and Boomer generation managers very frustrated with Generation Xers simply because they do not understand them. Many times the prior generation managers misinterpret Generation Xers as being lazy and not caring about their jobs. The reality is that Generation Xers are just different from the prior generations. They view authority differently, they work differently, they think differently, but they do have their eyes on the ball and they do get things done. An example of these differences is in schedules and working hours.

"Most of us don't have any particular problem with staying late; we just have a life outside of work. I've come in on weekends, stayed late, to get a project done. But I don't like to do it. Life wasn't meant to be spent at work; it was meant to be enjoyed with people you value. If we estimated the job correctly in the first place, there'd be no need to stay. Personally, I married my wife so that I could be with her; I'm not convinced that staying at work will bring me marital satisfaction."[42] So there you have it, from the perspective of Generation Xers, their parents lived to work but they expect to work to live. Therefore, Generation Xers demand balance in their lives, and if you are a manager of Generation Xers, expect them to leave no later than 5:00 PM, almost every day. Welcome to the world of the Generation Xers.

4. Their approach to authority is casual.

When the Generation Xers were growing up, "they had an egalitarian rather than a hierarchical relationship with their parents."[43] Their relationship with their parents (the ultimate authority) was one of equality. This generation being parentless most of the time, by necessity became very independent and self-reliant. Therefore, they were not dependent upon their parents like the prior generations were. They also witnessed authority figures (their parents, the president, televangelist, etc.) fall from grace and sometimes go into the gutter. The result of these influences on Generation Xers is that they are not so much against authority as they are simply not impressed by it.[44]

The following example will make the point. "A Boston company recently hired a new company president. He was making his way around the building, meeting with each department. In one such meeting, a Gen X employee asked the new president where he lived. After the president responded, the young guy said, 'Alright! I can get a ride to work with you.' And that's what happened! Boomers and Veterans would not have asked the question; for them, there's a certain aura around leadership that dictates what is appropriate and inappropriate to say and ask. Not so for this younger cohort, who would tell us we all put our Dockers on one leg at a time."[45] When the Generation Xers were growing up, on a daily basis they saw aggressive, hard-nosed reporters asking people in authority the tough questions. These visual experiences only confirmed to them that people in positions could and should be treated more or less as equals. So, the concept of formal hierarchical relationships is a difficult if not impossible concept for Generation Xers to understand. They just don't get it.

5. They like informality.

Generation Xers' casual approach to authority and their inability to grasp the concept of formal hierarchical relationships, cause them to expect informality in the workplace. They fail to understand any relationship between formality and getting the job done. Their focus is on the objective (getting the job done), not what hours they work or how they dress and so on. Anything that makes the work environment less "corporate" is a good thing from their perspective. They want to see the corporate world loosen up. Casual days are a big thing to Generation Xers. Generation Xers "just want to be comfortable at work, be able to avoid some of the politics, and just act like themselves."[46]

They see no relationship between all the formalities and the important things in their life.

6. They are skeptical and distrust both business and government.

In the 1980s when the young Generation Xers were entering the workforce, "the traditional 'understood' job contract was being torn up and redrafted to fit the new 'downsized,' no-stability employment model."[47] They watched as their parents were laid off in the downsizing of the 1980s, and the concept of retiring with a company pension went out the window. "Generation X learned that work is no guarantee of survival, that corporations can throw you out of your job without warning, logic, or even an apology."[48]

> "Loyalty is dead. Corporations killed it. In the 1980s, GM, IBM, AT&T, US West, and others cut 3.4 million jobs in the United States. Call it 'downsizing, right-sizing, or reengineering;' whatever you call it, the massive layoffs of the 1980s and subsequent recession cut a deep gash in America's security blanket. The millions who lost their jobs weren't just 'unnecessary overhead;' they were Gen Xers' parents."[49]

With the combination of the downsizing of the 1980s, a failing Social Security system, the Vietnam War, the Watergate scandal, and Richard Nixon's resignation, it becomes easy to understand why this generation is skeptical and does not have trust in corporations or the government of America. The result is that this generation "learned not to place faith in others, to be very careful with their loyalty and commitments for fear of getting burned."[50] Generation Xers "are careful and guarded in their personal and professional relationships, withholding their optimism and excitement for fear that things won't work out quite as planned."[51] It is not surprising that this generation does not trust anyone in a large corporation, especially the Fortune 500. "You will never hear them gripe about company loyalty: it's as foreign to them as buggy whips are to Boomers."[52] They do not expect loyalty from corporations and they do not expect to give it. In the current corporate work environment, for Generation Xers, work is just a "McJob" with no loyalty expected or given.

7. Generation Xers Can Parallel Process

"Generation Xers have been accused of having little to no attention span. However, some researchers believe that Generation X is the first parallel-processing generation. The theory is that while this generation was growing up, they were exposed to various types of media such as photography, television, movies, computers and video games. Because of this, the researchers 'claim that the different media a child is exposed to actually physically change the brain's neural networks.' The result is that this generation can parallel-process, they can do two things at the same time, and they do work in ways that are totally foreign to the prior Boomer and Veteran generations. **'This under-30 generation thinks and sees the world in ways entirely different from their parents.'"**

> Here's a scenario that illustrates the point. Bob sits at his desk while Ann, a Veteran coworker, explains the details of a very important project. Bob turns away to type some e-mail, glancing up from the screen occasionally to make eye contact with Ann. Soon, though, Ann stalks off in anger, saying, "I'll tell you about this later. It's clear this isn't important to you." Ann's interpretation of his behavior was that he didn't care about her or what she was saying because he wasn't looking at her, facing her directly, nodding his understanding. And who can blame her? But to him, listening intently to Ann could be done easily while typing some unimportant e-mail. He was "parallel processing," which he says is the best way for him to concentrate. As he sees it, he is occupying his surface consciousness with trivial information so he can focus his deeper consciousness on more complex tasks.[53]

Because of the Generation Xers' ability to parallel-process and their nontraditional orientation about time and space, most Generation Xers are misunderstood by their Veteran and Boomer generation managers. These managers think that the Generation Xers are goofing off, have a short attention span, are not focused on their jobs, etc., when in reality, the Generation Xers are not slacking off, they are just doing work differently. They think differently, they work differently, they have different expectations and, as a result, their perceived "work ethic" is different.

"If you're searching for the Generation X work ethic, don't look through the traditional lens. You won't find it. If you want to tap into it, give them a lot to do and some freedom regarding how the work gets done. You'll probably be surprised how much these 'slackers' can accomplish and still walk out the door at 5:00 P.M."[54]

8. They are independent and will not hesitate to find another job.

As we have seen in the seven earlier characteristics, Generation Xers have a casual attitude toward authority, are self-reliant and independent. Because of these characteristics, Generation Xers are not intimidated by the old approaches utilized by many of the managers who were trained to manage in the bureaucratic management system and its reliance upon fear to keep employees in line. **"After reading about the characteristics of Gen X employees, can we agree that 'fear' as a motivational technique will no longer be as effective as it was on the past generation? After all, what do the Gen Xers have to be afraid of? Losing their jobs? The facts clearly demonstrate that finding a new job, or losing a job, is not intimidating to members of Generation X. Some do not even respect having a job."[55]**

Generation Xers are far more independent than most managers think. "They are independent, and if that means going out and getting a new job every time they do not feel comfortable with you, well then, so be it, from their perspective."[56]

Summary

The Generation Xers got off to a rocky start when compared to the prior generations. They had to deal with divorced parents or two working parents, which meant that they become very independent and self-reliant at an early age. They had to fend for themselves and grow up much more rapidly than their parents. These absentee parents left them looking for a surrogate family either with their friends, or on the job. They developed an egalitarian relationship with their parents and that caused them to have a casual approach to people in positions of authority, to be informal, to rebel against micromanagement and to mostly ignore the hierarchical authoritative structure in business today. Events such as Watergate, the Vietnam War and the massive layoffs of the 1980s caused them to have little or no loyalty to the companies they work for, to demand balance in their lives, and to simply quit if they were not satisfied with the job or the way they were being managed.

Generation Y — 1980–2000

Generation Y, also known by other names such as Millennials, Nexters, Internet Generation, or Echo Boomers, are the first generation to grow up in the digital world. As a group, they have not known a home without a PC in it nor without access to the Internet. They are the first generation of the digital, networked, 24/7 information age environment. The norm for them is instant information via Google, instant messaging, instant music of their preference via iPods, and all of this on a 24x7 basis. They make Generation X look like technology has-beens. As just one example, they believe that a library is a museum for information. In fact, almost any librarian will tell you that the books on the shelves are starting to collect dust. If a Gen Yer does check out a book, it is only for a day or two so they can get the required excerpt or two to satisfy the requirement that some number of works be listed in their papers for school. They rarely read the book. As a result, many librarians today no longer carry the title of "librarian." They are called librarian technologist, or even better, media and information specialist. Today, they spend much of their time teaching Gen Yers how to maximize database searches rather than where to find a book. There is another characteristic of this generation that bears special attention. That is the fact that Generation Yers can process huge volumes of information in parallel. The combination of their digital, information-age skills and the ability to parallel-process large volumes of information puts this generation in a position to accomplish work in ways that cannot be conceived of by the prior generations. Because of this, they have huge potential to be extremely productive employees in the future.

So what is Generation Y like? Well, they can be described as a generation that:

- Has a new confidence, is upbeat and full of self-esteem.
- Is the most educated-minded generation in history.
- Is paving the way to a more open, tolerant society.
- Is leading a new wave of volunteerism.[57]

Also, Generation Yers are:

1. Talented
2. Think education is cool
3. Techno-savvy
4. Open-minded and socially conscious
5. Service-oriented
6. Independent with a "get off my back" attitude
7. Natural entrepreneurs
8. Hard workers
9. Eager for responsibility
10. Attuned to innovation
11. Self-confident
12. Optimistic
13. Goal-oriented
14. Not loyal to organizations
15. Loyal to people[58]

Generation Y, just like all the prior generations, have had their characteristics and values impacted by the significant events that occurred during their young, impressionable years. Their significant events are listed below:

1. Child focus
2. Violence: Oklahoma City bombing
3. Technology

4. Busy, over-planned lives
5. Stress
6. Clinton/Lewinsky
7. Columbine High School massacre
8. 9-11-2001 Twin Towers destroyed
9. Enron[59]

The parents of Generation Y consist of about one-third unwed mothers and many others who postponed having children until their late thirties or early forties. This latter group, now that they have children, is determined to do everything possible to provide the best opportunities for their children. These parents want well-educated and well-rounded children, and they are applying all their efforts and resources to make that happen. Because of this child focus by most of the parents (two-thirds of them), Generation Y will probably be as influential in the twenty-first century as the Boomers were in the twentieth century. At approximately 70 million strong, there are as many Gen Yers as there were Boomers. In addition to their numbers, the core values of Generation Y give some clues as to how influential they will be.

Generation Y Current Core Values

1. Optimism
2. Civic Duty
3. Confidence
4. Achievement
5. Sociability
6. Morality
7. Street Smarts
8. Diversity[60]

Generation Y, with these core values and their expertise in the digital age, are positioned to make a huge impact on society. "Economists are predicting a dramatic increase in productivity with the arrival of the Nexters. It looks like they'll be hard working, dedicated, and **ready to sacrifice personal pleasure for the collective good**."[61] Business must pay attention to the core values of Generation

Yers as they will carry these values into the workplace. Three of these values are of special importance; civic duty, morality and diversity. Gen Yers will use these values to evaluate prospective employers. If they are not satisfied with the company's reputation and past performance in these areas, they will look for employment elsewhere. In all probability, employers will not even get a chance to talk to Gen Yers if they have a poor reputation in these areas. That is because the Gen Yers, with just a click of a button, can poll all their friends for information and recommendations regarding a company and their reputation prior to applying for a job. If the Gen Yers don't like what they hear from their friends, or their friends' friends, they won't even apply. They will just cross that company off their list. That is the reality of today's connected generation. This generation is in high demand by corporate America. While the labor shortage is just beginning to make its presence known, corporations are already aggressively competing for the services of Generation Y. "College students are recruited to attend evening open houses, where big corporations ply them with Corona and chips, hoping to entice them into the workplace with signing bonuses and attractive benefits packages."[62]

In their book, *Managing Generation Y*, Carolyn A. Martin, Ph.D. and Bruce Tulgan provide a list of the fourteen expectations that Generation Y has of management and the work environment. These fourteen items provide an excellent foundation for companies that are trying to understand what it will take to attract and retain this generation:

1. Provide challenging work that really matters.
2. Balance clearly delegated assignments with freedom and flexibility
3. Offer increasing responsibility as a reward for accomplishments
4. Spend time getting to know staff members and their capabilities
5. Provide ongoing training and learning opportunities
6. Establish mentoring relationships
7. Create a comfortable, low-stress environment

8. Allow some flexibility in scheduling
9. Focus on work, but be personable and have a sense of humor
10. Balance the roles of "boss" and "team player"
11. Treat Yers as colleagues, not as interns or "teenagers"
12. Be respectful, and call forth respect in return
13. Consistently provide constructive feedback
14. Reward Yers when they've done a good job[63]

For Generation Y, the Internet and the digital age is normal. They take to it like ducks to water, and they are far ahead of their elders in this area. "My current boss usually manages my work in whatever way I suggest, because she recognizes that she does not have the expertise to contradict me. Her expertise is in public policy, not IT. She describes the ends that she wants the technology in the office to create; then she leaves me relatively free to implement her vision."[64] The digital gap between Generation Y and the prior generations is one of many major strengths that Generation Y has to offer. Generation Y will find new digitally based methods to increase productivity in the workplace. "I did this myself" and "I am pushing the envelope."[65] Generation Yers are focused in on the future. For them, "Slow, unwieldy processes are out; streamlining is in. 'One size fits all' is out; customization of anything is in. Passive learning is out; interactivity is in."[66] **This group is ready and capable of changing the world as we know it, if they are just given the opportunity**.

Managing Gen Yers will be a big challenge for supervisors who are steeped in the bureaucratic management mentality. Gen Yers **"…know how they want to be managed, and they won't accept it any other way."**[67] Remember, Gen Yers are an independent lot and have a "get off my back" attitude. These "…younger adults will leave rather than put up with being treated poorly."[68] "Like anyone with an ounce of self-respect, the typical Gen Yer doesn't respond well to management by intimidation. Domineering people with short, hot tempers leave this generation cold. Condescending people who yell and scream lose their loyalty instantly."[69] In the minds of Gen Yers, the seven worst traits of managers are:

1. Close-mindedness
2. Ineffective delegation
3. Lack of knowledge and organizational skills
4. Inability to train or to facilitate training
5. Disrespect of young people
6. Intimidating attitude
7. Overemphasis on outward appearance[70]

During the industrial age, companies could overlook the domineering, short-tempered managers, because the employees (Veterans and Boomers) would put up with them. Gen Xers and Gen Yers will not put up with them; they will just leave and find another job. Then management will be left wondering why their turnover rate is so high and be no doubt complaining about all those "young whippersnappers." It is important to remember that for Gen Yers, *"Positions and titles mean little to this generation. Rather the person who has hands-on knowledge and who can help them get the job done and accomplish their goals wins their loyalty and admiration."*[71] The managers who are looking for respect based solely on their position in the hierarchy will find managing Gen Yers difficult, if not impossible. "Gen Yers don't base their respect for authority figures on mere titles. They respect those who are confident and knowledgeable, who care about them, and who understand the importance of mutual respect."[72] Gen Yers are looking for bosses who are "'nice,' 'laid-back,' 'easygoing,' and 'not condescending'; in short, managers who make them feel 'comfortable.'"[73] Gen Yers are "out with the terms 'manager,' 'superior,' 'supervisor,' (and) in with 'coach,' 'team leader,' 'colleague,' (and) 'associate.'"[74]

The Gen Yers are eager to change the world and make it better. The question is whether or not the management of American business will be able to respond to the Gen Yers with a work environment that will capitalize on the potential they present. It is clear, however, that those companies who plan to hire and retain Gen Yers must make changes in the way they manage their employees. The old ways of managing will leave the Gen Xers and Gen Yers cold. If you want Gen Yers to work professionally, then you must address them professionally. If you want the best out of Gen Yers, then you must expect the best, and that is what you will get.[75]

"Together, these two generations are now redefining how organizations can get the best work done by the best talent. Gen X and Gen Y already make up nearly half of the American workforce, 55 million strong."[76] These two generations cannot be ignored. **Gen Yers "join an organization not because they have to, but because they really want to, because there's something significant happening there."**[77]

Summary

Generation Y has grown up in the information age and is connected to their friends and the virtual world 24/7. They have had the latest technology and they will expect any company who hires them to provide the same. They are more diverse then all prior generations. Approximately one third will be either biracial or from a non-white minority. The majority will be well-rounded, well-educated young adults. Having grown up when the economy was good and jobs were plentiful, they have high expectations for their careers and potential earning power. They expect to be better off financially than their parents. They are concerned about the environment and volunteer in the communities in which they live. They are more like the Veterans than any other generation, and **the values of honesty and integrity are important to them.** More than anything else, they want to make a difference in the world. They are looking for jobs that provide them more than just a paycheck. They want a job that has meaning and a purpose to it. They want to be part of a committed team of high-quality people working together to improve the world.

Hiring and Retaining Generations X & Y

Companies that want to hire and retain Generations X & Y must, at a minimum, address six specific items in the work environment if they hope to be successful.

1. Transparency and Trust

Management must establish a relationship between themselves and these generations based on trust. Generation X does not trust business or management, and therefore management must take the initiative to overcome this issue. When information is not readily available from management, Gen Xers feel like management has something to hide. Honesty and integrity are important to both generations, but especially to Generation Y. Both generations expect to deal with management on more of an egalitarian or equal relationship. Further, if they do not feel like they can trust the management, they will simply leave.

2. Work that has Purpose

These generations are looking for companies whose values are in alignment with their values. These generations value the community, the environment and diversity. Companies must ensure that these generations have opportunities to volunteer in their communities, and participate in activities that improve the environment either on the job or off. Companies must also show by their actions that they support diversity in the work place and take all reasonable measures to ensure that discrimination does not occur. Finally, companies must communicate to these generations what they stand for and what they are in business to do. They must communicate to these generations what their purpose is. By doing this, they can give meaning and purpose to the work so that Generations X & Y don't feel like they are stuck in a "McJob."

3. Clear Objectives and Freedom

Generations X & Y both are looking for managers that will give them clear objectives, but then give them the freedom to do the work their way and on their schedule. Both generations are independent and have specific ideas as to how they want to be managed. Neither generation wants to be micromanaged or bogged down with a lot of rules and formalities. This is a very critical point because these generations do work differently than the prior generations. They can multi-task, parallel-process and utilize those skills to create new and different ways to improve productivity if they are only given the freedom to do so. Remember, just tell them "why the water is important," and they will take care of the rest.

4. Low-stress Work Environment

Casual Friday will not cut it for these generations. Every day is casual day for them. Companies must create work environments that are informal, comfortable and without a lot of stress. This means a much less restrictive dress code, workplace amenities such as an exercise room, child care or possibly on-site health care. It also means that the management team cannot be the type that instills fear. Generation Yers are looking for managers that they can trust, that show them respect and that can be both a manager and a trusted team member.

5. Balance

Both Generations, but especially Generation X, will demand balance between their work life and private life. This means flexibility in schedules and not a lot of evening or weekend duty. Some is acceptable, but to expect it on a regular basis will not work. Success in achieving a low-stress work environment will go a long way in addressing the issue of balance.

6. Management

Companies must ensure that their managers are not threatening, intimidating, disrespectful, manipulative or coercive with these generations. Generations X & Y simply will not put up with managers who have these kinds of characteristics. They are independent, they know how they want to be managed, and Generation X in particular does not fear losing a job. Therefore, when these generations become dissatisfied with the way in which they are being managed, they will simply quit.

At first glance, the above six items may appear quite difficult for today's management to address. However, as we will see later, there are solutions for these issues that have been demonstrated by such leaders as Jack Strack of SRC Holdings. Jack has the following to say on this area of concern, "The population will keep on aging, the employee pool will keep on shrinking, and the competition for talent will intensify. If companies want to maximize shareholder value over the long term, they have to focus on the growth and retention of their people."[78]

Chapter 3
The Information Age Challenge

To fully understand the challenge that the arrival of the Information Age is presenting to businesses today, it will be helpful to gain some perspective and insight into the history of management systems. One key element of this insight is the relationship between new technologies and management systems. To gain this understanding, we will examine three different time periods.

1. 5000 +BC to 1850 AD
2. 1850 to 1920
3. 1989 to today

5,000 +BC to 1850 AD

The first time period to be examined is the 5,000 +BC to 1850 AD. The beginning date of 5,000 +BC is rather arbitrary because the exact date of the first businesses that had employees is not clear. So, for the purposes of this book, the date of 5,000 +BC was chosen. The actual date could be as much as 5,000 or 10,000 years earlier, but that is hard to tell. However, the establishments of interest during this early period are those that grew to such size that the owners were able to hire one or more employees. When these businesses hired their first employees, the role of the owner(s) changed. They were no longer just owners; they were now managers as well. The management system that was utilized by these early establishments is named the Autocratic Management System. This is one in which the owner(s) make all decisions unilaterally. Once a decision is made, it is final. Under this system, it is up to the employees to do as they are told. Period. End of story. While this generalization is not true in all cases, the general thesis is accurate. Under this management system, the owner/manager has all of the power and makes all of the decisions. Some managers may take input from the employees into

44

consideration, but that does not alter the fact that in the end, the management makes all of the key decisions.

In the United States, the business establishments during the colonial period and through the 1840s were predominately single proprietorships with a few partnerships. In these enterprises, a single owner or up to several partners operated a blacksmith shop, general store, bank, or manufacturing company that was in a single building. These small enterprises were single-function in nature, and these establishments were owned and managed by the same person(s). Because these enterprises were small and had just a few employees, the Autocratic Management System was sufficient for their needs.

The primary element that prevented these enterprises from growing in size was the sources of power available to them. The source of power for these enterprises was fire, manpower, animal power, and wind power. These sources of power, combined with the use of primarily hand tools for production, did not generate so much output that it could not be handled by the small one-owner enterprises. Most manufacturing was conducted in the owner's house. In the towns, however, artisans could have one or two apprentices or journeymen. Because the source of power was limited to human, horse, wind, or water power, the rate of industrial production was quite low. Once a product had been produced, the ability of the producer to ship the product to other regions of the country was very limited and expensive.

Transportation during the colonial period was unscheduled and infrequent at best. The options available for shipment of goods were ferries, the stagecoach, and wagon lines. The stage coaches hauled mostly passengers and mail but only a little freight. As a result, the primary shipping option for goods was the unscheduled wagon lines. The wagon lines, being horse-drawn, did not operate year-round. This was particularly true in the parts of the country where mountains and winter closed the roads for several months each year. Shipments between the United States and Europe were also slow and irregular. Depending on the wind and the weather, a trip between the continents could vary from three weeks to three months. The transportation, communication, and manufacturing technologies prior to the 1850s made it impractical, if not impossible, to economically build any type of large enterprise. The exception was, of course, those enterprises that were built using slave labor.

1850 to 1920

In the 1850s, the dynamics of business in the colonial United States began to make a dramatic change. The dramatic change was driven by the arrival of several key new technologies and a new source of power. The first key new technology was the use of coal as an energy source to power steam engines. It was the steam engine replacing wind and water power that first enabled the year-round manufacture of large quantities of goods in a single location. This, however, would have been of little benefit without the two other key technologies, the railroad and the telegraph. The first railroads were built in the 1830s, and the telegraph was invented in 1844. As the railroad companies acquired rights-of-way for their tracks, the telegraph companies would use the rights-of-way for their telegraph lines. As a result, the railroad and telegraph spread over the country somewhat in unison.[79] For the first time, it was not only possible to move freight and people faster than by horse, but it could also be done year-round and on a regular schedule. Thus, the combination of steam-powered industrial equipment and steam-powered railroad engines made it economically and technically feasible to produce large volumes of goods at a single location and distribute them across a large geographic area. It was also possible, for the first time, to build a large enterprise spanning a large geography and then control it from a single central point. This was first done by the railroad companies.

As the companies grew in size and geography, it became immediately obvious to the owners that the Autocratic Management System was no longer capable of meeting their needs. The first large companies that felt the need for a new management system were the railroads. Therefore, it was the new technologies of the industrial age that changed the business environment to such a degree, that it rendered the Autocratic Management System obsolete. As a result, the large businesses of the day began the development a new management system that was designed for the new industrial-age business environment. That new management system would be called the Bureaucratic Management System (BMS).

This is a key point and bears repeating. What caused the demise of the Autocratic Management System as the primary management system in the industrial age? It was the arrival of the new industrial-age technologies and the impact that those new technologies had on the business environment. With the new technologies (steam power, railroads, etc.), it was now possible to produce large quantities of product at a single site, distribute that product over a large geographic area on a year-round basis, and finally, control the entire organization from one single point. These companies then could have hundreds of employees who were spread throughout the country. The end result was the obsolescence of the Autocratic Management System and the need for a new system to replace it. The lesson to be learned here is that when a rash of new technologies dramatically alters the business environment, the management system must be changed to address the realities of that new environment. Now, on with the story.

The development of the Bureaucratic Management System in the U.S. began in the 1850s and for all practical purposes was completed in the 1920s. It was during those seventy years that the BMS evolved into the management system as we know it today. In the 1920s, Alfred Sloan Jr. of General Motors created and implemented the multi-divisional, decentralized business structure, which completed the evolutionary development of the BMS.[80] Since that time, there has been little change in the BMS concepts or structure. The business environment of the late 1800s into the early 1900s had the following four key characteristics:

1. The producer had the marketplace power.
2. The management had the knowledge power base.
3. The rate of change was slow.
4. The work was simple.

1989 to Today

Since the early days of the industrial age, the business environment in the United States has gone through a dramatic shift. This shift has taken it from the industrial age into the information age. These shifts are not small, insignificant shifts, but are huge shifts. In fact, these shifts are 180-degree shifts! This evolution can be understood by examining the following seven changes or shifts that have occurred since the 1900s:

1. The marketplace power base shift from the producer to the consumer;
2. The dramatic increase in the rate of change;
3. The digitalization of all forms of information, music, video, etc.;
4. The speed and volume of digitalized information communications;
5. The information explosion;
6. The increased job complexity driven by new technologies and the information explosion; and
7. The knowledge power base shift from management to the employees.

1. The Marketplace Power Base Shift from the Producer to the Consumer

During the first three to four decades of the development of the BMS, the consumer had virtually no marketplace power. The consumer at that time had to buy the products that were available from the nearest store(s). Their transportation was by foot and horse. It was an all-day, sometimes several-day, trip to "town" to make their purchases for the next few weeks or months. Even in the larger cities of the time, the choices were few. In this environment, the producers did not have to be concerned with the consumer's desires or preferences. The producers were much more focused on distribution channels. If the producers could get their product to the store(s) that the consumer frequented, the consumer either had to buy the product or do without. With this as a beginning environment for the BMS, it is not surprising that the graphical representation of the BMS does not allow for or show the consumer (customer or market). Even today, when a person is asked to provide an organization chart for their company, the consumer will not be on it. If the consumer is added to the pyramid organization chart, where would the consumer be on that chart? The answer is this—at the bottom next to the front-line employees. See Figure 3.1.

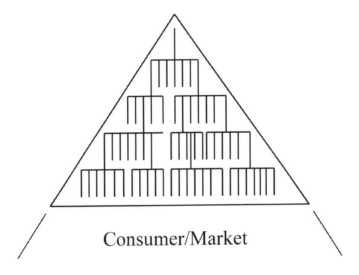

Fig. 3.1

During the time when producers had the marketplace power, they could and did become highly successful even though they paid little attention to the consumers. Today, however, that has all changed. The consumer now holds the marketplace power because the consumer now has CHOICE! Today, the consumer can no longer be held hostage by the producers. Not only can the consumers choose between many domestic suppliers for a product, they can now choose from many foreign suppliers as well. In the prior figure (Figure 3.1), the consumer was at the bottom, which is representative of the lowest level of power. In the BMS, the greater the power, the higher the level. Power flows from the top to the bottom. Again, this worked in the 1800s when the BMS was created. Today, however, if we add the consumer to the organization chart and give the consumer the level that their power now commands, the consumer will be at the top of the chart. See Figure 3.2.

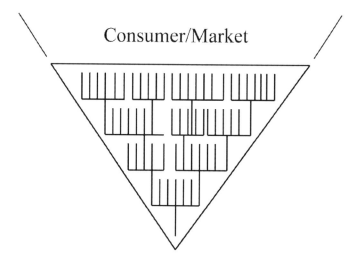

Fig. 3.2. Today's organization chart

With this chart inverted, a number of things have happened. First, the consumer is graphically represented with their proper level of power. Secondly, there has been a 180-degree shift in the orientation of the BMS organization chart. Thirdly, the role of management has shifted from one of command and control to one of support and enablement. This third point represents a huge change in the role management will play once the change has been made to recognize the power that the customer holds today. This recognition not only turns the BMS pyramid upside-down, but as we will see, it changes everything.

2. The Dramatic Increase in the Rate of Change

Beginning in the early 1850s and then accelerating in the1900s, change in the world and the business environment began to take place and at an ever-increasing rate. Using transportation as an example, from the time of recorded history to 1900, the primary mode of transportation was either by foot or by riding animals. In the early 1900s, automobiles began to appear in small numbers and the Wright brothers made the first successful heavier-than-air flight in 1903. Then, as noted earlier, in just the next sixty-six years, man went from mere heavier-than-air flight to landing on the moon! Even more amazing is the fact that from the time the Russians put the first satellite in space in 1959, until the United States landed the first man on the moon was only ten years! In the 1900s, communications went from the telegraph to the telephone with a hand crank and party lines to rotary dial phones to touchtone phones to mobile phones to 1G, 2G, and now 4G cell phones—eight generations of phones in less than one hundred years. In the 1940s, the first computers were created using vacuum tubes. Then came the solid-state transistor, television, the Internet, DNA research, plastic, nylon, air conditioning, and on and on and on. When a person begins to reflect on the inventions and changes that have taken place in the years since 1900 as compared to the 10,000 years prior to 1900, it is absolutely astounding! It is almost unbelievable how much change has taken place and how rapidly things are changing today.

These changes have not been limited to the industrial segment of our society. Other changes just as profound have taken place. Women's rights, the end of segregation, women in the workplace, and immigration are just a few examples of events that have dramatically changed the workforce. The advances in medicine with vaccines, organ transplants, open-heart surgery, CAT scans, and many other new medical inventions provide a good example of the rate of change that continues to increase. When a person pauses and looks back at the changes over the past five to ten decades and compares that change to all the changes in the prior recorded history of man, the recent rate of change can be overwhelming.

The dramatically increased rate of change over the past one hundred years and the information explosion since the 1980s have combined to completely reshape the environment in which business must operate today and the environment in which managers must manage today. These changes are permanent and are increasing at an alarming rate.

3. The Digitization of Information

The digitization of information began with the invention of the first digital computer in the late 1940s. Computers store information that is represented in a format of zeroes and ones. In the digital world, either a switch is on or off. If it is on, that represents a one. If it is off, that represents a zero. These on-off switches (they are called "bits" in computer jargon) can then be combined in groups to represent more complex data. For example, four bits can be combined to represent any number from zero to nine. Eight bits can be combined (eight bits are called a "word" in computer jargon) to represent alphabetic characters. It is this representation of information or data in the digital format that people are talking about when they speak of the digital age. Once the information has been captured in the digital format, it can be stored, transmitted and reproduced at very high speeds by computers and their associated input/output devices such as displays, tape and disk storage. Prior to the digital age, data and information were stored in a wave form which is an analog format.

In the 1960s, with the introduction of IBM's System 360, the rate of computerization of the business world began to accelerate so that by the late 1970s, most medium and large businesses had been "computerized." Also in the early 1980s, a number of personal computer manufacturers emerged and began the process of "computerizing" the individual in the home. Today, most homes have at least one personal computer and many homes have two or three.

During the last twenty-five years, the cost of computers has dropped dramatically while the performance has increased at an astounding rate. Since 1980, the power of the processor in the personal computer has doubled approximately every eighteen months, but the cost has been decreasing. In the early 1980s, a PC with a slow Intel processor, two diskette drives (no hard drive), and 64K of memory could cost as much as $5,000 in 1980 dollars. Today, however, a PC with CD-ROM drive, 80-GB hard disk, 512K of main memory, and a fast processor can be purchased for under $500.00.

This combination of lower cost with higher performance of the processors available today has enabled what is called "pervasive" computing. Pervasive computing is when computers are imbedded into products and not used as stand-alone computing systems. Today, computer chips are imbedded into all kinds of industrial, medical and personal-use products. As just a few examples of the digitization process, today we have digitized cameras, music, television, 3D medical pictures (MRI and CAT scans), phone service known as VOIP (Voice over Internet Protocol), and the list just goes on and on.

Carly Fiorina (the former CEO of HP) speaks of this information as being "digital, mobile, virtual, and personal." By digital, she means that all analog information—from photography to entertainment to communication to word processing to architectural design to the management of a home lawn sprinkler system—is being digitized, and when that happens, the data can then be manipulated electronically, stored electronically, and distributed via satellites, fiber-optic cables, and the Internet, which all use the digital information format rather than the older analog information format.[81]

As pervasive computing continues to expand, more and more information is captured digitally. Today, it is not only possible for these imbedded computers to capture volumes of information digitally, but they can send you reports on it. For example, it is now possible for your car to send you an email and let you know if it is ok or if it needs some attention.

Pervasive computing and the digitization of our world is reaching into every aspect of our lives. The world is moving from the analog (an electronic wave signal) world to a digital (zeros and ones) world. It is the capture of information in this digital form that computers and digital communication networks use that is driving the information-age revolution. It is the advent of today's cheap computer processors, however, that has made the digitization of our world possible.

4. The Speed, Volume, and Availability of Digital Information

In addition to the integrated computer chip and satellite communications, there are another four new technologies that are changing the way work is getting done in business today. These new technologies are also changing the basic structures of business. These four new technologies are:

    A. Fiber-optic Cables
    B. The Internet
    C. Internet Search Engines
    D. Wireless Communications

The first technology that is bringing dramatic changes to the business world environment is the fiber-optic cable. In the 1990s, many companies invested heavily in fiber-optic cable networks to meet the projected needs of the Internet for high-speed, broadband communications. The demand did not materialize at the rate projected, and as a result, a huge surplus of communications capacity was created. Further, the amount of information that can be carried on each single fiber of an optical cable continues to increase. "Advances in fiber optics will soon allow a single fiber to carry 1 terabit (a terabit is one trillion bits) per second. With 48 fibers in a cable, that's 48 terabits per second. Henry Schact, the former CEO of Lucent, which specialized in this technology, pointed out that with that much capacity, you could 'transmit all the printed material in the world in minutes in a single cable. This means unlimited transmitting capacity at zero incremental cost.'"[82] These fiber-optic networks are making it possible to communicate large amounts of data around the world quickly and at low cost.

The second technology that is changing the business world is the Internet. The power of the Internet lies in the fact that anyone on the Internet can communicate with anyone else on the Internet. All that is required to establish the communications link is the IP (Internet protocol) address for that person. With the Internet, for just a few dollars a month (or less), anyone, anywhere in the world can communicate with anyone else anywhere in the world. The Internet address can be for a pc used by an individual person or it can be for a large mainframe computer attached to the Internet. These mainframe computers (now more commonly called servers) make all types of information available to anyone on the Internet. This information can be virtually anything from books to medical information to vacation and flight scheduling to financial information. The information available is virtually limitless.

The third technology that is changing the business world is the Internet search engines that are available from companies such as Yahoo and Google. It is these search engines that make the world's information available in a manageable manner for anyone around the world. These search engines allow a person to become their own self-directed researcher for any type of information that that person is interested in, both personal and business. Instantly available is a person's background for employment screening or the complete description of a competitor's products. Google is also usable in over one hundred languages.[83] Therefore, the street goes both ways. Not only can a person easily acquire information on a competitor's products, anyone around the world can do the same thing and in many different languages. "Never before in the history of the planet have so many people—on their own—had the ability to find so much information about so many things and about so many other people."[84] Are you new to a large city and want to eat Chinese but don't know where to go? Just go to Google and key in "Chinese restaurant" with your zip code, and up will come a list of Chinese restaurants for your consideration. Any information you want to find, just select your favorite search engine and, most likely, the information is just seconds away.

The fourth technology that is dramatically changing the business environment is wireless communications. Wireless communication is making it possible to utilize the three previous technologies from almost anywhere at any time. The most common use of wireless technology today is the cellular phone. Other wireless devices, such as laptop PCs, PDAs, iPaq, the Blackberry and the iPhone, are only the beginning of the wireless movement. With the aid of miniaturization, a continual new stream of products will allow a person to do many types of work from anywhere in ways that we have not yet thought of. In Japan, for example, NTT DoCoMo is working on cell-phone technology that will allow a person to have a two-way video conference, scan barcodes to buy products, pay bills by using the cell phone as a credit card, and access personal medical records by using the cell phone as an authentication system.[85] As the infrastructure supporting wireless communications grows in geographic coverage and interoperability between vendors, and as broadband capability increases, the worker will no longer be tied to an office. No longer will companies be tied to a building. The communications that now exist between person and person, person and computer, and computer and computer will continue to grow and expand and, at the same time, change the structure of the business world.

For example, suppose that you are flying across the ocean near Greenland in a Boeing 777 and one of the Rolls-Royce engines is hit by lightning. Normally, when an engine is hit by lightning, you would have to land the plane, fly in an engineer to do a visual inspection, and make a decision about what damage was done and what repairs, if any, must be made before the plane could fly again. This delay, however, would be very inconvenient for the passengers and the airline. The airline would have to make arrangements for the passengers; they would lose their flight position and also have to find new crews. All of this would also be quite costly. But what happens today? "That Rolls-Royce engine is connected by transponder to a satellite and is beaming data about its condition and performance, at all times, down to a computer into Rolls-Royce's operations room. Thanks to the artificial intelligence in the Rolls-Royce computer, based on complex algorithms, it can track anomalies in its engine's performance while in operation. The artificial intelligence in the Rolls-Royce computer knows that this engine was probably hit by lightning and feeds out a report to a Rolls-Royce engineer."[86] The engineers are able to analyze and monitor the engine's performance in real time and therefore to determine what actions must be taken before the plane lands. If they can determine, based on all the information that they have, that no action or even inspection is required, then the airplane can remain on schedule, saving the passengers and airline time and money.[87]

The arrival of all these new technologies and the ways they can be combined to do things in new and different ways than in the past are causing turbulence and chaos in the business world. They are causing a dislocating, disruptive revolution that is changing everything. They are flattening the old hierarchies of the industrial age. "The whole world has changed in profound ways. But there is something about the flattening of the world that is going to be qualitatively different from other such profound changes: the speed and breadth with which it is taking hold."[88] "To put it another way, the experience of the high-tech companies in the last few decades who failed to navigate the rapid changes brought about in their marketplace by these types of forces may be a warning to all businesses, institutions, and nation-states that are now facing these inevitable, even predictable, changes but lack the leadership, flexibility, and imagination to adapt—not because they are not smart or aware, but because the speed of change is simply overwhelming them."[89] The changes being brought on by these new technologies are happening with such dramatic speed that those companies that are unable or unwilling to adapt may not survive.

5. The Information Explosion

During the past five to six decades, the rate at which information has been created has accelerated at an exponential rate. A primary contributor to this information explosion has been technology in the form of the computer, communications networks, pervasive computing and most recently, the Internet. Different authorities on this matter have slightly different metrics for this information explosion, but in general, they all agree that it is happening and that the rate will increase as time goes on. Remember the statement from chapter one, *Ninety percent of all information that exists today has been created in the last fifteen years. That information is expected to double in the next five years!* Stephen M. R. Covey in his book *The Speed of Trust* makes the following assertion, "The world's fund of information now doubles every two to two-and-a-half years."[90] A person needs to reflect on the previous statements in order to get some perspective as to how the world is changing today and the rate at which it is changing. As some anonymous person said, *"There has been an alarming increase in the number of things that I know nothing about."*

Because of this information explosion and its integration into the work of today's employees, it is no longer possible for the manager to know how to do all of the jobs that their employees do. There is so much new information and knowledge that is coming at such a fast rate, it is difficult, if not impossible, for the employees to keep up with it, much less the managers. The fact is that knowledge is being created faster than it can be acquired. This information explosion is having a profound effect on the business environment. Examples such as the military and Wal-Mart in Chapter One show some of these effects. In particular, those two examples show how the speed and volumes of information in the information age are forcing tactical decision-making from the mid and lower levels of management to the employees.

The challenge for management today is to find a way to "manage" these front-line employees who must now make decisions that were only made by management in the past. The speed and volume of the information flow enabled by the new technologies of today make it impossible for the manager to absorb and process those volumes of information. Only the employees have any chance of doing that. Therefore, even if management was inserted into the line of information flow, the manger could not handle the volume of information. So, there is no choice. The front-line employees must be empowered to make many decisions that in the past were made by management only. Somehow, employees must start acting and thinking like owners and management.

These examples clearly show three key impacts that the information age and its new technologies are having on the business environment.

1. The volume and velocity of digital-based information is forcing the removal of layers of management and the flattening of the organizational structure.

2. The explosion of information is driving the tactical decision-making down in the organization from middle and upper levels of management to the first-line managers and their employees.
3. The business-operational knowledge base has shifted from management to the employees.

In the information-age environment of today, only the first-line managers and their employees have the knowledge required to make the tactical decisions that must be made in order to control costs and improve productivity, because they are the only ones that have the information. There is just too much information coming at such a fast rate that the involvement of the upper levels of management in the decision-making process at the operational level is all but impossible. This transfer of the operational knowledge power base from upper management to the first-line managers and their employees is just another example of the profound impact that the information age is having on the business environment and the ways that work is being done.

6. The Increased Job Complexity Driven by the Information Explosion

The digital revolution and the resulting information explosion have combined to dramatically increase the level of complexity of today's jobs. Most jobs today require that the employees interact with a computer system and the software that drives it. That software can require extensive training to use properly, and it is constantly changing.

Another factor is the growth of pervasive computing. As an example, the new car you buy will contain multiple computers. Computers control the engine, transmission, and, if your car has it, onboard navigation. Computers soon will be embedded in many products that the consumer purchases, from cars to games to television to appliances. As the pervasive trend continues, a side effect is that the products become more complex. As a case in point, just think for a moment about all of the functions that are provided to today's consumer with the cell phone. Think about the knowledge and training required to use all of the functions (storing phone numbers, setting the ring tone/sound, taking and sending pictures, checking one's email, sending text messages, accessing files, etc.) that new cell phones provide. Think about all of the capabilities that the new digital cameras provide. Take, review, and delete pictures before they are ever printed. You can review, size, and change the color of each picture, and print only the ones desired. This means a lot of new capability for the consumer, but it also requires more knowledge on the consumer's part.

The same thing is happening in the workplace. As computers become more pervasive in industry, the functions available to the workforce increase, and along with those increased capabilities are increased knowledge levels. The result is increased job complexity. Again, we have another 180-degree shift from jobs that are simple with a slow rate of change in the industrial age to jobs that are complex with a high rate of change in the information age.

All of these changes have combined to bring about another 180-degree shift that is the most important shift of all. That shift is a change in *what* the company is considered *to be*. In the industrial age, the company was considered to be the facilities and materials that the company owned. When you bought the "company," you bought the facilities and materials. The employees were not considered to be part of the company because they were only labor. They provided labor that could be replaced on short notice. The jobs were simple and had little knowledge or information content. That is no longer the case. A quantum shift has taken place. Today, for many and soon most companies, **the value of a company lies in the knowledge or "intellectual property" held by the employees.** Should all of the employees decide to leave en masse, the company would cease to exist. In the early decades of the industrial age, if all the employees left en masse, it was possible to replace all of them in short order, but not anymore. Today, it would not be possible to hire all new employees and regain the lost knowledge and information. There would be no one to teach the new employees how to perform the work as that knowledge left with the employees. A computer software company is a classic example of this. In a software company, only the employees hold the detailed software-application knowledge and expertise required to design, develop, test, deliver, and support the software application. The management can no longer possess all of this knowledge. There is just too much to know, and it is changing too fast for management to keep up with it. This is a clear example of the knowledge power-base shift from management to the employees. Today, the company can no longer be considered the facilities and materials. **Today, a company must be viewed as being the employees and the detailed knowledge that they and only they possess.** This is a 180-degree shift of monumental proportions!

7. The Knowledge Power Base Shift from Management to the Employees

During the early industrial age, few people had any formal education. The few that were educated (doctors, lawyers, engineers, etc.) became the management of the first large industrial organizations. This held true into the early 1900s. For example, in 1903, only 6% of the workforce could read. The fact that the knowledge resided with the management and not the labor force of the time fit well with the command-and-control structure of the BMS. The labor force of the day did not have the education to know what to do, so they had to be instructed (managed/controlled) by the managers. The work was also fairly simple in nature with a slow rate of change, so it was possible for the managers to have and maintain the knowledge required to be able to instruct the employees on what to do and also how to do it.

From 1900 to 1950, the labor force became much more educated. The work to be done became increasingly complex and required higher levels of education so that by the 1950s, a high school education was required for most positions in the labor force. These changes began the shift of the knowledge power base from management to the employees. This trend of increasing information and knowledge content has continued and accelerated, demonstrated by the fact that product cost used to be 80% materials and 20% knowledge; now it's split 70/30 the other way.[91] This dramatic increase in knowledge as a percent of the cost of a product clearly shows the impact of the information age on the business environment. Because of the dramatically increased knowledge content in current jobs and the information explosion, management just cannot keep up. The amount of knowledge required by a manager's employees is just more than the manager can handle. Management no longer has the knowledge power base and therefore is not in a position to "manage" the employee.

Under the Bureaucratic Management System, a manager has three responsibilities that must be fulfilled. The manager is responsible for:

1. Explaining to the employee what the job is;
2. If necessary, showing the employee how to do the job; and
3. Explaining to the employee how to improve performance when required.

Because of the information explosion and the subsequent shift of the knowledge power base from management to the employees, the manager is no longer able to dispatch the three responsibilities of a manager. Most managers can still dispatch responsibility number one, but responsibilities two and three are now beyond the capabilities of many managers. They simply no longer have the job knowledge to be able show an employee how to do the job or to tell the employee how to improve performance. It is now clear that the knowledge power base has shifted from the management to the employees. Thus, another 180-degree shift has taken place. This shift has been driven by new technologies of the information age and has rendered most of today's managers incompetent. They can no longer dispatch their three responsibilities.

Summary—The Challenges Facing Business Managers Today

Business managers today are facing a combination of challenges that no other managers in history have ever had to deal with:

1. The labor shortage that will be created as the Baby Boomers retire;
2. The issues related to attracting and retaining Generations X & Y; and
3. The arrival of the information-age technologies and their impact on the business environment.

1. The labor shortage that will be created as the Baby Boomers retire

As the Baby Boomer Generation retires from the workforce, the management of every business will be faced with the need to significantly increase the productivity of the workforce. This will be necessary to sustain the current level of economic activity and the current standard of living as the workforce invariably shrinks in size. If management is not able to increase productivity at a rate sufficient to counterbalance the declining work force, then the overall economy will shrink and a recession will take place. As a result, the question facing management today is this. How does business significantly increase productivity?

2. The issues related to attracting and retaining Generations X & Y

As we now know, there are many issues related to attracting and retaining Generations X and Y. There is Generation X that does not trust business, does not respect having a job and will not hesitate to quit when they become unhappy. Then there is Generation Y with their "get off my back" attitude and their high expectations of career earnings, management and the work environment. For companies to be successful in attracting and retaining Generations X and Y, they must find a way to create a work environment that has the following characteristics:

1. Open and transparent management that Generations X and Y feel they can trust;

2. Challenging work that has meaning and purpose to it;
3. Clearly stated objectives with the freedom to do the job their way without being micromanaged;
4. Ongoing learning and educational opportunities;
5. An environment that is informal and comfortable with low stress;
6. Balance between personal and professional life with flexibility in hours and scheduling; and
7. Leadership/management that is not threatening, intimidating, disrespectful, manipulative or coercive.

The companies that are successful in creating a work environment with these characteristics will have Generations X and Y flocking to their door.

3. The arrival of the information age

Describing the changes that management must make in order to deal with the new realities of the information age can be stated rather simply. Management of companies today must provide the leadership required for their companies to move from today's industrial age business model that has been in use since the 1800s to a new business model that is designed for the information age. The implementation of the new business model must address the three challenges facing management today: significantly increasing productivity, creating a work environment that is attractive to Generations X and Y, and addressing the many 180-degree shifts that have occurred since the industrial age. The first step will be finding a solution that will address all of these issues.

Chapter 4
Finding a Solution

The previous chapters have raised a number of issues that business must find a way to deal with. No doubt there is a wide array of actions that could be taken, but which ones will be effective and provide the best outcome? To find an answer to these questions has required about twenty years of research, followed by a close examination of four different categories of companies:

1. The companies that have made the transition from average performance to superior performance;
2. The best financially performing companies;
3. The most productive companies; and
4. The premier companies that have stood the test of time.

The purpose of examining these four categories of companies is that these companies represent the absolute best in business; as a group, they are the top one hundredth of one percent. All of these companies are doing things that are making them highly successful. The purpose of the examination will be to find out if there are any things that are common across all of these categories of companies and, if so, what they might be. Such things would be of significant interest.

Category 1. Companies that have made the transition from average performance to superior performance

The source of information for the category-1 companies is the book *Good to Great,* written by Jim Collins. Jim and his staff of researchers identified eleven companies that made the transition from what he calls "good" performance to "great" performance. The criteria for inclusion in this category was as follows: "Fifteen-year cumulative stock returns that were at or below the general stock market, punctuated by a transition point, then cumulative returns at least three times the market over the next fifteen years."[92]   The companies that made the cut are listed below under the heading "Transition Companies." The second column with the heading "Comparison Companies" is the list of companies that were in the same industry as the transition companies, had the same opportunity to achieve great performance, but for some reason or reasons, did not make the transition from average to great performance.

Transition Companies	Comparison Companies
Abbot Laboratories	Upjohn
Circuit City	Silo
Fannie Mae	Great Western Financial
Gillette	Warner-Lambert
Kimberly-Clark	Scott Paper
Kroger	A&P
Nucor	Bethlehem Steel
Philip Morris	R. J. Reynolds
Pitney Bowes	Addressograph
Walgreens	Eckerd
Wells Fargo	Bank of America

The terms "good," "average" and "great" have been used to describe the performance of these companies, but the question is this: As a group, what kind of performance were these companies able to produce after their point of transition? Figure 4.1 shows the performance of the stock of the transition companies as compared to the comparison companies and the market in total. This comparison covers a span of 35 years from 1965 to 2000.

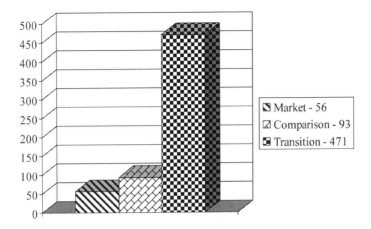

Fig. 4.1. $1 Invested from 1965–2000.

Figure 4.1 is showing that one dollar invested in the market from 1965 to 2000 would be worth $56. One dollar invested in a mutual fund consisting of the comparison companies would be worth $93. However, one dollar invested in a mutual fund consisting of the transition companies would be worth $471. This shows that the stock of the transition companies outperformed the general market by 8.4 times and the comparison companies by 5 times.[93] The astounding thing is that the transition companies did *something* that allowed them to outperform their competitors by a factor of five to one. Their competitors were in the same industry, operating in the same economic environment, selling in the same geographies, but the transition companies were still able to outperform them by a factor of five to one! Not 10, 30, 90 or 150%, but 500%! There is something going on here! The question is, what is that something?

In his analysis of these companies, Mr. Collins discusses what he calls the "Hedgehog Concept." This consists of three circles that intersect which represent the following three items:

1. What are you deeply passionate about?
2. What can you be the best in the world at?
3. What drives your economic engine?[94]

The observation that Mr. Collins makes is that the transition from average or below performance to great performance occurs after the companies have gained an understanding of the items in the three circles, and then made them their new number-one priority. So, all of the companies in this study were able to dramatically improve their financial performance and profitability when they shifted their focus from profit as the number one objective to a focus on what they were passionate about, what they could be the best at, and what would drive their "economic engine." That is a very interesting observation. The profits increased when the number one priority of management shifted FROM PROFIT to SOMETHING BEYOND PROFIT. It was not that profits were no longer important, it was just that profits were no longer the number-one objective.

Another observation that Mr. Collins and his team made while doing the research on these companies was very surprising to them, and it had to do with the unique characteristics of the CEOs of these companies. The title of his book is *Good to Great*, so he refers to the CEOs of these companies as good-to-great leaders. Here is what he had to say about them: "We were surprised, *shocked really*, to discover the *type of leadership required for turning a good company into a great one.* Compared to high-profile leaders with big personalities who make headlines and become celebrities, the good-to-great leaders seem to have come from Mars. Self-effacing, quiet, reserved, even shy—these leaders are a paradoxical blend of personal humility and profession will."[95] It is interesting that he says that this type of leadership is "required" for turning a good company into a great one. It is also hard to believe that every company that made the transition from good to great just happened to have a CEO with these characteristics by accident. But, for whatever reason, the CEO of each company seemed to be cut from the same mold.

Category 2. The best financial-performing companies

The source of the information on the companies that have the best financial performance for category 2 is the book, *Think Big, Act Small* by Jason Jennings. The companies in this category are those companies, either public or private, that have been the best at consistently growing revenues. More specifically, in order to be included in this category, a company had to achieve the following:

1. Increase revenues by over ten percent per year for over ten years.
2. Increase operating profits or earnings per share by over ten percent per year for over ten years.

After starting with 50,000 prospective companies, the list was finally reduced to seventeen companies and then a final list of nine companies. These nine companies are in the top one hundredth of one percent of all American companies. An elite group indeed! Here is the list:

1. Petco Animal Supplies
2. Koch Industries
3. Cabela's
4. Medline Industries
5. Sonic Drive-In
6. O'Reilly Automotive
7. Dot Foods
8. SAS Institute
9. Strayer Education

Only three of the companies, O'Reilly Automotive, Strayer Education and Sonic Drive-In were publicly held companies from 1998 to 2003, so they are the only ones whose stock was used to create the chart in Figure 4.2. However, the chart does show that in only five years, the return on a $10,000 investment in the market was $3,425 while an investment of $10,000 in the three selected companies was $23,539, or 6.8 times greater. Of the two other companies that are publicly held, PETCO began public trading for the second time on February 26, 2002, and Cabela's started trading on June 25, 2004.

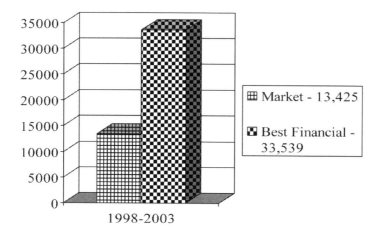

Fig. 4.2. ROI of $10,000 in 5 years.

Mr. Jennings and his researchers made many interesting observations of these nine companies, but two of them are of particular interest. First, they made this observation: "We believe that the companies included in the book are the best contemporary business models in existence."[96] That is a pretty strong statement. The *best contemporary business models* in existence? One characteristic of these business models was that they included a formalized statement of the company's "reason for being" or "purpose," so to speak. For example, Koch Industries has their ten guiding principles[97] and Sonic Drive-In has their four "Rules of the Road."[98] Because these companies had formalized their "purpose," the number one priority of the management team was to focus on the company "purpose" rather than merely profit. Again, that is not to say that profits are not important for these companies, it is just that it is not the number-one focus. Their "reason for being" or "purpose" is the number-one focus.

The second observation was concerning the unique characteristics of the CEOs of these companies. When speaking of these CEOs, Mr. Jennings says: "You won't find a single slick, swashbuckling sales type leading any of the companies that do the best job of consistently increasing revenues. In fact, you'll find just the opposite: very humble people leading and managing equally humble enterprises."[99] Then he went on to say, "After each interview, we'd end up discussing the same subject: *what was the magic* that allowed these companies to be the top revenue performers in the nation? And we always ended up with the same conclusion: the unassuming nature of the people who head these companies is central to the enterprise's ability to consistently grow revenues."[100] It is interesting to note that these findings are almost identical to what Jim Collins found in his research.

Category 3. The most productive companies in the world

The companies in Category-3 are the most productive companies in the world. Not just in the U. S., but in the world. The source of the information for the Category-3 companies is from the book *Less is More* again by Jason Jennings. The companies in this category must have been in business for ten years or more and then were selected based on their performance against the following four performance measures:

1. Revenue Per Employee
2. Return on Equity
3. Return on Assets
4. Operating Income Per Employee[101]

There were three companies—Nokia, Southwest Airlines and Harley-Davidson who made the final cut, but were not included in the analysis because the researchers felt that they had already been widely written about. Then they did their best to scrutinize the financials of the others to see if there were any potential "Enrons" before they made their final list.[102] After all the research and other considerations were taken into account, here is their final list of the most productive companies in the world:

- Nucor
- The Warehouse
- Lantech
- SRC Holdings

- World Savings
- Yellow Freight
- Ryanair
- IKEA

How productive are these companies?   Here are just a few examples of the kinds of productivity that these companies have been able to achieve:

1. Nucor's employees increased the steel output at the Darlington South Carolina plant from thirty tons per day to one hundred tons per hour![103]

2. The Warehouse is making double the profit per dollar of sales when compared to Wal-Mart.[104]

3. Ryanair carries eight times more passengers per employee then the industry average.[105]

4. IKEA creates twenty-five times more profit per employee than the industry average.[106]

With these kinds of productivity as compared to their peers, it is easy to see why these companies were selected as the most productive companies in the world. Just as in the prior two categories of companies, these companies are not just a little better or a little more productive than their competition; they are more productive by a factor of magnitudes, anywhere from 2X to 25X! Twenty-five times more profit per employee than the industry average, that is astonishing!

One characteristic of these companies that Mr. Jennings noted was that all of these companies were focused on, in his terms, "One Simple Big Objective."[107]   For SRC Holdings, their simple big objective was captured in the term "89-to-1."[108] The 89 stood for the $8,900,000.00 of debt that the company had as compared to the $100,000.00 in equity when the company was purchased.   Prior to becoming SRC Holdings, it had been a business unit of International Harvester that had been on the edge of bankruptcy for some time. Jack Stack and twelve other managers scraped together $100,000 and then borrowed $8,900,000 to buy the Springfield Remanufacturing Corporation from International Harvester.[109] The company rebuilt old broken-down engines to make them like new. Jack Stack became the CEO of the new company and explained to the employees that a company with a debt-to-equity ratio of 89-to-1 was basically brain dead. So, the "simple big objective" before them was to turn that number upside down to $100,000 in debt and $8,900,000 in equity! If they could do that, then they could all keep their jobs and prosper.[110]

For Nucor, Ken Iverson, the CEO, stated their simple big objective as follows: "Build a company where people will earn according to their productivity, will have a job tomorrow if they do it properly today, and a company where everyone... will be treated fairly."[111] The key observation is that each of these companies had their "simple big objective" as their number one priority and focus. As in the prior categories, profit was still important and a company cannot survive without it, but it was not the number-one priority for these companies.

A second common characteristic of these companies that Mr. Jennings and his staff couldn't help but notice was that these CEOs were not as they were expected to be. Here is what Mr. Jennings had to say about the CEO's of these most productive companies in the world. "Having had the opportunity of collectively spending many hundreds of hours with the people who lead and manage these highly efficient organizations, there's an observation that applies across the board—an observation that stands in stark contrast to what most people witness while moving about the upper echelons of business: there's simply no bullshit and bluster, *no sense of self-importance, about any of these people.*"[112] Then, later in his book he observes *"each is a model of humility and modesty* and acts as a responsible guardian of their investors' money."[113] In each case, these CEOs were cut from a different mold than the typical CEO. Their humility, modesty and lack of self-importance set them apart from what most people would expect.

Category 4. The companies that have stood the test of time

The source of information for the Category-4 companies is the book, *Built to Last*, written by Jim Collins. This book is about the companies he calls "Visionary Companies." What is a visionary company? Jim describes these companies as follows: "Visionary companies are premier institutions—the crown jewels—in their industries, widely admired by their peers and having a long track record of making a significant impact on the world around them."[114] In selecting the companies that would be used in their research, Jim and his staff created the following criteria:

1. Premier institution in its industry
2. Widely admired by knowledgeable businesspeople
3. Made an indelible imprint on the world in which we live
4. Had multiple generations of chief executives
5. Been through multiple product (or service) life cycles
6. Founded before 1950[115]

Jim also describes the companies that were selected as being "the best of the best in their industries, and have been that way for decades."[116] Then, as part of the research effort, a group of comparison companies were selected. These companies are good companies, but just not up to the standards of the visionary companies. As Jim describes the comparison companies: "they are good companies, having survived in most cases as long as the visionary companies and, as you'll see, having outperformed the general stock market. But they don't quite match up to the overall stature of the visionary companies in our study. In most cases, you can think of the visionary company as the gold medalist and the comparison company as the silver or bronze medalist."[117] As you read the list of the visionary companies and the comparison companies, you will see that they are some very well-known companies.

Visionary Companies	Comparison Companies
3M	Norton
American Express	Wells Fargo
Boeing	McDonnell Douglas
Citicorp	Chase Manhattan
Ford	GM
General Electric	Westinghouse
Hewlet-Packard	Texas Instruments
IBM	Burroughs
Johnson & Johnson	Bristol-Meyers Squibb
Marriott	Howard Johnson
Merck	Pfizer
Motorola	Melville
Philip Morris	RJR Nabisco
Sony	Kenwood
Wal-Mart	Ames
Walt Disney	Columbia[118]

How much difference in performance is there between being a visionary (gold medal) company versus being a comparison (silver or bronze medal) company? Some insight into this question can be gained by comparing the performance of the stocks of gold companies to that of the silver and bronze companies. This data was tracked from 1926 to 1990 and is shown in Figure 4.3.

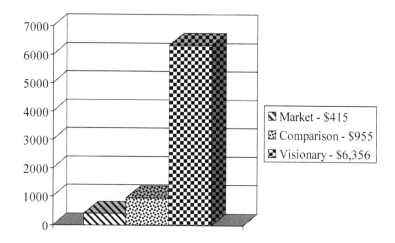

Fig. 4.3. $1 invested from 1926 to 1990.

Figure 4.3 shows the difference in performance between the silver/bronze companies and the gold companies over a period of sixty-four years. Over that time span, the stock of the silver/bronze companies outperformed the market by a factor of 2.3 times. However, the stock of the gold companies outperformed the market by a factor of 15.3 times, and it outperformed the stock of the silver and bronze companies by a factor of 6.6 times![119] Just as in the previous categories, the gold companies have outperformed their peers not by just 30, 50 or even 100 percent; they have outperformed them by 660 percent! What can account for such a huge difference?

Could the huge difference in performance between the gold companies and the silver/bronze have been as a result of superior leadership or possibly a hot product? To answer this question, we will focus on criteria numbers four and five that were used to select the gold companies.

Number four on the list of criteria is that the company must have had multiple CEOs. This is important because it means that these companies have been able to sustain their high levels of performance despite changing CEOs several times. Therefore, the success of the company cannot be attributed to the charisma or leadership of a dynamic or inspirational leader. That is not to say that these companies did not have good, competent CEOs, it is just that the research did not find any significant information that would lead to the conclusion that the performance of these companies could be attributed primarily to the CEOs.

Then number five on the list of criteria is that the company must have gone through multiple product life cycles. Therefore, the continued high performance levels of these gold companies cannot be attributed to the success of a specific product or service. These companies have found a way to be the best in their industries over a long period of time despite having multiple CEOs and going through the life cycle of multiple products or services. Therefore, these companies must have something else working for them that explains why they have been able to become and remain the premier companies and leaders in their industries over such a long period of time.

One characteristic that does separate the gold companies from the silver and bronze companies is that all of the gold companies have a formalized core ideology. This core ideology consists of two parts, "core values and a sense of purpose beyond just making money."[120] For these gold companies, it is their core values and their "sense of purpose" that serves as the guidepost for all decisions and, in the end, sets the focus and priorities of the company. These companies can best be described as "purpose-driven" companies. That is because these companies are all about the pursuit of their purpose and upholding their values as the number-one priority. There can only be one number-one priority, so these companies relegate the pursuit of profit to a position lower than number one. So, once again, we have a category of the most elite companies in industry that has something other than the pursuit of profit as their number-one objective.

Mr. Collins discusses the issue of whether or not profit should be the number one objective as being one of twelve myths. He says that this myth says: "The most successful companies exist first and foremost to maximize profits." The reality according to Mr. Collins and his research is that, "contrary to business-school doctrine, 'maximizing shareholder wealth' or 'profit maximization' has not been the history of gold/visionary companies. Gold/visionary companies pursue a cluster of objectives, of which making money is only one—and not necessarily the primary one. Yes, they seek profits, but they're equally guided by a core ideology. Yet, paradoxically, the gold/visionary companies make more money than the purely profit-driven comparison companies."[121]

During their research, Mr. Collins and his staff also made this observation: "A high-profile, charismatic style is absolutely *not* required to successfully shape a visionary company. Indeed, we found that some of the most significant chief executives in the history of the visionary companies did not have the personality traits of the archetypal, high-profile, charismatic, visionary leader."[122]

One example of this is William McKnight, a man most people have never heard of and yet the company he guided for fifty-two years has earned fame and admiration around the world. That company is known as 3M.[123] The few people who did write about Mr. McKnight described him as "a soft-spoken, gentle man; a good listener; humble and modest."[124]

Then Mr. Collins goes on to say: "McKnight is not the only significant chief executive in the history of the visionary companies who breaks the archetypal model of the charismatic visionary leader. Masaru Ibuka of Sony had a reputation as being reserved, thoughtful, and introspective. Bill Hewlett reminded us of a friendly, no-nonsense, matter-of-fact, down-to-earth farmer from Iowa."[125] Further insight into the minds of these unique CEOs can be gained by reflecting on the following quote by Sam Walton, the founder of Wal-Mart: "I have concentrated all along on building the finest retailing company that we possibly could. Period. Creating a huge personal fortune was never particularly a goal of mine."[126] Here is yet another example from the CEO of one of the premier companies in industry that has been hugely successful even though the maximization of profits was **not** the number-one objective.

Analyzing the four categories of companies

A review of these four categories of companies reveals that a total of forty-four companies were selected as the most elite of the elite. Nucor made the list twice, so there were a total of forty-three companies in the combined list. Further, the analysis revealed that all of these companies shared two characteristics that were not expected, and that these two characteristics set the gold companies apart from the silver and bronze companies. Those two characteristics were:

1. Maximizing profits was *not* their number one objective.
2. They did not have what is considered a "typical" CEO.

These characteristics will be examined in more detail, but first, it will be necessary to give these elite companies a name or description. Therefore, these companies will be called "purpose driven" or "management by purpose" companies. That is because these companies are pursuing some purpose that is beyond profit as their number-one objective. For example, the purpose of Wal-Mart is "to give ordinary folk the chance to buy the same things as rich people," and that is their number-one objective, not maximizing profits.[127] Now we can identify the two types of companies based on their number-one objective:

- Profit-driven (the pursuit of profit maximization)
- Purpose-driven (the pursuit of something beyond profit)

Next, we need a name or label to distinguish between the "typical" CEOs of the comparison or profit-driven companies and the "non-typical" CEOs of the "purpose-driven" companies. To accomplish this, we will use the analysis and description of leadership by Jim Collins in his book *Good to Great.* In that book, Mr. Collins identifies the following five levels of leadership:

Level 1	Highly Capable Individual
Level 2	Contributing Team Member
Level 3	Competent Manager

Level 4   Effective Leader
Level 5   Level 5 Executive

CEOs are found at levels four and five on the leadership scale, so those are the two levels that we are interested in. As it turns out, the "typical" CEO closely fits the description of a Level 4 Effective Leader, and the "non-typical" CEO closely fits the description of a Level 5 Executive. Mr. Collins describes these levels as follows:

<u>Level 4 — Effective Leader</u>: Catalyzes commitment to and vigorous pursuit of a clear and compelling vision, stimulating higher performance standards.

<u>Level 5 — Level 5 Executive</u>: Builds enduring greatness through a paradoxical blend of personal humility and professional will.[128]

The analysis to this point shows that in all four categories of companies, the companies that are the premier companies, the companies that made the transition to greatness, the companies that have the best financial performance and the most productive companies are all (or at one time were) purpose-driven companies with Level 5 or Level 5-like Executives! Unfortunately, this can change over time. On the other hand, all of the comparison companies are profit-driven companies with Level 4 Effective Leaders.

However there is one more item that must be covered before continuing. In the section on the Category-2 companies (the best financially performing companies), Mr. Jennings made the claim that those companies had "the *best contemporary business models in existence*." Earlier it was also noted that to find a solution to the issues facing businesses today, it would require twenty years of research and the examination of the four categories of companies just discussed. The result of the years of research and the examination of the companies in the four categories reveals that indeed, the purpose-driven companies do in fact have a different business model than the profit-driven companies. The description and explanation of the two business models will be covered in detail later, but first they must have a label or name. Those names are as follows:

1. The Industrial Age Profit-Driven Business Model.
2. The Information Age Purpose-Driven Business Model.

Each of these business models has five parts:

Part 1. Leadership
Part 2. A Management System
Part 3. A Measurement System
Part 4. A Performance-Evaluation System
Part 5. A Compensation System

In the following chapters, the five parts of both business models will be examined. By going through the process of examining each of the five parts of the two business models, the reasons for the huge differences in performance between the gold purpose-driven companies and the silver/bronze profit-driven companies will become clear. Additionally, this examination will reveal that the solution to the issues facing businesses today can be addressed by making the transition from the Industrial Age Profit-Driven Business Model to the Information Age Purpose-Driven Business Model. This transition will allow companies to address the coming labor shortage, dramatically increase productivity, create a work environment that is attractive to Generations X and Y, and much more.

Chapter 5
The Industrial Age Business
Model – Leadership

This chapter begins the first of four chapters that will describe the five parts of the Industrial-Age Profit-Driven Business Model. In doing so, the reasons which cause the companies that utilize this model to have such mediocre performance will become clear.

The first part of this model that will be covered is *executive management and leadership*. The research shows that today most companies have maximizing profit as their number one objective and that they also have level-4 or level-4-like executives. So, here are three questions that are just begging to be answered:

1. Why do most companies have maximizing profit as their number one objective?
2. Why do most of these companies have Level-4 or Level-4-like CEOs?
3. What is a Level-4 Effective Leader?

Question Number 1. Why do most companies have maximizing profit as their number one objective? There are two answers to this question. One has to do with the history of the Industrial age business model; the second has to do with today's publicly held companies and the perceived roles of the board of directors and top management.

First, during the early decades of the industrial age, large businesses were owned by individuals and not stockholders. These individuals raised the capital necessary to buy the equipment, buildings, land, and so on necessary to grow their companies by selling bonds in the financial centers of New York and Europe. As a result of selling the bonds, the owners of these companies were bound to make regular interest payments and other payments on a scheduled basis to the bondholders. If they were unable to do so, then they would be in default and would lose their company to the banks and bondholders. Also, during this time, the producers held the marketplace power so these owners did not have to concern themselves very much with the preferences of the customers. As a result, the primary focus of the owners was to manage and control their businesses such that enough profit was generated to make the scheduled and required bond payments. Therefore, it was very natural for them to make maximizing profit their number one objective.

In addition, they were supported by the economic thinking of the industrial age. In 1776, Adam Smith wrote his famous book *The Wealth of Nations,* which puts forth the idea that the purpose of business was to utilize land, labor and capital in the most efficient manner possible so as to maximize the profits for the owners/investors. The maximization of the profits was desired because that would then allow the profits to be used for the benefit on the community as well as the owners. In this context, the maximization of profits was viewed as admirable and for the benefit of all. So the initial industrial-age business model had, and still has, the maximization of profits for the benefit of the owners/stockholders as the number one priority of the company.

Moving ahead to today's business environment, almost all medium to large companies are now publicly held companies with a board of directors, stockholders and a team of professional, senior-level managers hired to run the business. The role of the board of directors is to select the CEO, to oversee the actions of senior management, and to do so in the best interest of the stockholders. Most stockholders however, are interested primarily in one thing. That one thing is the stock price, and to ensure that the stock price goes up as much and as quickly as possible. After all, that is how they make money on their investment. The stock price, however, is tied to the profits of the company. Therefore, the number one objective and focus of the stockholders, the board of directors and the senior-level managers is on the quarterly profits. The senior-level managers have two reasons for being so focused on the quarterly and annual profits. First, they were hired and put in their jobs for the sole

---

purpose of generating profits for the stockholders. But secondly, and more importantly, the largest part of their compensation is tied to the appreciation of the stock in the form of stock options granted to them by the board of directors in their compensation contract. Therefore, the senior-level managers in the publicly held companies are also MAJOR STOCKHOLDERS! It is not uncommon for the CEO of a publicly held company to be the owner of hundreds of thousands or even millions of shares of the companies that employ them. Since they own or have options on so many shares, every dollar increase in the price of the company's stock is worth a lot of money to them. Therefore, it would only be natural for them to be focused on the stock price. Further, simple logic would lead most people to come to the conclusion that if you want to maximize profits, then profits should be the number one objective. The data shows that "some 60 percent of executive pay is now tied to stock options, up from just 2 percent in 1980."[129] With so much of their compensation tied to the price of the stock, it is not surprising that so many CEOs place so much focus and emphasis on achieving the quarterly profit objectives.

Question Number 2. Why do most of these companies have Level-4 or Level-4-like CEOs?

The primary reason that these companies have level-4 CEOs is that the Industrial Age model creates a business environment with requirements that match the characteristics and personalities of level-4 executives. The company culture is a derivative of the purpose of the company, so when the purpose of the company is to maximize profits, then the company culture reflects that. The pursuit of profit in and of itself has no particular redeeming value associated with it. It does not stir any particular human emotion except one: greed. Therefore, when a company's purpose is to maximize profit, then the company culture that grows out of that purpose is one where there are no stated company values; it is every person for him/herself.

The drive by management to reduce expenses in every area possible in order to maximize profits then leads to an antagonistic relationship with all of the various constituencies of the company. The company will have an adversarial relationship with its suppliers, employees and unions if they have them. Also, one characteristic of profit is that it is by nature short-term. It is not possible to measure profit or to make profit in the future. Profits can only be achieved by completing a sales transaction today. Not tomorrow, but today. Therefore, profit can only be measured and evaluated as one aspect of PAST performance. Because of this, companies which have the maximization of profits as their number one objective will be internally focused on the numbers in the short-term. It is just the nature of profits and the culture that is derived from the pursuit of it. So, to deal with these antagonistic and adversarial relationships and the short-term focus of the profit objectives, the board of directors will look for a hard-driving, fear-instilling, self-serving, "make the numbers happen" type of CEO.

The current paradigm among boards of directors today is that it takes a strong, hard-driving, aggressive management team to whip the company into shape and to make sure that the company achieves its financial objectives for the benefit of the stockholders. This paradigm fits very well with the seven characteristics of the Level-4 Effective Leader.

Question Number 3. What is a Level-4 Effective Leader?

There are seven characteristics that define an executive as a Level-4 Effective Leader. Those seven characteristics are as follow:

1. Thinks in the short-term;
2. Is hard-driving and instills fear in the organization;
3. Is often very egocentric;
4. Is excessive about self-enrichment;
5. Takes all the credit for success and blames others for failures;
6. Is not concerned about successors; and
7. Has ambition for (only) him/herself.

1. Level-4 Effective Leaders think in the short-term.

The typical industrial-age thinking executive believes very strongly that the maximization of profit is the correct and proper number-one priority of the company they work for. In addition, the board of directors has made it very clear to the CEO that the primary reason they have been selected for the job is that the board has every confidence that the CEO will meet or exceed the quarterly and annual financial objectives of the company. As an incentive for the CEO to make the financial objectives, the board may put financial targets in the CEOs employment contract and give the CEO additional stock options for each time that the quarterly and annual targets are met. Further, the CEO understands that if the quarterly and annual financial targets are *not* met, that the board will see it as their responsibility to then find a new person to be the CEO. With these pressures put on the CEO by the board of directors, it is easy to understand why the CEO would be very focused on tracking and reporting the financial numbers on a regular and short-term basis. Then, based on the revenue performance of the company, the CEO can manage the expense side to ensure that the quarterly profit objectives are met. To accomplish this, the CEO may decide to defer optional expenses such as the purchase of new equipment or software, or the investment in other parts of the business, such as employee education.

The key point is that the Level-4 Effective Leader will primarily make all decisions based on the impact that the decision will have on the quarterly earnings. So, if the decision has a short-term negative affect on the employees, customers or some business partner, then that is just the way it has to be. The profit that affects the CEO's bonus and job security comes first. "A study by the National Bureau of Economic Research found that most managers would not make an investment that offered an attractive return if it meant that they would miss their quarterly earnings target. Shockingly perhaps, more than 80 percent of executives would cut marketing and R&D expenditures for the same reason, even if they truly believed that doing so would hurt the company in the long run."[130] It is clear from the above data, that the priority that management of American business today has placed on short-term profits is having a negative effect on the long-range health of the businesses that they manage. This is evidenced by the fact that out of the companies that made the Fortune 500 in 1955, only 71 of them were still on the list in 1995.[131] Over time, decision after decision for short-term gain at the expense of long-term survival will usually lead to short-term mediocrity and long-term failure!

2. Level 4 Effective Leaders are hard-driving and instill fear into the organization.

Level-4 Effective Leaders as a group utilize a two-step approach to achieving the objectives that they have set out for the company. Step one is to pass down to the managers and the employees below them a set of objectives that will ensure that the CEO's objectives are achieved at a minimum. After the objectives have been passed out, the CEO will then make it clear to everyone that the expectation is that all of the objectives will be achieved, and if not, then the CEO will utilize several techniques to manipulate the managers and employees to achieve the objectives. The techniques may include positive incentives, negative incentives or a combination of both. These incentives can have a wide range of forms, but some common types of incentives are sales promotions, additional sales bonuses tied to specific levels of achievement, loss of bonuses, lower performance evaluations, and contests. If the first incentives are not successful, then more aggressive incentives can be used such as reductions in pay or threats of layoffs. In the end however, fear is and always has been the primary tool used by upper management to coerce the employees into achieving the objectives as set out by senior management. It is fear that provides the power behind the incentive tools that are used by the Level-4 Effective Leaders.

Some CEOs can be so aggressive and forceful, that the employees refer to them as tyrants. As an example, Stanley Gault was the CEO of Rubbermaid, and when he was accused of being a tyrant he responded by saying, "Yes, but I'm a sincere tyrant."[132] When the CEO is a tyrant, such as the case of Mr. Gault, the middle managers and employees become so focused on what the CEO might think and do, that they lose sight of the real world outside of the company. In this situation, the environment inside the company becomes reality for them and the real world outside of the company becomes only a secondary consideration. They become more concerned about what the CEO might do to them than what their customers will do to them.

The fear that a tyrannical CEO instills into a company causes many negative things to happen. The company becomes very rigid and goes by the book because everyone is afraid to make any decisions. There is so much fear in the organization that it becomes paralyzed. As the level of fear goes up, the level of trust goes down, and then everything within the company slows down. When this happens, productivity, customer satisfaction, employee satisfaction and financial performance all go down in the long run. The focus is internal on the company and its politics rather on the customers and their needs. This is not a healthy situation and leads to mediocre performance as evidenced by the performance of the comparison companies shown in chapter 3.

3. Level-4 Effective Leaders are often very egocentric

In the minds of the Level-4 Effective Leaders, the world revolves around them. They believe that the success of the organizations that they manage is a direct result of their leadership and the outstanding decisions that they make. Because they believe that the profits of the company can be attributed to their leadership, they feel entitled to compensation that the majority of the public views as excessive. Many of these CEOs receive as much compensation in one working day as many employees receive in one year! In 1980, the average CEO received 42 times more compensation than the average employee. In 1990, that number increased to 107 times, and in the year 2005, it was 525 times.[133] If the minimum wage and worker pay had increased at the same rate as CEO pay, then in 2001, the minimum wage would have been $21.41 and worker pay would have been $101,156 instead of $25,467.[134] In 2005, the average CEO of a Standard & Poor's company received $13.51 million in total compensation, which was an increase of 16.14% over 2004.[135] A compensation package of $13.51 million per year divided by 260 working days (five days/week times fifty two weeks) results in earnings of $51,961.00 per day or $5,196.00 per hour, assuming a ten-hour day. For an executive to legitimately feel that they have earned and are worth $5,196 per hour would require a rather large ego. However, for most of these executives, the money is just a method of keeping score. It is the way they judge their personal success versus their peers. Therefore, it is not really about the money itself so much as it is about how much money they receive (their score) when compared to their peers. Every true level-4 CEO wants to earn more money (have a higher score) than their peer CEOs. Because of this competition, there is no rational upper limit for CEO compensation because they are all trying to receive more compensation and thus a higher score than their peers. It is a never-ending spiral! The data speaks for itself.

4. Level-4 Effective Leaders are excessive about self-enrichment

The Level-4 Effective Leaders are not shy when it comes to self-enrichment in many forms. In addition to the very large compensation packages that average well over ten million dollars per year for the larger publicly held companies, these executives see fit to give themselves many additional benefits and perks. Free medical coverage, company jets, vacations, extravagant parties, executive-only bathrooms, executive-only dining rooms, a large support staff, reserved parking spaces and of course the obligatory large corner office on the top floor of the building. Then if they should lose their job because of the poor performance of the company, there is the "Golden Parachute" or severance package. For example, Robert Nardelli left Home Depot after only five years with a package estimated to be worth $210 million.[136] That is an average of $42 million per year of service. $42 million divided by 260 working days per year yields an astounding severance benefit of $161,538 per day worked! To be fair, however, this is not all of Mr. Nardelli's doing. It was the board of directors of Home Depot that agreed to the contract that gave Mr. Nardelli the $210-million payout. It is customary, however, for CEOs of companies to sit on the boards of other companies.

So in that case, there are Level-4 CEOs on the boards of directors deciding on the compensation packages for the Level 4 CEOs that they hire. This in turn leads to a conflict of interest because the compensation of any CEO is influenced by what their peer CEOs are making. So CEOs that are sitting on boards of directors that increase their CEOs' compensation, are raising the standard by which their own compensation will be judged.

In addition to issues regarding compensation, twenty-three companies came under government scrutiny for providing false or misleading information to investors and "cooking" the books. These are companies such as Enron, Global Crossing, Tyco, WorldCom and Dynegy. The data for these companies shows that from 1999 to 2001, the compensation of their CEOs averaged $62,211,916 while the average CEO compensation of the other S&P 500 companies was $36,500,000.[137] This data is very revealing and demonstrates that when the purpose of a company is to maximize profits, situations occur where egocentric CEOs can enrich themselves at rates that appear to be unconscionable.

5. Level-4 Effective Leaders take all the credit for success

Perhaps an example is the best way to make this point. This example is a little extreme, but it is a real example. Scott Paper hired a CEO whose name was Al Dunlap. Scott Paper had been bumping along in mediocrity or worse, and the board of directors hired Mr. Dunlap to turn things around and put the company on the road to better performance. Mr. Dunlap was the type of CEO who would "loudly beat his own chest, telling anyone who would listen (and many who would prefer not to) about what he had accomplished. Quoted in *Business Week* about his nineteen months atop Scott Paper, he boasted, 'The Scott story will go down in the annals of American business history as one of the most successful, quickest turnarounds ever, [making] other turnarounds pale by comparison.'"[138] The turnaround that Mr. Dunlap was so proud of was accomplished primarily by actions such as cutting the R&D Budget in half and then reducing the workforce to get the stock price up and to prepare the company for sale. The company was sold and Mr. Dunlap received a great deal of money. According to Business Week, Mr. Dunlap received $100 million for the 603 days he spent at Scott Paper. That translated into $165,000 per day on the job.[139] Mr. Dunlap was so proud of himself and all of his accomplishments, that he even wrote a book about it. This example is from Jim Collins book *Good to Great* and here is what Mr. Collins had to say: "Granted, the Scott Paper story is one of the more dramatic in our study, but it's not an isolated case. In over two thirds of the comparison cases, we noted the presence of a gargantuan personal ego that contributed to the demise or continued mediocrity of the company."[140] The quote from Mr. Collins makes several key points that must be remembered. One, it is not an isolated case for a CEO to have a huge personal ego; it is common. Two, the huge egos of these CEOs contributed to either the continued mediocrity or the demise of the companies they managed. Not only do the Level-4 Effective Leaders take all of the credit for their successes, but they also will blame others for all of the failures. When the company experiences difficulties of any type, the CEO will blame the failures or difficulties on anyone but himself.

6. Level-4 Effective Leaders are not concerned about their successors

Level-4 Effective-Leader CEOs with large egos, as a group, are not particularly concerned with what happens to the company when they leave. In fact, from their viewpoint, if the company does poorly after they leave, that is just more evidence to prove that they were great leaders and that the company's success during their tenure was attributable to them. Therefore, the Level-4 Effective Leaders will often choose a weak successor. One example of this was Stanley Gault at Rubbermaid. During Mr. Gault's tenure at Rubbermaid, the company experienced forty consecutive quarters of earnings growth. By some measures, that would be considered great performance. However, Mr. Gault did not prepare the company to be successful after his departure. "His chosen successor lasted only one year on the job and the next in line faced a management team so shallow that he had to temporarily shoulder four jobs while scrambling to identify a new number-two executive. Gault's successors found themselves struggling not only with a management void, but also with strategic voids that would eventually bring the company to its knees."[141] This case is not as isolated as most people might think. In his research for the book, *Good to Great*, Mr. Collins made the following observation: "In over three-quarters of the comparison companies, we found executives who set their successors up for failure or chose weak successors, or both."[142] There you have it! The research shows that the Level 4 egocentric leaders set up their successors for failure, or chose weak successors or both, over 75 percent of the time! Clearly, this kind of activity by Level-4 leaders is not uncommon.

7. Level-4 Effective Leaders have ambition for themselves

The bottom line for Level-4 Effective Leaders is that they are self-serving and have ambition only for themselves. This is clearly demonstrated by the fact that the feeding of their egos is more important to them than the future of the companies they work for, the customers of those companies or the employees of those companies. The fact that over 75 percent of the executives in Jim Collins' research study either chose a weak successor or set the successor up for failure or both provides indisputable evidence that their egos are more important to them than the companies they lead. Also, the research showed a negative correlation between the larger-than-life, egocentric CEOs and the results that they produced.[143]

So why do so many egocentric, hard-driving, tyrannical, Level-4 executives become CEOs? There are two primary reasons for this to occur. The first reason is that it is a natural outcome of the Industrial-Age Profit-Driven Business Model. Under this business model, the sole purpose of the company is to produce as much profit as possible for the benefit of the stockholders. The pursuit of profit does not have any inherent long term aspects to it, so the focus within this model is on the short term and the numbers. As a result of this short term focus on the profit numbers, it is natural to look for a CEO who has demonstrated an aggressive nature that can "drive" the company forward and thereby "maximize" the profits for the stockholders.

That is just the way the business model is designed. It is designed to focus on results, results, results, quarter-by-quarter-by-quarter. Period. In this environment then, it is natural to expect that a hard-driving, tyrannical individual would be the best choice to produce the desired quarter-by-quarter results. When this business model design is coupled with the fact that the CEO's primary compensation comes from stock options which are tied to the stock price which is tied to earnings, then the Level-4 executive will be very focused on the quarterly results, at the expense of almost everything else. The reason for this is that as the CEO achieves the quarterly objectives, it feeds the CEO's ego. The Level-4 CEOs are also prone to measure their self-worth and status by the amount of money they make. Therefore, as the profits go up, so does their compensation and thus, so does their ego.

The second reason for so many Level-4 executives becoming CEOs is that the boards of directors in business today are operating under the false assumption that they must hire a larger-than-life egocentric leader (usually from the outside) to take the company from just average performance to outstanding performance.[144] It is the old "expert from afar" syndrome. Most boards of directors seem to operate from the assumption that they must bring in an outsider, try something new and different, or somehow stir up the pot to get the profits headed in the preferred direction.

Corporate Culture and CEOs

There is an old business saying, "Management is the carrier of the culture." What this means is that the CEO and a few top executives of the company will determine what the culture of the company will be. The culture is a reflection of themselves, and there is a lot of truth to that statement. However, the statement is not quite correct, and here is the reason. It is the company purpose that determines what the company culture will be like, AND the type of CEO that the company will hire. If the company purpose is to maximize profits, then that will result in a Level-4 Effective Leader as the CEO and one type of company culture. If however, the company purpose is the pursuit of something beyond profit, then that will almost always result in a Level-5 Executive (Level 5 Executives will be described later) as the CEO and a quite different company culture. The sequence of events is this. The company purpose will determine the type of CEO that the company will hire. Then the combination of the CEO's characteristics and the company purpose will determine the type of company culture the will be formed. Therefore, the fact is that the company purpose determines BOTH the type of CEO that the company will hire and the type of company culture that the company will have.

In the case of the Industrial-Age Profit-Driven Business Model, where the company purpose is to maximize profit, the company's board of directors will seek out and hire a Level-4 Effective Leader. When that occurs, the company culture will be a reflection of the company purpose and the characteristics of the CEO. The pursuit of profit as a company purpose has no inherent values or long-term aspect associated with it. Therefore, the culture that is derived from it is typically short–term focused and not associated with any particular company values other than greed. Then when the Level 4 Effective Executive is hired, the characteristics of the CEO are added to the inherent short-term and valueless nature of the purpose, which is the pursuit of profit. When the company culture is created from these sources of input, then the company culture will have the following characteristics:

1. Executives feel superior to the employees
2. High levels of fear
3. Very little teamwork
4. Poor human resources practices
5. Antagonistic relationship with constituencies
6. Low employee morale
7. High turnover rates
8. Low levels of trust and productivity
9. Little risk taking, innovation, adaptability or responsiveness
10. Internally focused and self-serving

The culture will be morally impoverished, self-serving and internally focused. This can many times lead to low levels of customer satisfaction and ethical lapses. In this environment, the company expects loyalty, but does not give it. The company expects the employees to work hard to increase profits, but does not share those profits with the employees. The company attempts to minimize the wages paid to the employees because that is perceived to add to the amount of profits. The same goes for such things as health benefits for the employees.

Sometimes, the top executive is the owner, or the CEO of a publicly held company who comes to view himself/herself as an owner. The CEO owns a lot of stock, has options on much more stock, so he/she is an "owner." When the top executive either is the owner or views himself/herself as the owner, then they may feel that they have "special privileges." They can do whatever they want. They can go where and when they want, say what they want and act as they want. After all, they are the owner and everyone else (in their view) are just hired hands and not on their same level. When this occurs, and the top executives feel and act as if they can do pretty much as they please. One CEO refers to this behavior as "playing the owner card." "People become very passive when the owner card is played. They may be angry, but they don't fight back. Instead they clam up. They shut down. They just obey. You don't get any creativity and engagement from them. They do what they're told to do and nothing more."[145]

The above characteristics and top executives who play the owner card create a company work environment that is not very attractive to the employees. The employees in these companies work there because they have to have a job. They are not there because they want to be there; they are there because they feel they have no other choice. The employees working in this type of company culture are rendered ineffective because of the high levels of fear within the organization and the facts that there is a low level of trust and they are not allowed to make any meaningful decisions. Jack Stack, the CEO of one of the most productive companies in the world, refers to these employees as "the living dead." The innovation, creativity, and drive that the employees could provide to the company are stifled by the management and the resulting company culture.

Chapter 6
The Industrial Age Business Model – Management System

Part Two of the Industrial-Age Profit-Driven Business Model is the management system. That system is commonly known as the Bureaucratic Management System (BMS). In order to understand why the BMS was implemented the way it was and why it has become ineffective and obsolete, it is important to have a more detailed understanding of four key elements of the business environment during the time of its development. It is also important to understand how these four elements have changed over time. Those four key elements are:

1. Who holds the marketplace power base?
2. Who holds the knowledge power base?
3. What is the level of work complexity?
4. What is the rate of change?

Tracking these four key elements over time will help explain why the Industrial-Age Profit-Driven Business Model was an efficient management model in its first seventy years of existence. It will also help explain why and how it has become an obsolete and inefficient business model in today's business environment.

Beginning in 1850, the BMS was implemented in the U.S. and, for all practical purposes, reached its final form in the 1920s. There has been little change or improvement since that time. The BMS worked well during this period because the business environment had these four key business characteristics.

1. Marketplace Power Base

In 1850, the producer had nearly 100% of the marketplace power. That was true because consumers were limited to the buying options available to them within their travel space. The consumer of the time was traveling primarily by foot or horse, so the buying opportunities were limited to a small geographical space, which was most often the local general merchandise store. The majority of the population at that time lived in a rural setting. "In 1790 only 202,000 out of the 3,930,000 Americans lived in towns or villages of more then 2,500, and of the 2,881,000 workers, 2,069,000 labored on farms."[146] Because of these demographics, the consumer had almost zero marketplace choice. The consumer had to purchase the items available at the local store or do without because there just were not any other feasible alternatives.

Department stores had their beginnings in the larger cities in the 1860s and 1870s.[147] While this gave the city dwellers a little more choice, it did not do much for the majority of the population because they were still living on the family farm. It was not until later when the new transportation and communication infrastructure was in place and the mail-order house came into being that the consumer had much choice. The first large mail-order house was Montgomery Ward, which was formed in 1872. By the 1880s, Montgomery Ward was doing a nationwide business, and in 1887, its catalogue of 540 pages listed over 24,000 items.[148] Montgomery Ward specialized in items for the farm community and had almost no competition until Sears Roebuck & Company began selling watches by mail in 1887. Sears soon expanded and by 1899, had twenty-four departments of items. Sales went from $138,000 in 1891 to $2,868,000 in 1905.[149] With the exception of the mail-order houses, the consumer still had to physically go to the establishment of the supplier in order to make a purchase. Therefore, the consumer was beginning to have some choice and marketplace power, but their marketplace power was still almost nonexistent.

2. Knowledge Power Base

Within the business environment, it was the owners and managers who were the educated ones, and they held the knowledge power base. By far, the majority of the labor had only some elementary level of education, if any. As late as 1903, only 6% of the labor force could read. So it was management that knew how to run the business, knew how to do the work that was required, and knew how to organize the enterprise. The managers, therefore, held the knowledge power base. The majority of the employees were hired for their physical capabilities and nothing more. The management in the industrial age then came to view these employees that were hired for manual labor as "things." These "things" could be hired and let go at will with little regard for the individual. This mindset then led to poor labor relations in the larger companies and the eventual union movement.

3. Simplicity of Work

The work requirements for the jobs in the 1800s were simple, and most required no formal education at all. This simplicity allowed the jobs to be filled with uneducated and unskilled workers. It was not until 1895 that Fredrick W. Taylor delivered his first paper on what soon would be termed "scientific management."[150] Taylor's work began with time and motion studies that resulted in the manufacturing processes being broken down into small steps. Each step was simple in nature and could be performed by unskilled labor. With this manufacturing structure, a manager could, in a short amount of time, explain to the new employee what was required to do the work and show them how to do it, if necessary. This structure worked quite well in the growing manufacturing industry. During this time, most work was accomplished with hand tools. In all cases, however, the work remained relatively simple and required almost no knowledge or formal education on the part of the worker.

4. Rate of Change

In 1850, the rate of change was still relatively slow but was beginning to speed up. In the years prior to 1850, there had been almost no change in the business environment for thousands of years. The arrival of the industrial age began an increase in the rate of change, which has continually increased to this day. Driven by new technologies such as the railroad, telegraph, steam power, and new industrial steam-powered machines, the industrial output of the country was rising dramatically. New communication and transportation infrastructures were being developed in some parts of the country, but most of the population could not reach them. Thus, for the few who lived in the larger cities and the more densely populated Northeast, there was significant change, but for many, they were still without all the "new conveniences." For example, in 1903 only 14% of homes had a bathtub and only 8% had a telephone. Most women only washed their hair once a month and used borax or egg yolks for shampoo. Drugs as we know them today were nonexistent. Marijuana, heroin, and morphine were all available over the counter at the local drug stores. According to one pharmacist, "Heroin clears the complexion, gives buoyancy to the mind, regulates the stomach and the bowels, and is, in fact, a perfect guardian of health."

Thus, for the period from 1850 to 1920, the four key business elements had these characteristics:

1. **Marketplace power base—held by the producer**
2. **Knowledge power base—held by management**
3. **Work—simple, little knowledge required**
4. **Rate of change—slow**

The next period of time that we need to examine is the period from 1920 to 1950. During this period, the market and knowledge power bases began their shifts and the rate of change continued to speed up.

1. Marketplace Power Base

From the 1920s to the 1950s, the automobile, truck, and road infrastructure gave the population and business a great boost in the ability to conduct business and to travel. A greater percentage of the population now lived in cities. With the expansion of department stores, mail-order houses, the increased speed of transportation, and the telephone, the consumers were gaining power in the marketplace.

Their choices were increasing compared to their 1800s counterparts. However, their choices were still limited. For example, when buying a new car in the 1950s, most buyers had only three choices. They could buy a car from Ford, General Motors, or Chrysler. In the larger cities, there were other choices such as Studebaker or Packard, but not many. Products from outside the country were still few in number and expensive due to transportation costs and import duties. While the choices for consumers were still limited, they were increasing all the time. The consumer was gaining power due to the increase in choices available to them, but the producer was still in control and had the marketplace power.

2. Knowledge Power Base

The labor force was becoming more educated. During this period, over half of the labor force had graduated from high school. World War II had concluded, and the GI Bill was financing a college education for thousands of GIs. Managers still had the knowledge to do the work of the employees under their direct supervision. While the knowledge power base still resided with management, the knowledge gap between management and labor had narrowed substantially.

3. Work

As industry continued its development, businesses became more sophisticated and began to create a much greater number of jobs that required a high school education in order to be considered for employment. Much more advanced industrial equipment and production processes required math and reading skills. Jobs requiring a college education in fields such as accounting, finance, engineering, etc. were being created in much greater numbers. The complexity of the work was increasing, and the knowledge required of the worker was much greater.

4. Rate of Change

In 1903, there were 8,000 cars and only 144 miles of paved roads. The speed limit in most cities was 10 miles per hour. More than 95% of births took place at home. Ninety percent of all U.S. physicians had no college education. Only 6% of adults had graduated from high school. By 1950, paved roads spanned the United States north to south and east to west and the speed of travel increased over six times. The average household had a car. More new technologies were invented. The propeller-powered airplane became common, and then the jet engine was invented. The black-and-white television and the first electronic computer were produced. Many households now had their first refrigerator, washing machine, and telephone. Graduation from high school became the norm in education. The rate of change continued to increase with no signs of slowing down.

Therefore, during the period from 1920 to 1950, the four key business elements had these characteristics:

1. **The marketplace power base was still held by producers, but it was weakening.**
2. **The knowledge power base was still held by management but was weakening.**
3. **Work was now more complex and required higher education levels.**
4. **The rate of change continued to speed up.**

For the period from 1950 to today, the shift that started in the 1920-to-1950 time period continued and is now complete. Today, the four key business elements have these characteristics:

1. **The marketplace power is now held by the customer because they have choice.**
2. **The knowledge power base is held by the employees because there is so much information to be absorbed that management can no longer keep up.**
3. **Work is now complex because of the high knowledge content.**

4. The rate of change is fast because of the information-age impact.

This represents a 180-degree shift between the business environment of the industrial age and the business environment of the information age that we have today.

The Industrial-Age Paradigm

Another characteristic that is key to understanding the industrial-age business model is the industrial-age mechanistic paradigm. The period from the 1800s up to the early 1900s was the time in which this paradigm evolved into the mass psyche of the American population. Within this paradigm, everything was viewed and treated as if it were a machine. One element of this industrial-age paradigm that is particularly important is the one-way system view of the production and delivery process within business. The managers involved in manufacturing, as an example, viewed the process in the following form:

Design it. Make it. Sell it.[151]

For those companies in the service sector, it was viewed as follows:

Design it. Sell it. Deliver it.

What is significant about this one-way view was that there was no feedback from the consumer. That small detail is not a problem as long as the producer has the marketplace power.

A second important element of the industrial-age paradigm is that *almost everything was viewed from the mental image of a machine.* For example, James Champy, in his book *Reengineering Management*, speaking of Henry Ford of Ford Motor Company said, "There's not much question what word Ford would have chosen to describe his 'great business.' He would have called it a *machine*."[152] Henry Ford's competitor, Alfred P. Sloan of General Motors, "thought of a great business in terms of the machine metaphor."[153] When the machine metaphor is used for companies, then the company is viewed as operating independently of the community or the environment in which it operates. Therefore, the management teams that still have the industrial-age mechanistic paradigm will not feel that the company has any particular responsibilities to the community, environment, or any other constituency that may be affected by its operations. Their view is that the company is responsible only to the owners or stockholders.

The organizational structure of the first companies was heavily influenced by the military, the Catholic Church, and the industrial-age mechanistic paradigm. The result was a rigid hierarchy structure that when drawn graphically resembled a pyramid. Still today, if one hundred people were asked to draw a sketch of the organizational structure of the business they work for, no doubt the drawing would look like a pyramid when completed. The pyramid is the current paradigm for what an organizational structure would look like. See Figure 6.1.

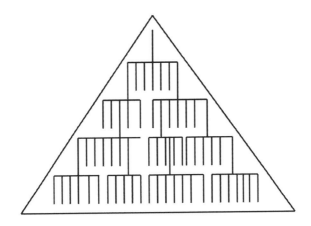

Fig. 6.1. The BMS Organizational Structure.

The railroads were the first to implement the formal organizational pyramid structure in the U.S. The pyramid structure was created as a result of a series of railroad accidents, and it was this structure that became the blueprint for all organizations that followed. In 1841, the Western Railroad experienced a series of accidents that culminated in a head-on collision of passenger trains on October 5, 1841, killing a conductor and a passenger and injuring seventeen others. The particular line involved had been constructed by three separate teams of Western employees, and after construction was completed, each team continued to operate their section of the line. A lack of overall coordination of the entire line, which was 150 miles long, contributed to the accident.[154] As a result of the accident, the Massachusetts legislature launched an intensive investigation into the operation of the railroad. A committee was formed to find a solution to the ongoing problem of railroad accidents and, in particular, the ones at Western. The solution as described in the committee's report titled "Report on Avoiding Collisions and Governing the Employees" was to fix "definite responsibilities for each phase of the company's business, drawing lines of authority and communication for the railroad's administration, maintenance, and operation."[155] From these recommendations, the Western Railroad created a new organizational structure. The new organizational structure "called for a comparable set of functional managers on each of the three geographically contiguous operating divisions and then the creation of a headquarters to monitor and coordinate the activities of the three sets of managers. Each division had its assistant master of transportation (later called division superintendent), its road-master, and its senior mechanic or foreman in charge of roundhouses and shops."[156] Thus was formed the "first modern, documented, and defined internal organizational structure used by an American business enterprise."[157] This internal organizational structure was the beginning of the Bureaucratic Management System in the U.S.

The BMS with its rigid hierarchy structure, functional organization, and distinct lines of authority was now formally documented. The manager's industrial-age mechanistic paradigm and the rigid hierarchy structure of the new BMS were in alignment. This alignment made the industrial-age managers quite satisfied. These managers were very comfortable in a rigid command-and-control business model with clearly defined lines of power and authority because it fit their industrial-age mechanistic paradigm.

The managers operating with the industrial age paradigm view things as if they are a machine. The rules of this paradigm say that when a part of the "machine" is malfunctioning, the malfunctioning part must be replaced. This paradigm is still alive and well today. When management determines that part or all of the organization is not producing the desired results, what is the solution to the problem? Many times the solution is to "replace the bad part," and this is accomplished by *REORGANIZING!* By reorganizing, management thinks they have removed the "bad part" and replaced it with a new "good or better part." The problem is that in most cases, the organizational structure was not the cause of the problem that management was trying to fix. As a result, the problem does not go away and reappears again somewhere else and possibly in a new form. Attempting to solve problems by reorganizing is not only an industrial-age phenomenon, as evidenced by the following quote:

"We trained hard, but it seemed that every time we were beginning to form up into teams, we would be reorganized.

"I was to learn later in life, we tend to meet any new situation by reorganizing, and a wonderful method it can be for creating the illusion of progress while producing confusion, inefficiency and demoralization." – Found on a scroll written in AD 66 by Petronius Arbiter.

After the reorganization, if things have not improved, the conclusion of management would probably be that the first reorganization was an improvement, but that it was not done quite right. Then, after a period of time and study, another reorganization would be announced. The use of reorganization after reorganization in an attempt to solve problems is really a subconscious response to the industrial-age mechanistic paradigm that is still prevalent today.

This industrial-age mechanistic paradigm also applies to boards of directors and helps explain their tendency to bring in a new CEO from the outside when things are not going as well as expected. Replace the bad part (CEO) with a new and better part (the new CEO from the outside).

The dynamics of what happens within the BMS organizational pyramid also provides greater insight into the inner workings of the BMS system and how it operates. The organizational pyramid is the perfect structure with which the rigid command-and-control philosophy of the BMS could be implemented. The backbone, the essence of the BMS, is to first issue the COMMAND (Level 4's love to command), then after the command is given, to enforce the command with tight CONTROL. Level-4 executives also love to control everything. The top management of large business enterprises of the 1850s had good reason to implement a rigid command-and-control system—they were also the owners! It was their personal fortunes that were at risk in the businesses they were managing. Prior to the railroads, only a few of the largest textile mills or iron-making and metal-working factories were capitalized at over one million dollars. In contrast, the east-west railroad trunk lines—the Erie, the Pennsylvania, the Baltimore and Ohio, and the New York Central railroads—each cost from $10 to $17 million.[158] The developers of the railroads financed their businesses primarily through the issuance of bonds that were then sold in the financial centers of Boston, New York, and Europe.[159] For these managers, the success or failure of the business was also their personal success or failure, and that determined if they would add to their personal fortunes or lose it all. With so much at risk, they installed manual record-keeping systems that allowed them to keep close track of the operations on a daily basis.

For the BMS hierarchy structure to work efficiently, it was necessary to implement a rigid command-and-control system similar to the one used in the military. A key element of this structure was the clear and rigidly defined distribution of power. Therefore, the first dynamic of the pyramid structure to be examined is the distribution of power. Power within the organization is distributed based on the level within the organization. The top level has the most power, and as the levels drop, so does the power of the person at that level. Also, the power of a person at each level is conferred on them as soon as they assume the position, just like in the military. Power is not something that the person earns or something that is granted to them by the people that person works with. The power is dictated by their position in the hierarchy. This power and level within the pyramid is also tied to compensation. The logic is that the higher the level a person has, the more power they have and, therefore, the more pay they should receive. Thus, not only is power determined by a person's position within the pyramid, but also the level of compensation is determined by this position. It is this structure that causes employees to compete so vigorously to move up within the organizational pyramid. Some managers have been known to sabotage the careers of their peers in order to get promoted. This environment is not conducive to teamwork or trust.

A second key dynamic of the pyramid to be examined is the setting of objectives within the organization. Once a year, the top management will pass down to the level below them a set of objectives to be achieved in the coming year. As the objectives are passed from level to level, a number of things happen. The first is that the managers at each level will begin to **negotiate a safe objective, one that they know they can achieve.** Once they have negotiated a safe objective, they will then add a few percentage points to the objective (for insurance) before passing it to the employees below them in the pyramid. Then the managers **will do everything possible to exceed the goal, but just barely.** They exceed the goal by a small margin for two reasons. First, when the objective is exceeded by a small amount, the manager uses that as proof that the objective was set correctly and that it was only hard work by the manager and their employees that allowed the objective to be exceeded. Secondly, the manager knows that if the objective is exceeded by a large amount, the objective will be raised in the coming year. If the objective is raised by a large amount, especially if it should happen several years in a row, the objective would eventually be set so high that the manager could not reach it. That would not be good for either the manager or the manager's employees. So, **the plan is clear. Negotiate a safe goal and then exceed it, but just barely.** Under this system, the more forceful and hard-driving the Level-4 executive is, the more conservative the objectives will be, and thus the lower the performance of the company will be.

Another thing that happens in the goal-setting process is that the information is transformed. At the top of the organization the objectives are stated in financial terms, or dollars. But by the time the objectives reach the employees, the objectives have been translated into things to be accomplished, number of new accounts sold, products manufactured, etc.[160] Since the top management talks in terms of "dollars" but the employees talk in terms of "things",, they have difficulty communicating.[161] In the process of passing the information down through the levels of the organization and the transforming of the "dollars" format to the "things" format, a lot of breakage occurs.   As a result, the goals and direction of the employees at the bottom has very little in common with the goals and direction of senior management at the top. See Figure 6.2.

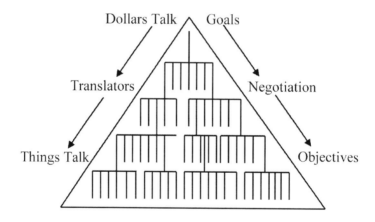

Fig. 6.2. Goal Translation

It is the breakdown in the communications between the top of the organization and the lower portion of the organization that leads to the rumor mills and talk around the water cooler. This is very counterproductive and expensive for the company. As one CEO commented, "Rumor mills cost money, lots of money. They are the most expensive form of corporate communications around. They breed fear, mistrust, divisiveness, unrealistic expectations, and ignorance. They take all the problems a company has and make them worse. For that, you pay through the nose."[162] Today, there is little symmetry between the directions at the department level of companies and the direction set by top management. Ideally, everyone in the organization would be going in the same direction. Ideally, all employees and all management would know what the company as a whole was trying to achieve and why, but because of the communications disconnect, they do not. The magnitude of this disconnect was clearly documented by the Harris Interactive data from Chapter One, which showed that only one in five employees had a clear "line of sight" between their tasks and the goals of the organization. With the employees and departments not acting in concert with the top of the company or each other, costs go up, and there is a huge negative impact upon the productivity of the overall organization. The result is that the employees and their immediate managers do not know what the company is trying to achieve and why. It is this disconnect that is the cause of a large amount of counterproductive activity at the departmental level in almost every business today.

The third key dynamic of the model to be examined deals with the "control" in the command-and-control philosophy of the BMS. The control is enforced by the collection of information on the performance of the organization on a scheduled basis. The information that is used for control purposes is collected first at the lowest levels of the organization and then passed from level to level until it reaches the top. Several things happen to this information as it flows from the lowest levels of the organization to the highest levels within the organization. The first thing that happens is that the information gets translated from the low-level "things" format into the high-level "dollars" format. A second and more important thing that happens is that if there is any bad news at the lowest level, the degree of badness will be lowered some degree for each level of management that the information passes through. Each level of management wants to look as good as possible, so each level will reduce the content of bad news before passing the information up to the next higher level. For example, the employees working on a project know that the project is three months behind schedule and have told their manager(s). As this information passes through each level of management, each level then claims that the lower level was too cautious, not aggressive enough, and with some extra effort, things will improve. That level then lessens the degree by which the project is behind schedule. By the time the information reaches the top management, the message that is delivered to top management is that "The project is on schedule and may even be completed ahead of schedule!"

It is only the bad news that is reduced or eliminated during the flow from the bottom of the pyramid to the top of the pyramid. Good news will flow to the top with no reduction at all and sometimes may be enhanced as it makes its way to the top. This phenomenon has been the subject of research by a number of researchers. Although the specific results of each research project were different to some degree, their conclusions were the same. The factual information (if it is negative) becomes distorted or eliminated as the information passes through each level of the hierarchy on its way to the top of the organization. See Figure 6.3.

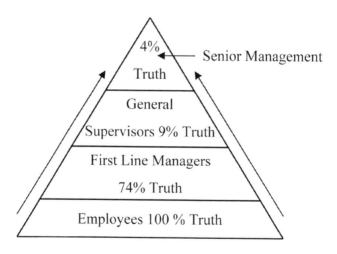

Fig. 6.3. Pyramid of Truth. Adapted from "Quality Improvement and TQC Management at Calsonic in Japan and Overseas" by Sydney Yoshida

The pyramid of truth makes clear the degree to which the bad news at the bottom is transformed into good news by the time it reaches the top of the organization. At the bottom, where the work is done, the workers know the truth. They know, for example, if the new product works as expected or if the project is on time or not, etc. However, as the data shows, they hide 26% of the bad news from their immediate manager. Then, as the information passes through more levels of management to the general or divisional manager, an additional 65% of the bad news is transformed or deleted. By the time the information reaches the top of the organization, only about 4% of the bad news (or truth) remains in the information. The other 96% of the truth has been removed. The employees have long wondered why the top management keeps making those dumb, stupid decisions. This happens not because the top management is dumb or stupid; it happens because they just do not know what the truth is. This low level of truth in the organization then leads to a low level of trust.

When a company is operating in a low-trust environment, the low level of trust will manifest itself in the form of office politics, hidden agendas, a lot of interpersonal conflict, interdepartmental battles and defensive/protective (CYA) communications. The level of trust in business today is lower than most people think. "A 2005 Harris poll revealed that only 22% of those surveyed tend to trust the media, only 8% trust political parties, only 27% trust the government, and only 12% trust big companies."[163] Research also shows that only 51% of employees have trust and confidence in senior management and only 36% of employees believe their leaders act with honesty and integrity. Further, over the past 12 months, 76% of the employees have observed illegal or unethical conduct on the job—conduct which, if exposed, would seriously violate the public trust.[164] "According to a 2005 Mercer Management Consulting study, only 40 percent of employees trust that their bosses communicate honestly."[165] Stephen M. R. Covey has written an entire book (*The Speed of Trust*) on just the topic of trust in business and its impact on business. He makes the observation that as trust goes down, the speed at which things happen will also go down, and then cost will go up.[166]

When the employees do not trust the management, and the management then in turn does not trust the employees, the lack of trust will manifest itself in a number of ways. Management will create a rigid hierarchy structure with multiple layers of management to oversee and control the employees. Rigid, cumbersome processes that require numerous management signatures will be created. This will result in the slowing down of all activities within the organization, decreasing productivity and driving up cost. Creativity, innovation, responsiveness, morale and customer satisfaction will also suffer. The typical bureaucratic malaise will be evident to everyone.

A real question that must be asked at this point is: Why do the employees and middle managers not tell the full and honest truth (leading to a low level of organizational trust) when there is bad news to be told? The answer lies in another industrial-age paradigm that is a part of the American mass psyche. Here is a question: **If 1,000 mistakes are made, how many of those 1,000 mistakes are made by people?**

History shows that the answer given by most people is 1,000. The commonly accepted paradigm is that people make all the mistakes, and therefore, if 1,000 mistakes were made, then people made all 1,000 of them. But is it really true that people made all 1,000 of the "mistakes"?

First, so there will be no misunderstanding, we must define what a mistake is. For the purposes of this example, a mistake will be defined as a decision made by a person that later is determined to be an incorrect decision based on the information available to the person at the time of the decision. This is to say that if a person makes a decision that is later determined to be a mistake, and that decision was based on faulty information, then the "mistake" should be blamed on the faulty information and not the person.

Performing a task, any task, regardless of whether it is simple or complex, involves a series of decisions. If the decisions made during the performance of the task are made correctly, then the result should be correct. If any of the decisions are made incorrectly, then the end result should be incorrect, or a "mistake."

The Israel Military Industries conducted a study to examine the cases where a non-conformance to specification (a mistake) was identified. The purpose of the study was to determine if the non-conformance should be attributed to the employee or if it was due to some other cause. In the study, over 900,000 "mistakes" were audited over a twenty-seven-month period. Out of the 900,000 mistakes studied, there were only 205 cases where the "mistakes" were determined to be the result of employee error. **That meant that the workers were not the source of the mistake 99.99978 percent of the time.**[167] This means that in 899,795 cases out of 900,000, the non-conformance to specification (the mistake) was caused by something other than employee error. Stated another way, the study showed that in the cases where a "mistake" was identified, the mistake was caused by something other than employee error 99.99978 percent of the time. And those were only the situations where a mistake was identified. That does not account for all the instances where no mistakes were found. When all events are counted, the employees are performing correctly at a rate far greater than 99.99978 percent of the time.

How could it be that so many mistakes are being blamed on the employees if they are not the cause of them? To understand this apparent confusion, some examples will be helpful. Suppose that we are in the widget-manufacturing business. The engineering department designs the blueprints for the widgets. The manufacturing production department then takes the blueprints and creates work instructions for the employees on the manufacturing floor to follow. In the manufacture of part number 184453, the work instruction says to cut the raw material to a length of 6.125 inches. So, a work order comes through the plant floor with the raw material, and the employee cuts the parts to a length of 6.125 inches long per the work instructions. Later, in the manufacturing process, when the widget is to be assembled, the inspector determines that the parts should be 6.375 inches long, not 6.125 inches long, and the parts are declared defective (a mistake). With some research, it is discovered that there was an engineering change that occurred after the first set of work instructions was created. The engineering change process within the manufacturing system failed to update the work instructions in a timely fashion. The time delay in updating the work instructions caused the non-conformance (the mistake) to happen. The non-conformance (mistake) was caused by a poorly designed engineering change process. The engineering change process was not exactly defective; it worked most of the time, but it could work better. Another way to say it is that there was a defect rate designed into the engineering change process. The employee did everything correctly, and yet the parts were defective.

But what happens at Widgets, Inc.? The manager informs the employee that the parts on work order 899456 for part number 184453 were cut .25 inches too short, and the employee is blamed for the error. The employee is also told that if this continues, the employee will be given three days off work without pay. The employee no longer has the work instructions to review and has no way of knowing what the real cause of the non-conformance to specification (the mistake) was. The employee just assumes that the manager knows the facts and therefore assumes that the manager is correct. The manager also assumes that the inspector that declared the parts defective was correct. Further, there is no real reason to expect that anything is askew here. After all, the paradigm says that if a mistake is made, it is made by people. With this industrial-age paradigm, no effort is made to find the real source or root cause of the problem. Everyone is too busy focusing on achieving their quotas (objectives) to worry about finding a root cause. To find a root cause of the problem would require some time and effort.

Here is another question. How many times have you left your place of residence and when returning to your place of residence, found yourself at the wrong place? The answer is probably never. Your decision-making while performing the task of returning to your place of residence has been perfect! The Israel Military Industries found that when "mistakes" did occur, the "mistakes" were caused by inaccurate, unclear, incomplete information given to the workers for them to use in the completion of their work tasks. The mistakes were not a result of defective decision-making by the workers. The source of the mistake was somewhere upstream in the system or process. The mistakes could have been caused by poor designs, worn gauges, incomplete work instructions, defective maintenance of equipment, poor training, engineering changes, substandard materials, etc. There is no end to the number of different things that could cause "a mistake" to occur. The study by the Israel Military Industries clearly shows that **most mistakes are caused by the system in which the employee works, not the employee.** The problem is that today, the mistake is blamed on the person present at the point where the mistake occurred. *That person at that point in the system is blamed even though he/she did not cause the problem in over 99% of the cases.*

Here is one more example to illustrate this point. In Houston, Texas, the most dangerous section of freeway with the highest accident rate is a six-mile section of Interstate 45 that runs north from downtown Houston to the 610 loop around Houston. This section of freeway is five lanes wide and is crossed by both loop 610 and Interstate 10. It has many curves. The local cross streets have elevated bridges crossing the freeway. The frontage roads and bridges are approximately twenty feet higher than the freeway, and the on-ramps are short and curvy. In many cases, the drivers entering the freeway cannot see the freeway traffic because of the height of the frontage roads and the bridges crossing the freeway. The drivers must drive down the short, steep on-ramps without knowing what traffic is coming and do the best they can to adjust. It is no wonder there are a lot of accidents on that section of freeway. To compound the situation, this section of freeway is heavily traveled.

But what does the state's Department of Transportation say about the accidents on this section of I-45? "Boy, look at all those dumb drivers having all those accidents on I-45 north in Houston. They must get stupid on I-45 north between downtown and loop 610!" Remember, if 1,000 mistakes are made, then 1,000 mistakes are made by people. If 1,000 accidents happen, then 1,000 accidents were caused by people. That is the current paradigm. The truth is that neither the drivers on the freeway nor the drivers entering the freeway have all the information necessary to make the correct decisions all of the time. They are forced to make the "enter the freeway" decision with the information they have and do the best they can to adjust. Sometimes, however, in spite of the best efforts of the drivers, accidents do happen. Most of those accidents are caused by the design of the freeway, not the poor decision-making of the drivers, **but the drivers are blamed for all of the accidents**. There is no question that people do indeed make mistakes. However, the data shows that they do not make nearly as many mistakes as managers blame them for.

Earlier the question was asked, "Why do the employees and managers not tell the full and honest truth when reporting information to upper management?" The reason is that if there is any bad news (mistakes), they will be blamed for it, even if they had nothing to do with it. The bad news may then result in some negative consequences, and it is the fear of those negative consequences that makes them hesitant to tell the truth. It is much safer for them to not tell the truth in hopes that the problem will go away or that someone other than themselves will be blamed.

So today, when a mistake (an error, a non-conformance to specifications, etc.) occurs, the employee is usually blamed for the mistake. That is due to the current paradigm. Since the root cause of the problem is not found and removed, the mistake occurs over and over and over again. Until management changes their paradigm and begins to look for the root cause of problems rather than blaming the employees, the problems will not go away. Finally, there is the fact that Level-4-type executives will deflect the responsibility for all problems away from themselves. Because of their large egos, they are sure that the problem has something to do with the employees, the competition, government regulations, or the weather; it surely couldn't be related to their decision-making. This is a problem for which industry must find and implement a solution. Not implementing a solution is costing industry untold millions of dollars every day.

The Arrival of Professional Salaried Management

Before the industrial age, when business enterprises were small, one-owner or two-owner partnerships, the business could easily be managed by the owners themselves. However, with the large businesses that were developed in the industrial age to produce all types of goods from food and farm equipment to textile and metal products, it was no longer possible for the owners to manage the companies themselves. The many activities involved in purchasing, producing, and marketing massive amounts of goods for national distribution and sale were more than they could possibly handle. The solution was to hire professional salaried managers that are known today as "middle management."[168] As a result, the creation of the middle-management positions and their responsibilities happened in parallel with the evolution of the Bureaucratic Management System.

The middle-management position had not existed in the U.S. business world prior to the Industrial Revolution and the evolution of the BMS. The creation of this position, along with the work of Fredrick Taylor, was the beginning of what is now called "modern management." Among the first pioneers of modern management was George B. McClellan of the Illinois Central Railroad. In the early 1850s, he authored some basic principles of general administration for the new "middle management" to follow while fulfilling the responsibilities of their positions. Those principles were as follows:

(1) **A proper division of responsibilities**
(2) **Sufficient power conferred to enable the same to be fully carried out, that such responsibilities may be real in their character [that is, authority to be commensurate with responsibility]**
(3) **The means of knowing whether such responsibilities are faithfully executed**
(4) **Great promptness in the report of all derelictions of duty, that evils may be at once corrected**
(5) **Such information to be obtained through a system of daily reports and checks that will not embarrass**

> principal officers nor lessen their influence with their
> subordinates
>
> (6) **The adoption of a system, as a whole, which will not
> only enable the General Superintendent to detect errors
> immediately, but will also point out the delinquent**[169]

These "principles of general administration" spelled out quite
clearly what the role of the "middle management" would be. After the
commands had been received from top management and passed down
to the worker, it would be the responsibility of middle management to
be prompt in "the report of all derelictions of duty" so that "evils may
be at once corrected." The method for detecting these derelictions
of duty would be "through a system of daily reports and checks,"
and these daily reports and checks would be constructed so as to
"point out the delinquent." This shows that from the beginning of
the BMS, the employees were being blamed for any mistakes that
might occur.

The middle managers of the 1800s were hired from the ranks of
the educated professionals of the day. The first middle managers by
training were accountants, engineers, and military officers. These
managers had a rather low opinion of the workers that they managed.
Most workers could neither read nor write. The view of the managers
was that the workers were naturally lazy and would not work unless
watched at all times. Additionally, the managers felt that most of the
workers did not focus on their work as much as they should, and
thus, they "made many mistakes." The lack of focus (in the opinion
of management) was because the workers were only thinking of
themselves and not the company.

These managers, in order to be able to "point out the delinquent,"
would form the organization along functional lines. Once the
functional organizations (departments) were formed, then each
department would receive their own set of objectives that were
countable. The department's production would then be counted and
reported daily, weekly, etc. to the upper levels of the organization. By
1880, these reports were quite detailed, so much so, that the workers
felt like they were always under scrutiny. "The minutest details of

cost of materials and labor in every department appeared from day to day and week to week in the accounts; and soon every man about the place was made to realize it. The men felt and often remarked that the eyes of the company were always on them through the books."[170]

In this environment, the management was forced to focus on the short-term and on their individual departmental objectives. Their responsibility was to meet the departmental objective set for them even if it had to be accomplished at the expense of other departments or the employees or the company in total. They would accomplish the objectives by making it clear to everyone "who is in charge." They may also be somewhat dictatorial. To ensure that they achieved their departmental objectives, the manager would first increase the objective and then spread it to all the employees and make it part of their performance plan. Once that had been accomplished, the manager would give clear marching orders to the workers, "**Make your objectives!!**"

Sometimes, however, despite the best efforts of the manager, the employees may not achieve the objectives set. The manager may then decide that it is time to motivate the employees to work harder. Management is sure that if the employees would just work harder, the objective can be achieved. The manager may try a number of things to motivate the workers: have a contest or maybe implement some type of bonus plan. If none of these actions work, the management may bring in a motivational speaker to get the employees going or threaten them with the loss of their job if they do not achieve the objectives. One CEO observed however, that when managers operate in this manner, "they are using fear and manipulation to force a certain behavior on people. Not only is that wrong, it is futile."[171] This CEO went on to say that "It is very hard to get anyone motivated to achieve someone else's goals."[172]

The typical industrial age manager also subscribes to the idea that "if it ain't broke, don't fix it." Maintain the status quo. Don't rock the boat. Changing things and trying new ideas is not an option. Change is considered to be a risky venture. Something bad may happen and the manager does not want to be responsible for any bad news. As we saw earlier, if there is any bad news, the employees will be blamed for it. So the least risky course to take is to make no changes at all. To try something new and have it not succeed could be interpreted as irresponsible, poor judgment, or dereliction of duty. In any case, it is not a good idea. If there is to be any significant change made, it will be as a result of instructions and decisions from higher up in the organization. Change may be implemented because of a change in strategic direction or a fine-tuning of the current company plan. Any change, however, will usually be implemented at the start of a new year, and it will come from top management. Because of this, change under the BMS occurs quite slowly. It is not a day-to-day, ongoing event.

The manager operating under the BMS will view their primary customer as being their own manager. Now think about that. Under the current business model, the middle managers view their most important customer as being their manager and senior management. That is where their focus is. This internal and upward focus is not a problem as long as the producer has the market place power. But as the consumer gains choice and thus the marketplace power, this becomes a larger and larger issue. So under the current business model, their focus will be inward at their departmental objectives and upward toward their primary customer: their manager and top management. Their focus will not be on customers. Due to this internal focus, they will spend a large amount of their time managing their careers. Their objective is to make things look good to upper management so they can get promoted to a higher level with higher pay. This "looking good" is accomplished by hiding all the bad news possible and going along with any ideas or directives from above even if they know they are unreasonable.

The managers may, however, still run into some problems as they attempt to achieve the objectives set for them. Sometimes, the departmental objectives are affected by the actions of other departments. The interdependencies between the departments may cause conflicts to arise between the departments. Some departments may even refer to other departments within the company as "the enemy." For example, at Widgets, Inc., the manufacturing department has as one of their objectives to keep the warranty cost below three percent of sales. Recently, the warranty cost has been creeping up and is now over three percent of sales. After some research into the issue, the manufacturing department discovered that one of the major causes of the rise in warranty claims is the failure of the control valves in the widgets. These control valves, they find, are coming from a new vendor selected by the purchasing department. So, the manufacturing department asks the purchasing department to return to the old vendor, whose control valves did not fail. The response from the purchasing department is a definite NO. The purchasing department says that the specifications of the control valves from the new vendor are identical to the specifications of the old vendor, but are almost 50% cheaper. Further, they claim, the expense of the control valves are a large part of the total cost of the widgets, and they cannot achieve their objective of keeping materials cost below 35 percent of sales if they have to switch vendors and return back to the old vendor. In addition, the purchasing department says that the old vendor just had a price increase of 12 percent. The battle is now on!

The goal of purchasing to buy at the lowest cost possible and the goal of manufacturing to keep warranty costs as low as possible are sometimes mutually exclusive. Conflicting goals such as in this example exist everywhere within a company that is managed under the BMS and its functionally oriented, fixed, numeric objectives. The interdepartmental conflict such as in the manufacturing and purchasing departments just described is designed into the BMS. It cannot be avoided. The objectives placed on one department invariably come into conflict with the objectives placed on other departments. These measurement conflicts will always drive costs up and increase the level of organizational infighting while lowering employee morale and productivity. As in the prior example, as the purchasing department tries their best to hold costs down, they may purchase lower quality raw materials and parts. However, a dollar saved on the purchasing side may add ten dollars to the manufacturing cost in the form of rejected products during manufacture. In addition, when the product reaches the consumer, the return rate may increase along with a decrease in customer satisfaction. However, none of this is of any concern to the purchasing department. Their job is to purchase items at the lowest cost possible, and they are doing their job. It is manufacturing's job to make defect-free widgets, not the purchasing department's.

The contradictions between the controls placed on different departments lead to many problems. First, the blame game enters the management process. The managers of the different departments will begin pointing fingers at the other departments and blaming them for the problems. They will make excuses like "If it weren't for them…everything would be fine. We are doing *our* job." Related to the blame-it-on-them strategy is the cover-your-rear mentality. When there are problems, the plan is clear. Attempt to blame the other departments for the objectives that are not being met, and, at the same time, start covering your rear just in case things do not go well. As a result, the disputes between the departments go on and on and cannot be resolved at the department-to-department level. The disputes only get resolved when upper management finally gets involved.[173] Once again, productivity is decreased.

When the objectives are set so high that they cannot be reached and enough pressure is applied from above, the managers and workers will start to "play the game" and fabricate compliance. They will fudge the numbers and start withholding information. This will lead to guarded communications and may cause the employees to be blatantly dishonest. For example, if a plant manager would say to all the employees, "If the reject rate of widgets ever exceeds two percent, I will fire everyone and hire all new people!" The chances are that plant the manager will never see a reject rate above two percent, even if it does occur. The employees will hide that fact from him.

The underlying driving force for all the behaviors that we have been describing is FEAR! The BMS is a fear-driven system. Everyone within the system is afraid of what will happen if the objectives are not met. Fear is what the upper management uses to control lower level management, and the lower level management uses fear to control the employees. Fear is the basis for control.[174] When the objectives are not met or mistakes are made, negative consequences soon follow.

The employees may suffer time off without pay, a reduction in pay, a demotion, or even termination.

The employees working in this fear-driven environment will be forced to focus on their own individual objectives, even at the expense of the company. In times of stress, they may do things to achieve their objectives at the expense of others. As the stress in the organization increases, the level of trust between the employees, their peers, and management will decrease. This lack of trust and the high levels of stress will lead to a low level of morale and productivity within the organization. In this kind of environment, the employees will feel like they are just putting in time. They will not feel like a part of the organization, and loyalty will also be low. There will be little if any sense of fulfillment from the work that they do. Without a sense of belonging or loyalty, the only motivation for the employees is money. If they find a higher paying job, they will be gone. The managers will also have a low level of credibility with the employees. The employees will know that the objectives are not realistic and will lose respect for the managers who continually urge them on and try to manipulate and motivate them to work harder to make the objectives.

When the managers have lost their credibility with the employees, they will become dictatorial and petty. The work environment will become highly political. Who you know and who is your friend will be of the highest importance. This happens when the objectives are not being met. When people are not meeting their objectives, they are all equally "bad." So, the difference maker becomes a matter of "who does the manager like?" The manager will then keep some people and let others go based on who the manager likes and does not like. The decisions will have little to do with keeping the best employees.

The environment that is created by the BMS in times of economic hardship is highly stressful and quite competitive. In times of economic hardship, the employees and management will develop a win/lose mentality. The win/lose mentality says that the only way I can win is if someone else loses. Consequently, one employee may sabotage another to look better. The employees and management will also view power as a finite entity. There is only so much power available, so to gain power, it must be taken away from someone else in the organization. Information is viewed as power, so one employee or manager may distort or withhold information from the other employees or managers. This withholding of information leads to peer mistrust. When employees and management no longer trust each other, the only way they can influence each other is through coercion and threat.

The managers in a time of economic hardship will be highly aggressive about finding out who they can blame for the failure to make the objectives and reducing cost. They will identify those who are "not getting the job done" and begin letting them go. The employees (not the managers) will be the first out the door. The managers will also look for ways to make the "numbers" look better which may lead to some questionable business practices. For example, they may devise ways to deceive the customer to increase profits. A couple of today's examples might be the hiding of high interest rates in car leases by car dealers, or food manufacturers reducing the quantity of product in a container without reducing the cost. To reduce cost, management may lay off the more skilled senior employees and hire less skilled younger workers at a lower salary, or reduce the salaries of the current employees. Management may also be more aggressive in their dealings with suppliers and other business partners to get reduced prices. The last action to be taken is to reduce the dividend to the stockholders.

There is a reason that a reduction of the stock dividend is the last cost reduction action to be taken. That is because the management under the current business model will assign priorities to the following constituencies as shown:

1. Stockholder
2. Management (my addition)
3. Customers
4. Suppliers/Vendors (my addition)
5. Public/community
6. Employees[175]
7. The environment (my addition)

This ranking of the seven constituencies of the company is in alignment with the industrial-age business environment and paradigm. The stockholder is the highest priority group because most management, and in particular, top management, own large amounts of stock and stock options. The top management must also keep the stockholders happy if they want to keep their jobs. If the stockholders become unhappy, their employment contract will not be renewed and they will lose their job. Most managers today also believe that the number one priority of the company is to maximize profits, so it is easy to understand why the stockholders are the most important group in the eyes of upper management.

Following the stockholders in second place is the management. They are making the ranking, so they can put themselves wherever they want to. Besides, since they are large stockholders, it just makes sense that they should be next in priority to the stockholders. The customers are third, because without customers, the company cannot exist. The fourth group is the business partners who are also known as suppliers. They provide products and services that the company cannot do without. The fifth group is the public, or public interest. Management cannot ignore the public and the laws of the land. Management may try to bend the rules, but in most cases, they will obey them. The sixth group on the priority list is the employees. They are sixth because they are viewed as expendable. This view is a holdover from the early days (1800s) of the industrial age, but the view has begun to moderate. However, many employees are still viewed by management as not being on the same level as management even today, or to use another word, they are *inferior*. Managers, because they are managers and hold a higher level with more power, conclude that they must be better, which is why they are the managers and why they receive all of the perks that they do. These managers operating under the industrial-age business model also view the employees as a line-item expense right along with all of the other line-item expenses in the financial reports. When expenses need to be reduced to protect the quarterly profits, then the salary line item will be cut right along with other line items with little thought as to the impact that it will have on the employees (people) and the company. This expense reduction for the salary line item may be called a layoff, downsizing, or a "resource action." Don't you just love that term, "resource action"? Management is not laying off people, you know, they are just implementing a "resource action." The last constituency, the environment, ranks so low within the industrial-age business paradigm, that it rarely will even be listed. The view of the industrial age is that the environment is there to be used at will. During the 1800s, the concepts of conservation and environmental damage were almost nonexistent.

The ranking of these constituencies also has a significant effect on the decision-making process of management. Since the employees have a low priority, they will be the first to go in times of economic hardship. The dividend that goes to the stockholders will be the last item cut since the stockholders (and the stock price) are of high importance to top management. Even more importantly, the management teams operating under this business model will use "A or B thinking." Since profit is the number one objective, then all decisions will be considered with respect to its impact on profits. From their viewpoint, they can, as an example (A) have increased profits OR (B) incur short-term expenses, or they can have (A) increased profits or (B) higher customer service. This is win/lose decision-making. In this case (A) the profits win, and (B) everyone else loses.[176] When management continually uses this A or B logic, and under-invests in new products, employees, customer service, etc. in the name of increased short-term profits, then eventually a negative feedback loop will be created between the company and its constituencies. The result of the negative feedback loop is at best, an average company with average performance. As was pointed out earlier, 80% of executives would cut short-term expenditures in order to protect the quarterly profit objectives, even though they knew that doing so would hurt the company in the long run. The negative impact on performance is exactly what the charts for the comparison companies is showing in Chapter four.

This type of thinking is what some authors refer to as zero-sum thinking. Zero-sum thinking is a mindset that leads to the conclusion that there is only a fixed amount of something. That something could be power, information, money or whatever. Regardless of what it may be, the managers who operate with zero-sum thinking believe that since there is only a fixed amount available, that the only way they can increase the amount that they have, is to take more from some other person or group. This is also called win/lose thinking. Whether it is called *A or B* thinking, *zero-sum* thinking or *win/lose* thinking, the end result is the same. One person or group is always trying to make gains at the expense of other persons or groups. These types of thinking are all elements of the industrial-age mechanistic paradigm, which is a paradigm of scarcity. The paradigm of scarcity says that there is only so much of anything to go around, so if you want more of it, you must take it away from someone else. This type of thinking is also the source of a great deal of competition. The more prevalent that this type of thinking is within an organization, the more competitive and combative the organizational culture will be. This in turn leads to the antagonistic relationship that a management team may develop with a union or suppliers. It is also the type of thinking that allows executives to maximize profits and their earnings at the expense of the other constituencies of the company such as the employees, customers and suppliers. Finally, true Level-4 Effective Leaders more often than not will utilize this type of thinking. It must be pointed out at this stage, that many CEOs are not true Level 4's and, by the same token, they are not true level 5's either. They are a combination of the characteristics of both.

Chapter 7
The Industrial Age Business
Model – Measurement System

The measurement system that is used in the Industrial-Age Business Model is derived from a company's annual business plan. The annual business plan is set by the top management and it is that plan upon which the accounting-based measurement system is based. On an annual basis, the top management will set the financial objectives for the company in the coming year. These objectives will then be distributed out to each functional area of the business. As these annual financial objectives are distributed down and out to the various departments, the objectives are divided, modified, translated, and finally delivered to each department manager. Within each department, every manager will receive the annual objectives that the manager is expected to attain with the help of the employees. The manager will then distribute the annual objectives to the employees in the form of individual annual objectives.

After these annual objectives have been distributed down to the employee level, it will be the immediate manager's responsibility to make sure that the employees achieve the objectives set. However, top management will not be satisfied if they have to wait until the end of the year to find out how things are going. Management will require that progress is reported each month at least. The purpose of the monthly reporting is so that management can determine on a monthly basis who is doing the job and who is not. To do this, the management will divide the annual objective by twelve to arrive at a monthly objective. It then becomes the responsibility of the first-line manager and the manager's employees to achieve the objective each month. That is the Industrial-Age Business Model's accounting-based measurement system. It is quite simple. All that is required is for the manager to divide the annual objective by twelve to get the monthly objective. Then the manager must review the numbers monthly to see if the employees exceed the objective or not. If an employee exceeded the objective, then he or she is a good employee. If the employee did not achieve the objective, then the employee is a bad employee. Above the bar is good; below the bar is bad. It is as simple as that.

For example, Joe the salesman's manager sets an annual quota of 1,000 units for Joe. Joe's manager will then divide the 1,000 by twelve to arrive at a monthly objective of 83.33 units per month. The manager then rounds the monthly objective up to 84 units per month for an annual objective of 1,008. Joe's manager always wants to add a little safety margin. Joe's manager then gives Joe the following annual objective.

Annual Objective 1,008 units

Monthly Objective 84 units

Joe's actual attainment on a monthly basis is as follows:

	Attainment	Variance	Result
Jan.	86	+2	Good
Feb.	78	-6	Bad
March	83	-1	Bad
April	94	+10	Really Good
May	82	-2	Bad
June	83	-1	Bad
July	86	+2	Good
Aug.	83	-1	Bad
Sept.	82	-2	Bad
Oct.	90	+6	Good
Nov.	75	-9	Really Bad
Dec.	86	+2	Good

It is easy to see from the numbers that Joe only exceeded his objective five months out of twelve. Joe was rated "really good" one month and "good" four months, rated "bad" six months and "really bad" one month. That is not a good performance. Joe only made his objective five of twelve months, less than half of the time. In fact, if times became tough and the manager was forced to layoff a salesman or two, Joe would probably be on the list. After all, Joe only made his objective less than half of the time, five out of twelve months. Joe is a below-average salesman. The manager, after all, expects every salesperson to exceed the monthly objective each month.

Now, let's look at Joe's performance with a slightly different measurement system. Rather than divide Joe's objective by the number of months in a year, let's divide the objective by the number of workdays in a calendar year and then multiply that number times the number of workdays in each month to reach a monthly objective based on the number of workdays in the month. We will then compare Joe's attainment to the new objective based on workdays in the month.

Now, Joe's manager says the following:

Joe, you are amazing! I don't know how you do it month after month. I am so happy to have you on the team and working in my department. You are just a great salesman!

How did Joe go from being a "below-average salesman" to being a "great salesman" based on the same actual attainment? Let's see how Joe performed against the new objectives rounded to the nearest whole number.

Annual Objective	1,008		
Workdays	257		
Daily Objective	3.922		

	Working Days	Daily Objective	Monthly Objective	Attainment
Jan.	22	3.922	86	86
Feb.	20	3.922	78	78
March	21	3.922	82	83
April	24	3.922	94	94
May	21	3.922	82	82

June	21	3.922	82	83
July	22	3.922	86	86
Aug.	21	3.922	82	83
Sept.	21	3.922	82	82
Oct.	23	3.922	90	90
Nov.	19	3.922	75	75
Dec.	22	3.922	86	86
Totals			1,005	1,008

With the new objectives, based on the number of workdays in the month, Joe was able to meet or exceed the objective every month! Perfect! Amazing! Just Amazing!

What did the second measurement system do that the first measurement did not do that made such a big difference? The second measurement system began to deal with something called **normal variation!** In this case, the variation was the number of workdays in a month. The real world varies. Anything measured in the real world varies. So, when you view the real world from the viewpoint of the Industrial Age Business Model accounting-based measurement system, which does not deal with normal variation, you will get a distorted view of reality. This occurs because the accounting-based measurement system does not deal with any variation. When using the accounting-based measurement system, any natural fluctuation above the bar is interpreted as success. A natural fluctuation far above the bar is cause for celebration, recognition, maybe even promotion. Perhaps a salesman might receive a salesman-of-the-month award or other type of recognition. The reality is that it was not anything special that the salesman did that caused the attainment to be so far above the goal, it was just normal variation. Several large transactions just happened to occur in the same month. That just happens from time to time; it is normal.

However, a natural fluctuation below the bar sends everyone scurrying for explanations. "What happened this month? Show me your business plan! What are you going to do to make sure that you

exceed the goal next month?" When this happens, a great deal of time
will be consumed in preparing for the review meetings. Much focus,
attention, and energy will be consumed by managers and employees
defending themselves from the effects of nature's normal variation.
All of the review meetings are really a complete waste of time and
achieve nothing! The real world will continue to vary regardless of
how many meetings are held and how many promises are made. The
meetings only succeed in driving up costs, lowering customer focus
and productivity.

Now, let's look at a third set of numbers for Joe. These numbers
show the amount of variance from the goal.

Annual Objective   1,008 units
Monthly Objective   84 units

	Monthly Objective Based on Workdays	Monthly Attainment	Variance	Percent Variance
Jan.	86	86	0	0
Feb.	78	78	0	0
March	82	83	+1	+1.2
April	94	94	0	0
May	82	82	0	0
June	82	83	+1	+1.2
July	86	86	0	0
August	82	83	+1	+1.2
Sep.	82	82	0	0
Oct.	90	90	0	0
Nov.	75	75	0	0
Dec.	86	86	0	0
Total	1,005	1,008	+3	+0.03% Avg.

These numbers reveal several things. First, Joe has figured out
how the game is played, and he is playing it. It is obvious that the

numbers are being juggled because Joe's attainment is always right on the monthly goal or slightly above the goal when it is calculated using days worked. Joe even made his objective during the months that he was on vacation. The natural variation of the real world would not produce the results shown. These numbers have been manipulated. Joe does not want his quota to be raised, so he is managing the numbers (by brute force) so that he either meets or exceeds the quota, but by a small amount. Joe is afraid that if he exceeds his objective by too much, the objective will be raised and that will put him at risk of possibly not being able to make the objective in the coming year. Since Joe met the objective each single month, it means Joe could have sold more than he actually did. *Joe is holding back production.* The chances are good that Joe has enough business sold to make his quota for the first month of the next year. Joe will not reveal this fact to his manager. He will keep the business in his secret file and pull it out as needed.

The example of the departmental objectives causing conflict between departments which caused many meetings to be held and time wasted, and the example of Joe, the salesman, holding back sales so that his quota will not be raised are two examples of: The Perversity Principle.

The Perversity Principle states:

If you try to increase productivity and decrease cost by imposing quantitative constraints on a system, you will only succeed in increasing your cost elsewhere in the system.[177]

A further examination of the sales example will make the Perversity Principle easier to understand. Figure 7.1 is a chart of the sales process at Widgets, Inc. where Joe, the salesman, works. Vertically, on the left side is a bar representing the number of salesmen with a certain level of attainment, and across the bottom is a scale for the actual attainment with a range from zero to some number N. As might be expected, the graph for all the salesmen looks like a normal distribution curve.

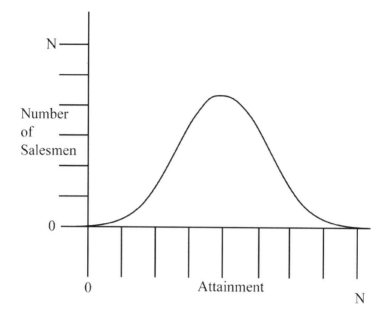

Fig. 7.1

This graph represents the sales process at Widgets, Inc. in its normal state. However, there is one thing missing. That one thing is the goal (also called a sales quota) for the salesmen. At Widgets, Inc., the sales management likes to motivate the salesmen to sell more. To accomplish this, on an annual basis, they hold a three-day meeting at a resort location for all of the salesmen and sales managers who make their goals. The management wants about seventy percent of the salesmen to qualify for the recognition event so the goal will have to be set low (left of center on the curve) so that at least seventy percent of the sales representatives will reach it. See Figure 7.2.

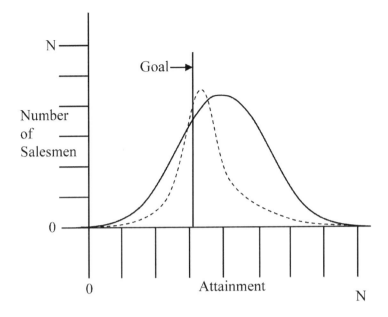

Fig. 7.2

The vertical bar is the goal, and the dotted line is the new attainment graph. It is now easy to see what the impact was when the goal (numeric constraint) was placed on the sales process at Widgets, Inc. The area under the dotted line represents the amount of attainment when the goal was introduced as compared to what the attainment could have been if there were no goal at all, allowing the sales process to take its normal course. The salesmen who could have far exceeded the goal are holding back, and that amount is represented by the difference of the amount of area between the two lines. The area below the dotted line is significantly smaller than the area below the solid line; this means lower sales. The chart shows clearly that the introduction of the goal has reduced the amount of sales substantially. In this case, about 30 percent of the salesmen are highly stressed because they failed to achieve the goal, and their jobs are at risk if they do not make the goal next year. The other 70 percent are feeling pretty good, but management is not happy with the sales volume. Also, the introduction of the goal has driven up the cost. A great deal of management's, staff, and salesmen time is consumed in setting, tracking, reporting, and other goal-related activities. The time consumed in these activities does not produce any sales, and the customers are not happy to have the salesmen tied up in meetings.

Management is not satisfied with the results and thinks they might be better if the goal was raised. Management's view is that a higher goal will challenge the salesmen and motivate them to work harder, so the goal is raised. See Figure 7.3.

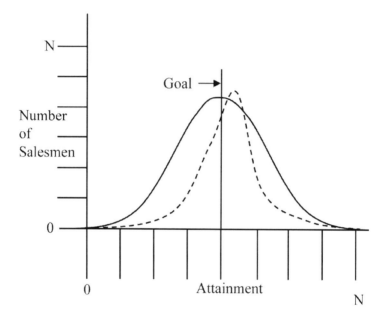

Fig. 7.3

With the goal raised to the middle of the distribution curve, the same problem still exists. There is still a large amount of lost sales, which are represented by the difference between the amount of area between the solid line and dotted line. In this case, since the goal was set at the midpoint of the distribution, one half of the salesmen will not make the goal. Some salesmen realize early on that they will not make the annual goal, so they start holding back early and saving business for the next year. They want to be sure to make the goal next year and keep their jobs. Saving some business this year for next year will help a lot. The other half of the sales force does achieve the goal and then stops selling, waiting for the coming year. In this case, half of the sales force is demoralized and the other half is holding back production. Management is disappointed because only half of the salesmen made the goal and many of the salesmen seem to have a bad attitude. The costs have also gone up because there have been a lot more meetings held to determine why half of the sales force is not reaching the goal. The salesmen are now spending even more time tracking the numbers and preparing for all the review meetings. After reviewing the current situation, management decides that the sales force needs a bigger challenge. They will raise the goal and introduce a large cash bonus for everyone who makes the new higher goal. That should motivate the salesmen and improve sales. See Figure 7.4.

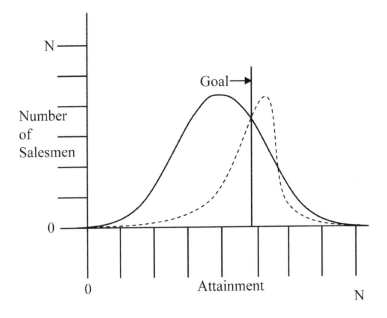

Fig. 7.4

In this case, only thirty percent of the salesmen make the goal. Another twenty percent try hard, but they just can't reach it. About fifty percent realize about the middle of the year that they will not be able to achieve the goal, so they start planning for next year by holding the business back. Again, management is disappointed in the lack of sales. Again, the lost sales are represented by the difference between the solid line and the dotted line. Again, costs are driven up because there are even more review meetings. It is clear now, that regardless of where the goal is set, it will cause the total sales attainment to be less than it would have been if there was no goal at all. That is the Perversity Principle in action! There is no way to avoid it. Any time a quantitative restraint in the form of a goal or objective or quota is placed on a system, the result will be lower production and higher costs. *Management believes that somehow the Perversity Principle can be circumvented, but it cannot be!*

The above "poor business decisions" are a product of the accounting-based measurement system, and it creates a number of severe problems. First, it distorts a person's view of the real world because it cannot explain normal variations. Because of this, untold effort and resources are expended in an attempt to explain and respond to these normal variations. All of those efforts are a complete waste of time and only serve to drive costs up. Secondly, when the measurement system is used for goal-setting purposes, it invokes the Perversity Principle which results in less production and higher costs. These problems then get compounded when the measurement system data are used for purposes of performance evaluation.

To solve these problems, a new measurement system will be necessary. The new measurement system must be able to deal with the normal variation of the real world in an easy-to-manage way and utilize a "common sense" approach.

Chapter 8
The Industrial Age Business Model
– Evaluation and Compensation Systems

The primary basis for performance evaluation under the Industrial-Age Profit-Driven Business Model is the objectives that are derived from the accounting-based measurement system. As was described in the previous chapter, the financial objectives for the company are translated and manipulated by the layers of management until they finally arrive at the employee level and are then incorporated into the employee's performance plan. These objectives are set as bars that the employee is expected to achieve. If the employee exceeds the goal, then the result will be a good evaluation. If the employee does not achieve the goal, then the employee's performance will result in a poor evaluation. This method of executing the employee's performance evaluation appears to make sense as long as you do not think about it. However, with just a little thought, it becomes clear that the current Industrial Age Business Model method of performance evaluation makes almost no sense at all. There are six major reasons for this:

1. The objectives that it is based on,
2. The built-in levels of performance,
3. The environment of mediocrity that it creates,
4. The way it confuses people with other resources,
5. The short-term focus, and
6. The way it destroys teamwork.[178]

Number One: The Objectives

The first problem is the objective that is set for the employee. When management sets an objective in the future (usually twelve months), it is clear that the objective cannot be "correct." This is explained by the fact that no one can see into the future with perfect clarity and predict with 100% accuracy what will happen. The setting of an objective is just an estimate of what management expects or wishes would happen. Normally, management will use past history as a guide to project or predict what the objective should be. They expect that the future will be reasonably like the past and, based on that assumption, will set objectives close to but almost always higher than the previous year's attainment. The logic is that if the employee attained X last year, that with a little more effort, the employee should be able to achieve Y this year. Therefore, it is clear that the objective is not an accurate statement of what the employee will achieve. It is only an educated guess or wish, and the only question is, how inaccurate is it? The objective is a derivative of a goal from the upper levels of the company, and it may have been uplifted by each layer of management. Taking this into consideration along with the fact that the objective has been projected twelve months into the future, it is clear that the degree of accuracy of the objective is relatively low. In other words, the objective is wrong. The only question is, how wrong is it? How far will it deviate from the year's actual attainment?

Currently, if an employee's attainment is substantially below the objective set, the employee will suffer significant negative consequences. If, on the other hand, the employee substantially exceeds the objective, the employee will receive significant positive rewards. **In both cases, the assumption is made that the objective is correct!** However, it is clear to everyone that an objective set twelve months in advance will not be and cannot be 100% accurate. However, when the objectives are used for the purpose of performance evaluation, the implied assumption is that they are 100% correct. If an employee achieves 90 or 95% of the objective, they failed; they did not achieve the objective. Does this really make any sense when the accuracy of the objective may be plus or minus twenty, forty, or even fifty percent? It is clear that management does not know the degree of accuracy of the objective. A better way of evaluating performance would be to use some "normal range" of performance measurement rather than the current above-the-bar-or-below-the-bar method.

For example, Joe, the salesman at Widgets, Inc., is given a sales objective of 1,000,000 widgets for the year. Now, let's think about the major elements that will determine how many widgets Joe will sell in the year. The major elements are such things as the size and content of Joe's sales territory, the price that the company has set for their widgets, the price of the competitors' widgets, the comparative quality and warranty of the company's widgets versus the competition, the overall economy, the health and growth rate of Joe's customers and prospects, the number and quality of Joe's competitors, and of course, Joe's sales skills and efforts. Each of the eight items just listed can vary month to month and year to year. With so many variables influencing the number of widgets that Joe can sell in a one-year period, it is clear that it would be almost impossible for a manager to forecast the future well enough to set an objective with any high degree of certainty. If a manager could predict/guess within plus or minus twenty percent, that would be pretty good. Joe's actual sales could be as low as 800,000 (80% of the objective and Joe is in trouble) or as high as 1,200,000 (120% of the objective and Joe is a hero) as a result of the normal variation of all of the variables involved in the sales process. When all of the variables that affect the sales volumes are considered, it seems irrational to assume that a fixed numeric objective set twelve months in advance could possibly be 100% accurate. Then, to use that numeric objective as a method to evaluate an employee's performance and to say that achieving 90 or 95% of the objective is unsatisfactory, is nonsensical. Again, the current method of employee evaluation appears to make sense unless you step back and really think about it a little, and then it almost seems to be irrational.

Number Two: Levels of Performance

The performance-evaluation systems in industry today have about four to ten levels of performance. Management feels these levels let the employees know how they are performing relative to the objectives set and to their peers. This, however, is just not the case. In practice, it is impossible to construct a performance plan and a definition of the levels of performance such that the manager can know exactly at which level the employee is performing. If it were possible to do so, the employee would know the level at which they have been performing before the evaluation took place. Because the definition of the levels of performance and the performance plan are somewhat disjointed, the manager is left with the task of deciding which level of performance to assign to each employee and then justifying that decision to the employee and upper management. In many companies, it is dictated that a fixed percentage of the employees must fall into the top and bottom categories of performance. Only X percent can be rated at the top level, and Y percent must be rated at the bottom level. This may serve the needs of management well, but it certainly does not serve the employee well, and it does not seem to be rational.

By placing a fixed percentage in these levels of performance, management is then able to distribute rewards (salary increases and/or bonuses, trips, etc.) and know ahead of time how many employees will qualify at each reward level. In any system where measurements are taken, there will always be numbers that are in the top ten percent and bottom ten percent. There will always be about one half below the average and one half above the average. There is no way to avoid the normal distribution of the measures. The problem is this: As was pointed out in the example of Joe, the salesman at Widgets, Inc., there were eight major variables in Joe's selling process. These eight variables have a large influence on what Joe's sales number will be for the year. These eight variables also have a high degree of variability from year to year and may cause Joe's number to fall in the top ten percent one year and in the bottom ten percent the next year in spite of the fact that Joe worked equally hard each year. It was the seven factors other than Joe's efforts that caused the large variation in results. Once it is understood that many other variables are causing the results to vary so widely, does it make any sense at all to use these same results as justification to place an employee in some specific performance level?

A system of performance evaluation that may appear to work well when viewed from a company level, simply breaks down when viewed from an individual employee level. From the company level, it looks fine. When the number of employees at each level of performance is plotted on a chart, a normal distribution curve is the result. There are a small number of employees at the bottom and at the top. Most of the employees are centered close to the middle or are average.

Management is happy. Joe, however, is unhappy. Joe just went from the top ten percent last year to the bottom ten percent this year and is worried about losing his job. At the individual employee level, the variation could be dramatic, and yet when the performance of all employees is plotted each year, it is always the same normal distribution curve that is the result. The variation at the individual employee level is lost.

Another problem is that each year, one half of the employees will fall into the bottom half of the performance-evaluation system. Approximately one half of the employees will be told each year that they are **"below average!"** Every year, the employees that fall in the "below average" category will be different due to the variation at the employee level, so over time more than half of the employees will be told their performance is "below average." This will have a highly negative effect on employee morale, company loyalty, and in many cases, future performance. Many employees will be completely demoralized and depressed after the performance review when they receive the news that they have been judged "below average." This may cause the employee to suffer from depression, and the result will be a lowered performance level and a higher level of anxiety.

Another example will help make this highly negative aspect of the current performance-evaluation system clearer. Suppose that the top one hundred high school graduates in a state were selected to compete for fifty all-expenses-paid college educations at the colleges of their choice. Let's further suppose that the method of determining the winners of the fifty scholarships will be done by taking a difficult entrance exam. Out of the one hundred students, the fifty with the top scores will get the scholarships. The exam is given and the top fifty students are selected. The bottom fifty students are notified that they were not selected and that they are **"below average!"** Now, it is true that the scores of the bottom fifty students were below the average of all the scores. However, it is also clear that all of these students are in the top one-tenth of one percent of all students nationwide. All one hundred of the students are outstanding individuals, and none are "below average" as individuals, and yet, no matter how good their scores are, half of them will be rated as "below average."

With the current method of performance evaluation in the business world today, about forty-seven percent of the workforce is being told (unfairly) that their performance is "below average" each year. They are told this despite the fact that their group, as a whole, may be among the most educated and brightest people in the country. When any group of people, scientists, engineers, doctors, etc. are ranked, there will always be a top ten percent, a bottom ten percent, and the half that are "below average." The problem is that the person only hears "bottom half" or "below average" and becomes depressed. The person does not hear "below the average of the cream of the cream" as in the case with the students. This practice needs to be corrected.[179]

Number Three: An Environment of Mediocrity

As the goals or objectives make their way from the top of the organization down to the lower levels, each level of management will begin a negotiation process that is intended to result in an easily achievable objective. It is in the interest of all management that the objectives of the organization are achievable. Their raises, promotions, bonuses, etc. all depend on them achieving the objectives set. Thus, in order to ensure that they can make the objectives, they lobby and negotiate to get the objectives set as low as they possibly can. This process results in a set of objectives for the employees that are not challenging and that most, if not all, of the employees can achieve. It should be clear that if more than 80 percent of the employees achieve the objective, that the objective was not a challenging one. The employees then reach the objective and start slacking off. They do not want to greatly exceed the objective because then the objective would be raised and possibly raised to the point where they could not make it. That would not be a good thing. This is the Perversity Principle at work again. In an attributes-type system, there is no way to avoid this problem. The problem is built into the system and is a natural part of it.

The employees who work under this system will show little initiative and not take any large amount of risk. The employees are forced to play it safe. If the employee does try something new and takes a risk but as a result, does not achieve the objective set, then he/she will pay the price. If what the employee tries turns out to be highly successful, then the employee may receive some small recognition or reward, and the manager will probably try to take much of the credit. Thus, trying something new and taking a risk has little upside potential and a large downside risk for most employees. Therefore, it is not in their best interest to take any risk or try anything new. The employees are better served by staying quiet, meeting the mediocre objectives (even though they know they could do a lot more), and thus keeping their jobs. Another way of stating this is that if you set objectives that over fifty percent of the employees can achieve, then by definition, the objective is "below average." *So, in essence, management is telling the employees to perform at a below-average level.*[180]

Number Four: Confusing People with Other Resources

During the performance-evaluation process, the employee is given some number of objectives to meet and that becomes the basis for the evaluation. The underlying assumption is that the employee is totally responsible for achieving the objective and that the employee has total control over all the elements necessary to achieve the goal. If this were not the case, then the employee could not justifiably be held responsible for achieving the objective. This underlying assumption, however, is false. The employee does not control all of the variables necessary to achieve the objective in almost every case.

A good example of this is Joe, the salesman at Widgets, Inc. In Joe's case, there were eight variables or elements that had a large impact on how many widgets Joe would be able to sell over a twelve-month period. Those elements were:

1. The size and content of Joe's sales territory
2. The selling price of the widgets
3. The price of the competing widgets
4. The quality and warranty of Joe's widgets

5. The economy
6. The economic health and growth of the customers and prospects
7. The number of competitors
8. Joe's selling skills and his selling efforts

It is clear that Joe has no control over the first seven major elements that determine how many widgets he will sell in a year. In addition, Joe only has control over part of element number eight. Joe can control his selling efforts as long as he is not interfered with, but he does not necessarily control his selling skills. To improve his selling skills, Joe may need some further education or training that would require time away from the job, and costs may be incurred. The education and training of the employees is a responsibility of management, not the employee. Therefore, Joe does not have complete control over his selling skills. Management has the majority of the responsibility in this area since they control education and training.

Joe's skills and efforts are just one element in the sales process at Widgets, Inc. The other seven elements we have listed above. Joe's sales attainment is determined by all of the elements of the system. All of the elements within the system, along with Joe's efforts, will determine the outcome of Joe's sales attainment for the year. However, when it comes time for the performance review, Joe will be held totally responsible for the outcome of the system as if he had complete control over it. Joe's attainment will be confused with the output of the system. There will be no separation of the system's contribution to the results from Joe's contribution to the results. This separation is lost in the confusion. This happens because management does not know whether Joe's attainment was caused by the system in which he works or by Joe. They *could* know that, but they do not have the measurement systems in place to tell them, so they just confuse the two and hold Joe totally responsible. Joe does not like this and does not agree with it, but he is just the employee and has no say or choice.[181]

Number Five: Short-Term Focus

The annual performance evaluation forces the management and the employees to focus on the short-term. While "short" is a relative term, almost all performance evaluations are based on twelve months or less. In most cases, the annual performance objectives are divided by twelve to arrive at a monthly objective. Then the focus drops from twelve months to one month. Many senior- and upper-level managers focus on each quarter or ninety days, but at the first-line manager and employee levels, the focus is usually on the month. In some industries, the focus is down to the week or day or even hour! The problem is that in almost all cases, it will take some short-term sacrifices in order to have long-term success. To succeed in the long term, the company may need to invest in additional plants, equipment, human resources, training, research and development, etc. The investment in these requirements for future long-term success may, however, hurt the short-term performance and measurements. It may be necessary to sacrifice short-term profits or production in order to ensure long-term survival. Thus, when the senior management asks the employees to sacrifice their attainment for the long-term good of the company, it will fall on deaf ears. The employees know that if they work for the good of the company at the expense of meeting their individual objectives, that at review time, their efforts for the good of the company will be overlooked and forgotten. The only question that will be asked is, why did you not make your objectives? Their willingness to work for the good of the company will put the employee at risk of receiving a low evaluation and could cost them their job. This happens because "working for the good of the company" is not normally part of the performance plan and usually cannot be measured. Since it is not part of the performance plan, the employee cannot get credit for it.[182]

Number Six: The Way It Destroys Teamwork

Organizations in industry are structured according to the industrial-age mechanistic paradigm, which produces an organizational chart that resembles a pyramid. Within the pyramid are numerous functionally organized departments such as sales, accounting, purchasing, production, etc. Each of these functional departments is then evaluated on functionally oriented objectives. Sales will be evaluated on how much product they sold. Purchasing will be evaluated on measures relative to the cost of goods purchased. Production will be measured on the amount of product produced, and perhaps, the cost of warranty repair/replacement, and so on for all of the departments. As each functional department strives toward making its functional objectives, their actions may have a negative impact on another department's efforts to achieve their objectives. Purchasing strives for low-cost supplies and materials while production requests and demands higher quality and higher cost supplies and materials. Production knows that the lower cost supplies and materials just drive up the production costs because of more rejected end products, but Purchasing refuses to listen to their complaints. As the functionally oriented measurements come in conflict with each other, tension arises between the departments. Some departments often have very negative things to say about other departments. The resulting battles between departments destroy any hope of cross-functional teamwork, and they drive up the company's overall cost.

These departmental and functional battles become intense because the managers and employees involved have a lot at stake. The actions that another department is asking to be taken will most likely have a negative impact on the department's and the employees' measurements. So, to the degree that the employees work in the spirit of teamwork and for the overall good of the company, they are sacrificing their own measures and future performance evaluations. The employees then have to make a choice. Do they work for the good of the company at their expense, or do they work for their own good at the expense of the company? Most employees are driven through fear to work for their own good at the expense of the company and of teamwork. The employee must put their own measurements ahead of the company's needs. The employee's bonus, pay raise, and the financial security of their family require it. The employee's desire is to work for the good of the company, but he/she is prevented from doing that. Any teamwork that may occur will happen in spite of the performance-evaluation system, not because of it. The conflict between the measures of the individual and the measures of the company is just another example of the Perversity Principle raising its ugly head.

Within the departments, the employees are also forced to compete with each other for the best evaluations. In this competitive environment, employees will view teamwork as benefiting the company and others, but there will be no benefit for the employee. If one employee compensates for another employee's weakness, they will only have less to show for themselves. Teamwork in this environment is a risky business for the employee. These barriers to teamwork within the company are designed into the performance-evaluation system.[183] . The Harris Interactive Survey data from Chapter One provided a spotlight on the lack of direction and teamwork that exists in companies today. It is the multilevel pyramid structure, measurement system and performance evaluation in combination that causes those types of results to exist. A graphical representation of this lack of teamwork that exists under the Industrial-Age Bureaucratic Profit-Driven Business-Model and its performance-evaluation system is shown in Figure 8.1.

Fig. 8.1. Teamwork under the Bureaucratic Management System

In the words of Stephen R. Covey, "Traditional performance appraisal is clearly one of the bloodletting management practices of our day."[184]

Summary

The current performance-evaluation system as implemented under the Industrial-Age Business Model has seven major defects:

1.   The numeric objectives within each employee's performance plan create barriers to departmental and interdepartmental teamwork. These barriers are far too great for the individual employee to overcome. The result is that true teamwork is not possible over any meaningful period of time.

2.   The numeric objectives and goals must be set low enough for the majority of the employees and managers to achieve them. This creates an environment of mediocrity.

3.   The number of levels of performance in the performance-evaluation system increases the perceived variability of employee performance. Ten levels of performance evaluation means ten levels of variance. No rational justification can be put forth that will define why one employee falls into one level and not the adjacent levels.

4.   The performance evaluation is completed with the implied assumption that the employee has total control over all elements that determine the attainment of their objective(s). However, the current measurement-evaluation system cannot distinguish between the contribution of the employee and the contribution of the system in which the employee works (the other elements) toward attainment of the objective. In the "Joe, the salesman" example, these other elements included the sales territory, the product, the competition, etc. Because the current evaluation system cannot distinguish the contribution made by one element (the employee) from the many other elements contributing to the overall attainment, it confuses the contribution made by the employee with the contribution made by all of the other elements.

5.   The performance evaluation forces all employees (managers and non-managers) to focus on the performance-evaluation horizon. This horizon is most often one and twelve months. This is detrimental

to planning and working toward long-term success and growth for the company.

6.   The numerical analysis of the attainment toward the objectives is demoralizing to the employees. In each measurement period, half of the numbers will be "below average." The employees are held 100% accountable for the attainment, and therefore, half of them are told that they are below average. This is both quite demoralizing and untrue. It is true that the measurement is below the average, but it is not necessarily true that "the employee" is below average.

7.   The numerical objective that is used for performance-evaluation purposes is assumed to be 100% accurate, when in reality, it is more likely to be in error by as much as plus or minus 20 to 50 percent.

The Industrial-Age Business Model performance-evaluation system forces the managers and employees to focus on their specific objectives if they wish to be successful and remain employed. They have no choice. It is designed into the model. This inward focus on individual objectives puts the organization on the Industrial-Age Profit-Driven Business Model spiral. See Figure 8.2.

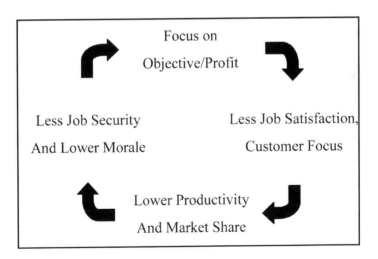

Figure 8.2. Industrial-Age Profit-Driven Business-Model Spiral

The managers and employees are forced by the performance-evaluation system to focus inward at their personal objectives. To the degree that pressure is applied by upper management to achieve the objectives, there will be less focus on customers (both internal and external) and lower employee satisfaction. This will, in time, lead to products and services that are not adapted to the customers' needs and wants, which will produce lower attainment and market share. The result will be lower sales causing financial hardships with less job security and lower employee morale. That will cause the employees to focus even more inwardly at their own objectives at a time when they and the organization should be more outwardly focused where the customers are. That is how the Industrial-Age Business-Model spiral works. This spiral speeds up and becomes more intense in times of economic hardship. This spiral also creates an organization with the following characteristics:

- Inward focus
- High level of fear
- Low level of trust
- Low employee loyalty and risk-taking
- Problems are hidden from management.
- Products and services are not customer-oriented.
- Teamwork is nearly nonexistent.
- Stress is high and rises sharply in times of economic hardship.
- Managers spend a lot of time politicking and managing their own careers.
- Upper management has all the answers and does not need input from employees or customers.
- The organization will also be rigid, inflexible, and have a go-by-the-book mode of operation. . Management will hold the employees accountable for all the problems and failures.

The objectives that are set for the low-level managers and employees are primarily the measures of output of various systems: the sales system, the manufacturing system, etc. To hold the employees responsible for the output of these systems, when management controls most of the system elements, does not make any sense. Managing a company with this methodology is equivalent to playing a basketball game while focusing only on the score rather than how the game is being played. To manage a company this way only makes sense if you don't think about it.

Finally, the evaluation system is tied directly to the employee's compensation, morale, and stress levels. Because of this, it is critical that the deficiencies of the current system be corrected. One basic problem with compensation in industry today is that for most employees, it has no relationship to productivity or profitability. If an employee works really hard and produces a lot, or if the employee decides to slack off, at the end of the pay period, the pay is the same. This is a problem that must be corrected.

This completes the description of the Industrial-Age Profit-Driven Business Model. In the following chapter, the Semco story will be told and then the Information-Age Purpose-Driven Business Model will be described in the later chapters.

Chapter 9
The Power of Values, The Semco Story

"The human mind once stretched by a new idea never regains its original dimensions."

– Oliver Wendell Holmes

In the previous chapters we have completed the description of the industrial-age profit-driven business model and its five parts. It is now time to describe the new information-age purpose-driven business model that will be used to replace the old industrial age business model. However, before we do that, it will be helpful to expand and open up the mind to new and different ways of organizing, managing and conducting business. This will be accomplished by including in this chapter a *Harvard Business Review* article written by Ricardo Semler, the president of Semco. The story of Semco Company and its management will reveal some new ideas and also show the importance of values to an organization. Semco is also an excellent example of how the implementation of a new business model can radically change the business fortunes of a company. The *Harvard Business Review* Article is included here in its entirety with the exception of the sidebars.

The Semco Company

Managing Without Managers
By Ricardo Semler

Harvard Business Review No. 89509
Adapted and Printed with Permission

In Brazil, where paternalism and the family business fiefdom still flourish, I am president of a manufacturing company that treats its 800 employees like responsible adults. Most of them—including factory workers—set their own working hours. All have access to the company books. The vast majority vote on many important corporate decisions. Everyone gets paid by the month, regardless of job description, and more than 150 of our management people set their own salaries and bonuses.

This may sound like an unconventional way to run a business, but it seems to work. Close to financial disaster in 1980, Semco is now one of Brazil's fastest growing companies, with a profit margin in 1988 of 10% on sales of $37 million. Our five factories produce a range of sophisticated products, including marine pumps, digital scanners, commercial dishwashers, truck filters, and mixing equipment for everything from bubble gum to rocket fuel. Our customers include Alcoa, Saab, and General Motors. We've built a number of cookie factories for Nabisco, Nestle, and United Biscuits. Our multinational competitors include AMF, Worthington Industries, Mitsubishi Heavy Industries, and Carrier.

Management associations, labor unions, and the press have repeatedly named us the best company in Brazil to work for. In fact, we no longer advertise jobs. Word of mouth generates up to 300 applications for every available position. The top five managers— we call them counselors—include a former human resources director for Ford Brazil, a 15-year veteran Chrysler executive, and a man who left his job as president of a larger company to come to Semco.

When I joined the company in 1980, 27 years after my father founded it, Semco had about 100 employees, manufactured hydraulic pumps for ships, generated about $4 million in revenues, and teetered on the brink of catastrophe. All through 1981 and 1982, we ran from bank to bank looking for loans, and we fought persistent, well-founded rumors that the company was in danger of going under. We often stayed through the night reading files and searching the desk drawers of venerable executives for clues about forgotten contracts long since privately made and privately forgotten.

Most managers and outside board members agreed on two immediate needs: to professionalize and to diversify. In fact, both of these measures had been discussed for years but had never progressed beyond wishful thinking.

For two years, holding on by our fingertips, we sought licenses to manufacture other companies' products in Brazil. We traveled constantly. I remember one day being in Oslo for breakfast, New York for lunch, Cincinnati for dinner, and San Francisco for the night. The obstacles were great. Our company lacked an international reputation—and so did our country. Brazil's political eccentricities and draconian business regulations scared many companies away.

Still, good luck and a relentless program of beating the corporate bushes on four continents finally paid off. By 1982, we had signed seven license agreements. Our marine division—once the entire company— was now down to 60% of total sales. Moreover, the managers and directors were all professionals with no connection to the family.

With Semco back on its feet, we entered an acquisitions phase that cost millions of dollars in expenditures and millions more in losses over the next two to three years. All this growth was financed by banks at interest rates that were generally 30%

above the rate of inflation, which ranged from 40% to 900% annually. There was no long-term money in Brazil at that time, so all those loans had maximum terms of 90 days. We didn't get one cent in government financing or from incentive agencies either, and we never paid out a dime in graft or bribes.

How did we do it and survive? Hard work, of course. And good luck—fundamental to all business success. But most important, I think, were the drastic changes we made in our concept of management. Without those changes, not even hard work and good luck could have pulled us through.

Semco has three fundamental values on which we base some 30 management programs. These values— democracy, profit sharing, and information—work in a complicated circle, each dependent on the other two. If we eliminated one, the others would be meaningless. Our corporate structure, employee freedoms, union relations, factory size limitations—all are products of our commitment to these principles.

It's never easy to transplant management programs from one company to another. In South America, it's axiomatic that our structure and style cannot be duplicated. Semco is either too small, too far away, too young, too old, or too obnoxious.

We may also be too specialized. We do cellular manufacturing of technologically sophisticated products, and we work at the high end on quality and price. So our critics may be right. Perhaps nothing we've done can be a blueprint for anyone else. Still in the industrial world whose methods show obvious signs of exhaustion, the merit of sharing experience is to encourage experiment and to plant the seeds of conceptual change. So what the hell.

Participatory Hot Air

The first of Semco's three values is democracy, or employee involvement. Clearly, workers who control their working conditions are going to be happier than workers who don't. Just as clearly, there is no contest between the company that buys the grudging compliance of its work force and the company that enjoys the enterprising participation of its employees.

But about 90% of the time, participatory management is just hot air. Not that intentions aren't good. It's just that implementing employee involvement is so complex, so difficult, and, not uncommonly, so frustrating that it is easier to talk about than do.

We found four big obstacles to effective participatory management: size, hierarchy, lack of motivation, and ignorance. In an immense production unit, people feel tiny, nameless, and incapable of exerting influence on the way work is done or on the final profit made. This sense of helplessness is underlined by managers who, jealous of their power and prerogatives, refuse to let subordinates make any decisions for themselves—sometimes even about going to the bathroom. But even if size and hierarchy can be overcome, why should workers care about productivity and company profits? Moreover, even if you can get them to care, how can they tell when they're doing the right thing?

As Antony Jay pointed out back in the 1950s in *Corporation Man*, human beings weren't designed to work in big groups. Until recently, our ancestors were hunters and gathers. For more than five million years, they refined their ability to work in groups of no more than about a dozen people. Then along comes the Industrial Revolution, and suddenly, workers are trying to function efficiently in factories that employ hundreds and even thousands. Organizing those hundreds into teams of about ten members each may help some, but there's still a limit to how many small teams can work well together. At Semco, we've found the most effective production unit to consist of about 150 people. The exact number is open to argument, but it's clear that several thousand people in one facility makes individual involvement an illusion.

When we made the decision to keep our units small, we immediately focused on one facility that had more than 300 people. The unit manufactured commercial food-service equipment—slicers, scales, meat grinders, mixers—and used an MRPII system hooked up to an IBM mainframe with dozens of terminals all over the plant. Paperwork often took two days to make its way from one end of the factory to the other. Excess inventories, late delivery, and quality problems were common. We had tried various worker-participation programs, quality circles, kanban systems, and motivation schemes, all of which got off to great starts but lost their momentum within months. The whole thing was just too damn big and complex; there were too many managers in too many layers holding too many meetings. So we decided to break up the facility into three separate plants.

To begin with, we kept all three in the same building but separated everything we could— entrances, receiving docks, inventories, telephones, as well as certain auxiliary functions like personnel, management information systems, and internal controls. We also scrapped the mainframe in favor of three independent, PC-based systems.

The first effect of the breakup was a rise in costs due to duplication of effort and a loss in economies of scale. Unfortunately, balance sheets chalk up items like these as liabilities, all with dollar figures attached, and there's nothing at first to list on the asset side but airy stuff like "heightened involvement" and "a sense of belonging." Yet the longer term results exceeded our expectations.

Within a year, sales doubled; inventories fell from 136 days to 46; we unveiled eight new products that had been stalled in R&D for two years; and overall quality improved to the point that a one-third rejection rate of federally inspected scales dropped to less than 1%. Increased productivity let us reduce the workforce by 32% through attrition and retirement incentives.

I don't claim that size reduction alone accomplished all this; just that size reduction is essential for putting employees in touch with one another so they can coordinate their work. The kind of distance we want to eliminate comes from having too many people in one place, but it also comes from having a pyramidal hierarchy.

Pyramids and Circles

The organizational pyramid is the cause of much corporate evil, because the tip is too far from the base. Pyramids emphasize power, promote insecurity, distort communications, hobble interaction, and make it very difficult for the people who plan and the people who execute to move in the same direction. So Semco designed an organizational circle. Its greatest advantage is to reduce management levels to three—one corporate level and two operating levels at the manufacturing units.

It consists of three concentric circles. One tiny central circle contains the five people who integrate the company's movements. These are the counselors I mentioned before. I'm one of them, and except for a couple of legal documents that call me president, counselor is the only title I use. A second, larger circle contains the heads of the eight divisions—we call them partners. Finally, a third huge circle holds all the other employees. Most of them are the people we call associates; they do the research, design, sales, and manufacturing work and have no one reporting to them on a regular basis. But some of them are the permanent and temporary team and task leaders, and we call them coordinators. Counselors, partners, coordinators, and associates. Four titles. Three management layers.

The linchpins of the system are the coordinators, a group that includes everyone formerly called foreman, supervisor, manager, head, or chief. The only people who report to coordinators are associates. No coordinator reports to another coordinator—that feature of the system is what ensures the reduction in management layers.

Like anyone else, we value leadership, but it's not the only thing we value. In marine pumps, for example, we have an applications engineer who can look at the layout of a ship and then focus on one particular pump and say, "That pump will fail if you take this thing north of the Arctic Circle." He makes a lot more money than the person who manages his unit. We can change the manager, but this guy knows what kind of pump will work in the Arctic, and that's worth more. Associates often make higher salaries than coordinators and partners, and then can increase their status and compensation without entering the "management" line.

Managers and the status and money they enjoy—in a word, hierarchy—are the single biggest obstacle to participatory management. We had to get the managers out of the way of democratic decision-making, and our circular system does that pretty well.

But we go further. We don't hire or promote people until they've been interviewed and accepted by all their future subordinates. Twice a year, subordinates evaluate managers. Also twice a year, everyone in the company anonymously fills out a questionnaire about company credibility and top management competence. Among other things, we ask our employees what it would take to make them quit or go on strike.

We insist on making important decisions collegially, and certain decisions are made by a company-wide vote. Several years ago, for example, we needed a bigger plant for our marine division, which makes pumps, compressors, and ship propellers. Real-estate agents looked for months and found nothing. So we asked the employees themselves to help, and over the first weekend, they found three factories for sale, all of them nearby. We closed up shop for a day, piled everyone into buses, and drove out to inspect the three buildings. Then the workers voted—and they chose a plant the counselors didn't really want. It was an interesting situation—one that tested our commitment to participatory management.

The building stands across the street from a Caterpillar plant that's one of the most frequently struck factories in Brazil. With two tough unions of our own, we weren't looking forward to front-row seats for every labor dispute that came along. But we accepted the employees' decision, because we believe that in the long run, letting people participate in the decisions that affect their lives will have a positive effect on employee motivation and morale.

We bought the building and moved in. The workers designed the layout for a flexible manufacturing system, and they hired one of Brazil's foremost artists to paint the whole thing, inside and out, including the machinery. That plant really belongs to its employees. I feel like a guest every time I walk in.

I don't mind. The division's productivity, in dollars per year per employee, has jumped from $14,200 in 1984—the year we moved—to $37,000 in 1988, and for 1989 the goal is $50,000. Over the same period, market share went from 54% to 62%.

Employees also outvoted me on the acquisition of a company that I'm still sure we should have bought. But they felt we weren't ready to digest it, and I lost the vote. In a case like that, the credibility of our management system is at stake. Employee involvement must be real, even when it makes management uneasy. Anyway, what is the future of an acquisition if the people who have to operate it don't believe it's workable?

Hiring Adults

We have other ways of combating hierarchy, too. Most of our programs are based on the notion of giving employees control over their own lives. In a word, we hire adults, and then we treat them like adults.

Think about that. Outside the factory, workers are men and women who elect governments, serve in the army, lead community projects, raise and educate families, and make decisions every day about the future. Friends solicit their advice. Salespeople court them. Children and grandchildren look up to them for their wisdom and experience. But the moment they walk into the factory, the company transforms them into adolescents. They have to wear badges and name tags, arrive at a certain time, stand in line to punch the clock or eat their lunch, and follow instructions without asking a lot of questions.

One of my first moves when I took control of Semco was to abolish norms, manuals, rules, and regulations. Everyone knows you can't run a large organization without regulations, but everyone also knows that most regulations are poppycock. They rarely solve problems. On the contrary, there is usually some obscure corner of the rule book that justifies the worst silliness people can think up. Common sense is a riskier tactic because it requires personal responsibility.

It's also true that common sense requires just a touch of civil disobedience every time someone calls attention to something that's not working. We had to free the Thoreaus and the Tom Paines in the factory and come to terms with the fact that civil disobedience was not an early sign of revolution but a clear indication of common sense at work.

So we replaced all the nitpicking regulations with the rule of common sense and put our employees in the demanding position of using their own judgment.

We have no dress code, for example. The idea that personal appearance is important in a job—any job—is baloney. We've all heard that salespeople, receptionists, and service reps are the company's calling cards, but in fact, how utterly silly that is. A company that needs business suits to prove its seriousness probably lacks more meaningful proof. And what customer has ever canceled an order because the receptionist was wearing jeans instead of a dress? Women and men look best when they feel good. IBM is not a great company because its salespeople dress to the special standard that Tom Watson set. It's a great company that also happens to have this quirk.

We also scrapped the complex company rules about travel expenses—what sorts of accommodations people were entitled to, whether we'd pay for a theater ticket, whether a free call home meant five minutes or ten. We used to spend a lot of time discussing stuff like that. Now we base everything on common sense. Some people stay in four-star hotels and some live like Spartans. Some people spend $200 a day while others get by on $125. Or so I suppose. No one checks expenses, so there is no way of knowing. The point is, we don't care. If we can't trust people with our money and their judgment, we sure as hell shouldn't be sending them overseas to do business in our name.

We have done away with security searches, storeroom padlocks, and audits of the petty-cash accounts of veteran employees. Not that we wouldn't prosecute a genuinely criminal violation of our trust. We just refuse to humiliate 97% of the workforce to get our hands on the occasional thief or two-bit embezzler.

We encourage—we practically insist on—job rotation every two to five years to prevent boredom. We try hard to provide job security, and for people over 50 or who've been with the company for more than three years, dismissal procedures are extra complicated.

On the more experimental side, we have a program for entry-level management trainees called "Lost in Space," whereby we hire a couple of people every year who have no job description at all. A "godfather" looks after them, and for one year, they can do anything they like, as long as they try at least 12 different areas or units.

By the same logic that governs our other employee programs, we have also eliminated time clocks. People come and go according to their own schedules—even on the factory floor. I admit this idea is hard to swallow; most manufacturers are not ready for factory-floor flextime. But our reasoning was simple.

First, we use cellular manufacturing systems. At our food-processing equipment plant, for example, one cell makes only slicers, another makes scales, another makes mixers, and so forth. Each cell is self-contained, so products—and their problems—are segregated from each other.

Second, we assumed that all of our employees were trustworthy adults. We couldn't believe they would come to work day after day and sit on their hands because no one else was there. Pretty soon, we figured, they would start coordinating their work hours with their coworkers.

And that's exactly what happened, only more so. For example, one man wanted to start at 7 A.M., but because the forklift operator didn't come until 8, he couldn't get his parts. So a general discussion arose, and the upshot was that now everyone knows how to operate the forklift. In fact, most people can now do several jobs. The union has never objected because the initiative came from the workers themselves. It was their idea.

Moreover, the people on the factory floor set the schedule, and if they say that this month they will build 48 commercial dishwashers, then we can go play tennis, because 48 is what they'll build.

In one case, one group decided to make 220 meat slicers. By the end of the month, it had finished the slicers as scheduled—except that even after repeated phone calls, the supplier still hadn't produced the motors. So two employees drove over and talked to the supplier and managed to get delivery at the end of that day, the 31st. Then they stayed all night, the whole workforce, and finished the lot at 4:45 the next morning.

When we introduced flexible hours, we decided to hold regular follow-up meetings to track problems and decide how to deal with abuses and production interruptions. That was years ago, and we haven't yet held the first meeting.

Hunting the Woolly Mammoth

What makes our people behave this way? As Antony Jay points out, corporate man is a very recent animal. At Semco, we try to respect the hunter that dominated the first 99.9% of the history of our species. If you had to kill a mammoth or do without supper, there was no time to draw up an organization chart, assign tasks, or delegate authority. Basically, the person who saw the mammoth from farthest away was the Official Sighter, the one who ran fastest was the Head Runner, whoever threw the most accurate spear was the Grand Marksman, and the person all others respected most and listened to was the Chief. That's all there was to it. Distributing little charts to produce an appearance of order would have been a waste of time. It still is.

What I'm saying is, put ten people together, don't appoint a leader, and you can be sure that one will emerge. So will a sighter, a runner, and whatever else the group needs. We form the groups, but they find their own leaders. That's not a lack of structure, that's just a lack of structure imposed from above.

But getting back to that mammoth, why was it that all the members of the group were so eager to do their share of the work—sighting, running, spearing, chiefing—and to stand aside when someone else could do it better? Because they all got to eat the thing once it was killed and cooked. What mattered was results, not status.

Corporate profit is today's mammoth meat. And though there is a widespread view that profit sharing is some kind of socialist infection, it seems to me that few motivational tools are more capitalist. Everyone agrees that profits should belong to those who risk their capital, that entrepreneurial behavior deserves reward, that the creation of wealth should enrich the creator. Well, depending on how you define capital and risk, all these truisms can apply as much to workers as to shareholders.

Still, many profit-sharing programs are failures, and we think we know why. Profit sharing won't motivate employees if they see it as just another management gimmick, if the company makes it difficult for them to see how their own work is related to profits and to understand how those profits are divided.

In Semco's case, each division has a separate profit-sharing program. Twice a year, we calculate 23% of the after-tax profit on each division income statement and give a check to three employees who've been elected by the workers in their division. These three invest the money until the unit can meet and decide—by simple majority vote—what they want to do with it. In most units, that's turned out to be an equal distribution. If a unit has 150 workers, the total is divided by 150 and handed out. It's that simple. The guy who sweeps the floor gets just as much as the division partner.

One division chose to use the money as a fund to lend out for housing construction. It was a pretty close vote, and the workers may change their minds next year. In the meantime, some of them have already received loans and have begun to build themselves houses. In any case, the employees do what they want with the money. The counselors stay out of it.

Semco's experience has convinced me that profit sharing has an excellent chance of working when it crowns a broad program of employee participation, when the profit-sharing criteria are so clear and simple that the least gifted employee can understand them, and, perhaps most important, when employees have monthly access to the company's vital statistics—costs, overhead, sales, payroll, taxes, (and) profits.

Transparency

Lots of things contribute to a successful profit-sharing program: low employee turnover, competitive pay, absence of paternalism, refusal to give consolation prizes when profits are down, frequent (quarterly or semiannual) profit distribution, and plenty of opportunity for employees to question the management decisions that affect future profits. But nothing matters more than those vital statistics— short, frank, frequent reports on how the company is doing. Complete transparency. No hocus-pocus, no hanky-panky, no simplifications.

On the contrary, all Semco employees attend classes to learn how to read and understand the numbers, and it's one of their unions that teaches the course. Every month, each employee gets a balance sheet, a profit-and-loss analysis, and a cash-flow statement for his or her division. The reports contain about 70 line items (more, incidentally, than we use to run the company, but we don't want anyone to think we're withholding information).

Many of our executives were alarmed by the decision to share monthly financial results with all employees. They were afraid workers would want to know everything, like how much we pay executives. When we held the first large meeting to discuss these financial reports with the factory committees and the leaders of the metalworkers' union, the first question we got was, "How much do division managers make?" We told them. They gasped. Ever since, the factory workers have called them "maharaja."

But so what? If executives are embarrassed by their salaries, that probably means they aren't earning them. Confidential payrolls are for those who cannot look themselves in the mirror and say with conviction, "I live in a capitalist system that remunerates on a geometric scale. I spent years in school, I have years of experience, I am capable and dedicated and intelligent. I deserve what I get."

I believe that the courage to show the real numbers will always have positive consequences over the long term. On the other hand, we can show only the numbers we bother to put together, and there aren't as many as there used to be. In my view, only the big numbers matter. But Semco's accounting people keep telling me that since the only way to get the big numbers is to add up the small ones, producing a budget or report that includes every tiny detail would require no extra effort. This is an expensive fallacy, and a difficult one to eradicate.

A few years ago, the U.S. president of Allis-Chalmers paid Semco a visit. At the end of his factory tour, he leafed through our monthly reports and budgets. At that time, we had our numbers ready on the fifth working day of every month in super-organized folders, and were those numbers comprehensive! On page 67, chart 112.6, for example, you could see how much coffee the workers in Light Manufacturing III had consumed the month before. The man said he was surprised to find such efficiency in a Brazilian company. In fact, he was so impressed that he asked his Brazilian subsidiary, an organization many times our size, to install a similar system there.

For months, we strolled around like peacocks, telling anyone who cared to listen that our budget system was state-of-the-art and that the president of a Big American Company had ordered his people to copy it. But soon, we began to realize two things. First, our expenses were always too high, and they never came down because the accounting department was full of overpaid clerks who did nothing but compile them. Second, there were so damn many numbers inside the folder that almost none of our managers read them. In fact, we knew less about the company then, with all that information, than we do now without it.

Today, we have a simple accounting system providing limited but relevant information that we can grasp and act on quickly. We pared 400 cost centers down to 50. We beheaded hundreds of classifications and dozens of accounting lines. Finally, we can see the company through the haze.

(As for Allis-Chalmers, I don't know whether it ever adopted our old system in all its terrible completeness, but I hope not. A few years later, it began to suffer severe financial difficulties and eventually lost so much market share and money that it was broken up and sold. I'd hate to think it was our fault.)

In preparing budgets, we believe that the flexibility to change the budget continually is much more important than the detailed consistency of the initial numbers. We also believe in the importance of comparing expectations with results. Naturally, we compare monthly reports with the budget. But we go one step further. At month's end, the coordinators in each area make guesses about unit receipts, profit margin, and expenses. When the official numbers come out a few days later, top managers compare them with the guesses to judge how well the coordinators understand their areas.

What matters in budgets as well as in reports is that the numbers be few and important and that people treat them with something approaching passion. The three monthly reports, with their 70 line items, tell us how to run the company, tell our managers how well they know their units, and tell our employees if there's going to be a profit. Everyone works on the basis of the same information, and everyone looks forward to its appearance with what I'd call fervent curiosity.

And that's all there is to it. Participation gives people control of their work, profit sharing gives them a reason to do it better, information tells them what's working and what isn't.

Letting Them Do Whatever the Hell They Want

So we don't have systems or staff functions or analysts or anything like that. What we have are people who either sell or make, and there's nothing in between. Is there a marketing department? Not on your life. Marketing is everybody's problem. Everybody knows the price of the product. Everybody knows the cost. Everybody has the monthly statement that says exactly what each of them makes, how much bronze is costing us, how much overtime we paid, all of it. And the employees know that 23% of the after-tax profit is theirs.

We are very, very rigorous about the numbers. We want them in on the fourth day of the month so we can get them back out on the fifth. And because we're so strict with the financial controls, we can be extremely lax about everything else. Employees can paint the walls any color they like. They can come to work whenever they decide. They can do whatever the hell they want. It's up to them to see the connection between productivity and profit and to act on it.

That concludes the Harvard Business Review Article by Ricardo. Next, is the sidebar from that article with Ricardo's unique view on compensation.

Ricardo Semler's Guide to Compensation

Employers began hiring workers by the hour during the Industrial Revolution. Their reasons were simple and rapacious. Say you ran out of cotton thread at 11:30 in the morning. If you paid people by the hour, you could stop the looms, send everyone home, and pay only for hours actually worked.

You couldn't do such a thing today. The law probably wouldn't let you. The unions certainly wouldn't let you. Your own self-interest would argue strongly against it. Yet the system lives on. The distinction between wage-earning workers and salaried employees is alive but not well, nearly universal but perfectly silly. The new clerk who lives at home and doesn't know how to boil an egg starts on a monthly salary, but the chief lathe operator who's been with the company 38 years and is a master sergeant in the army reserve still gets paid by the hour.

At Semco, we eliminated Frederick Winslow Taylor's segmentation and specialization of work. We ended the wage analyst's hundred years of solitude. We did away with hourly pay and now give everyone a monthly salary. We set salaries like this:

A lot of our people belong to unions, and they negotiate their salaries collectively. Everyone else's salary involves an element of self-determination.

Once or twice a year, we order salary market surveys and pass them out. We say to people, "Figure out where you stand on this thing. You know what you do; you know what everyone else in the company makes; you know what your friends in other companies make; you know what you need; you know what's fair. Come back Monday and tell us what to pay you."

174

When people ask for too little, we give it to them. By and by, they figure it out and ask for more. When they ask for too much, we give that to them, too—at least for the first year. Then, if we don't feel they're worth the money, we sit down with them and say, "Look, you make X amount of contribution. So either we find something else for you to do, or we don't have a job for you anymore." But with half a dozen exceptions, our people have always named salaries we could live with.

We do a similar thing with titles. Counselors are counselors, and partners are partners; these titles are always the same. But with coordinators, it's not quite so easy. Job titles still mean too much to many people. So we tell coordinators to make up their own titles. They know what signals they need to send inside and outside the company. If they want "Procurement Manager," that's fine. And if they want "Grand Panjandrum of Imperial Supplies," that's fine, too.

This completes the HBR Article. One thing you can say about Ricardo, he is certainly innovative! Following is some additional information about Semco from Ricardo's book *Maverick* which was published in 1993. The turnaround in the productivity and financial fortunes at Semco all came about when the management (in this case, Ricardo) decided to take a leap of faith and manage Semco utilizing three values: trust, democracy and transparency. The first value was trust, Ricardo put 100% trust in the employees. In Ricardo's own words, "We have absolute trust in our employees. In fact, we are partners with them."[185] He went on to say, "We simply do not believe our employees have an interest in coming in late, leaving early, and doing as little as possible for as much money as their union can wheedle out of us. After all, these same people raise children, join the PTA, elect mayors, governors, senators, and presidents. They are adults. At Semco, we treat them like adults. We trust them. We don't make our employees ask permission to go to the bathroom, or have security guards search them as they leave for the day. We get out of their way and let them do their jobs."[186]

Without his trust in his employees, all of the innovative actions that he and his employees have taken would not have been possible. The second value that is key to this story is democracy. One example of democracy at Semco is their profit-sharing plan. "Semco has a profit-sharing plan – but with a difference. Typically, companies hand down these plans like God handed Moses the Commandments. The owners decide who gets what, when. At Semco, profit-sharing is democratic. We negotiated with our workers over the basic percentage to be distributed—about a quarter of our corporate profits, as it turned out—and they hold assemblies to decide how to split it. It's up to them. *Profit sharing has worked so well that once, during negotiations over a new labor contract, a union leader argued that too big a raise would overextend the company.*"[187] You certainly would never hear a union leader make that kind of a statement in a company that was run using the industrial-age command-and-control business model, that is for sure.

The power of trust and democracy can readily be seen in how the relationship between Semco and the unions have changed since those values have been utilized within the company. With democracy also comes freedom, which then leads to flexibility and innovation.

When you eliminate rigid thought and hierarchical structure, things usually get messy, which is how our factories look. Instead of machines neatly aligned in long straight rows, the way Henry Ford wanted it, they are set at odd angles and in unexpected places. That's because our workers typically work in clusters or teams, assembling a complete product, not just an isolated component. That gives them more control and responsibility, which makes them happier and our products better. Nearly all of our workers have mastered several jobs. They even drive forklifts to keep teammates supplied with raw materials and spare parts, which they have been known to purchase themselves from suppliers.

The Metalworkers' Union at first resisted this flexibility. Long ago, organized labor was forced to adopt narrower and narrower job classifications as a defense against giant corporations that pushed ever harder for higher productivity and profits. Eventually the unions realized that they could turn the system against the corporate masters by refusing to allow any deviation from the rules without extra pay. With time, the system became more beneficial to labor than to management—but it really wasn't serving either side.

When the union realized that Semco had no intention of dismantling its power, that the higher profits our factories would generate would mean higher pay for its members, and that we were intent on giving workers a meaningful say in our business, obstructionism eased. We have been allowed to innovate—to let our employees innovate. We are all freer.[188]

Ricardo then went further. "I went ahead and asked our employees at each of our four business units to form committees comprised of representatives from every part of the operation but management. Machinist, mechanics, office workers, maintenance workers, stockroom personnel, draftsmen—every group would have a delegate on these committees, which would meet regularly with top managers at each plant."[189]   When the committees were formed, they were given instructions that "they were to look after the workers' interests. Members would even have time off, with pay, to dedicate themselves to their new job, which we fully expected would lead to demands for shorter hours, higher pay, improved working conditions, and maybe even better food in the cafeterias. We didn't want the unions to think the committees were designed to replace them, so we negotiated their charters with union leaders, and gave them a seat on each committee as well."[190]   As a result of these committees being formed at Ricardo's request, "When plants faced hard times, their factory committees would take the initiative and lower wages or increase hours, saving money and protecting jobs. When layoffs were unavoidable, the committees got involved in the sensitive and unfortunate task of deciding who would go."[191] Many managers and company owners have complained that they wished that their employees "would act like owners."   The Semco story shows clearly, that when management creates the appropriate working environment with trust, empowerment, and profit sharing along with the open sharing of all information, including the books (financial reports), that the employees will indeed take the initiative and "act like owners." They just have to be given the opportunity by management.

Ricardo's Take on Rules

With the implementation of the values of trust, democracy, profit-sharing, transparency, and the sharing of all company information, the need for a manual on corporate rules and guidelines mostly evaporated. Without the rigid, bureaucratic, command-and-control management structure, all of the costs associated with documenting and implementing a lot of rules can be for all practical purposes eliminated. Ricardo's view is that:

"Rules and regulations only serve to:

1. Divert attention from a company's objectives.
2. Provide a false sense of security for executives.
3. Create work for bean counters.
4. Teach men to stone dinosaurs and start fires with sticks.

The desire for rules and the need for innovation are, I believe, incompatible. Rules freeze companies inside a glacier; innovation lets them ride sleighs over it."[192]

As you might guess, all of the thick manuals on regulations at Semco are gone. "All that new employees at Semco get today is a twenty-page booklet we call *The Survival Manual*. It has lots of cartoons but few words. The basic message: use your common sense."[193] Ricardo's advice is to "take a deep breath, pluck up your courage, and feed the policy manual to the shredder, one page at a time."[194] Not only does this approach save the company money, but a less obvious side benefit is that "people begin to make more decisions on their own, **decisions they are usually better qualified to make than their supervisors.**"[195]

The implementation of truth as a company principle invariably leads to transparency on the part of management. "I know all the arguments against a policy of full disclosure. Employees will use the numbers to argue for raises in good times, or be frightened by the numbers in the bad times. Even worse, trade secrets will be leaked to the competition. But the advantages of openness and truthfulness far outweigh the disadvantages. And a company that doesn't share information when the times are good loses the right to request solidarity and concessions when they aren't."[196]

As Ricardo says,

> We always try to speak the truth and nothing but the truth. And on those rare occasions when the truth, for some special reason, cannot be told, we say nothing. We believe it is essential that all company

communications, especially those intended for the workers or the public, be absolutely honest. We even apply this policy to journalists. Reporters from all the television networks and major newspapers and magazines in Brazil can talk to whomever they want at Semco, no matter what they have reported in the past, and do. And our people speak their minds, without fear. We take another step to insure that communication at Semco flows. Two or three times a year we distribute a questionnaire called 'What Does the Company Think?' It gives workers another chance to tell us whether they are satisfied with their salaries, have any reason to leave the company, would ever support a strike, have confidence in management, and so on. The results are published for all to see (of course), and enable us to monitor our credibility as well as their concerns.

We even encourage civil disobedience in the company, though we do it subtly. If a request for some item gets bogged down in purchasing, for example, employees know that in a jam they can just buy it themselves and send us the bill. Workers have held protest in our cafeterias because they thought we should subsidize 100 percent of their meals, not just 70 percent. Some have refused to wear a uniform. Our reaction is to do nothing, except explain why things are as they are. If coexistence is impossible, they'll either eventually leave on their own or be slowly expelled from the system. But we have people who agree with very little of what we think and are still here, unapologetic and unfettered. So what if they don't wear a uniform, as long as they do their job.[197]

When employees are trusted and empowered by their management as in the case at Semco, then the employees are free to speak their minds, to be innovative and to take as much initiative as their good sense will allow. When the trust and empowerment is coupled with a profit-sharing plan that is straightforward and designed so that the employees can see a direct relationship between their production and the size of the profit-sharing check, then the employees will take the initiative. An example if this is what happened at the Hobart plant of Semco. "Soon every section of the Hobart plant boasted scoreboards above the shop floor that tracked the workers' current production against a monthly goal they themselves set. Managers didn't put the scoreboards up; the workers did. They even had a master scoreboard in the cafeteria that showed the whole plant's daily output, product by product. At first, setting goals and monitoring production was uncomfortable for some workers, who were accustomed to arguing that if management's quotas weren't met it was because executives hadn't planned correctly. Now, the workers couldn't mindlessly complain about how the factory was run, since they were helping to run it."[198]

Team members and managers

With the implementation of trust, self-directed teams or what Ricardo refers to as participative management, the employees have, through much of their own initiative, taken over many of the personnel responsibilities at Semco. At Semco, it is the teams that "recruit and expel new members of their teams,"[199] not management. "Today, anyone who applies to be a machinist at Semco will be interviewed by a group of machinists, not an executive, which is the worst thing that can happen to him, because he might be able to talk his way past a manager but not the people who know everything there is to know about being a machinist and who may one day be his co-workers. If they say yes, the candidate has a job. I've not heard of a case in which shop-floor workers have opposed someone and a manager has gone ahead and hired him. I can't imagine a Semco manager taking such a risk. Nor do I know of a case in which someone is approved by everybody on the shop floor but rejected by the manager. In our system it isn't possible for one person to overrule everyone else."[200]

At Semco, not only do the employees choose their teammates, they in essence also choose their "manager." Per Ricardo:

> Like so many innovations at Semco, I don't exactly know how it started. Initially, we just wanted to know why some people hadn't become the successes we thought they would be when we promoted them, and naturally asked those who worked for them. That led us to draw up a form subordinates now use to evaluate their managers twice a year. It has about three dozen multiple-choice questions designed to measure technical ability, competence, leadership, and other aspects of being a boss. The questionnaire is filled out anonymously, so no one is afraid to be honest. We weight the questions and answers according to their importance and calculate a grade, which is posted, so everyone knows where everyone stands. Seventy percent is passing, but most managers get between 80 and 85 percent. Managers who score below 70 are not automatically dismissed, but a low grade usually creates intense pressure on an individual to change. What we want to see is improvement from one year to the next. Supervisors meet with their subordinates to discuss their grades, so the process of change starts very quickly. This employee review builds on one of Semco's great strengths, our transparency. At our company people can always say what's on their minds, even to their bosses—even when it's about their bosses. It is instilled in our corporate culture that everyone should be willing to listen, and admit when they are wrong.[201]

Ricardo observes: "Does this mean workers can fire their bosses? I guess it does, since everyone who consistently gets bad grades usually leaves Semco, one way or the other."[202] You might say that at Semco, they have successfully inverted the pyramid, at least in this case they have.

Ricardo Semler in many ways is what Jim Collins describes as a Level-5 Leader. He has more ambition for the company than for himself. He does not require all of the ego satisfaction perks that a Level-4 Effective Leader would.

> In the lobby of our headquarters, a standard-issue office building with four floors of steel and glass, there is a reception desk but no receptionist. That's the first clue that we are different. We don't have receptionists. We don't think they are necessary, despite all our visitors. We don't have secretaries either, or personal assistants. We don't believe in cluttering the payroll with ungratifying, dead-end jobs. Everyone at Semco, even top managers, fetches guests, stands over photocopiers, sends faxes, types letters, and dials the phone. We don't have executive dining rooms, and parking is strictly first-come, first-served. It's all part of running a 'natural business.' At Semco we have stripped away the unnecessary perks and privileges that feed the ego but hurt the balance sheet and distract everyone from the crucial corporate tasks of making, selling, billing and collecting. Our offices don't even have the usual number of walls. Instead, a forest of plants separates the desks, computers, and drawing boards in our work areas. The mood is informal: some people wear suits and ties or dresses, others jeans and sneakers. It doesn't matter. If people want to emulate Thomas Watson and don white button-downs, that's fine. But turtlenecks and T-shirts are okay too. And I want our people to feel free to put their feet on their desks, just like me. I am pleased to report that more than once a group of Semco executives has been interrupted by people who wanted to use their conference room to hold a birthday party. It warms my heart to see vice presidents eating cake on little plates decorated with Mickey and Minnie. My office is on the fourth

floor—at least it was the last time I looked. I don't use it as much as other proprietors. Most mornings I work at home. I concentrate better there, despite two sheepdogs that like to bark when I'm on the phone with important customers. I encourage other Semco managers to work at home too. I also take two months off each year to travel, and I like to roam far. There are pictures in my office of two recent expeditions, a balloon safari in Tanzania and a trek through the Khyber Pass in Afghanistan. I never leave a number where I can be reached when I'm away and I don't call in. I want everyone at Semco to be self-sufficient. The company is organized—well maybe that's not quite the right word for us—not to depend too much on any individual, especially me. I take it as a point of pride that twice on my return from long trips my office had been moved—and each time it got smaller. My role is that of a catalyst. I try to create an environment in which others make decisions. **Success means not making them myself**.[203]

On the subject of status symbols, Ricardo says, "We don't condone symbols of power or exclusivity such as executive cafeterias or reserved parking spaces."[204]

When it comes to pay: "As a matter of corporate policy, we try to keep our top salaries within ten times our entry level pay, which is in stark contrast to the rest of the country. For the record…my salary reached a high of $300,000 in the heady days of 1989, but has been as low as $120,000."[205]

Finally there is this. "Nothing is harder work than democracy, I keep telling myself. I don't remember the last time I made a corporate decision alone, nor can I count all the times I've been voted down. But I gladly bite my lip when I disagree with a judgment made by consensus, because I believe that unfettered democracy is much more important (and even more profitable in the long run) then prevailing over our managers in a way that takes you back to the days in which seesaws and sandboxes were important parts of the world. There is an added benefit to having a democratically minded No. 1: the No. 2s, No. 3s, No. 4s and No. 5s can play meaningful roles right away. Too many vice presidents in traditional companies are made to feel like also-rans; when they can't move up they have to leave. An inordinate amount of talent is lost this way.

"With this in mind, and with Semco restructured in a way that made it much less vulnerable to the economy, I decided it was time to virtually eliminate another level of our hierarchy: mine. Instead of one person at the top, Semco would be run by a committee of our Counselors. They were, I believed, a particularly well-balanced team, professionally and personally."[206] One final observation from Ricardo: "No company can be successful, in the long run anyway, if profits are its principal goal."[207]

Have Ricardo's unorthodox approach to management and trusting of its employees been successful? In the years from 1980 to 1992, the employees raised the value of the goods produced per employee from $10,800 to $92,000, four times the average in Brazil and an average annual increase of 70% per year. In the same time period, *sales grew five times with one third the workers.*[208] This represents an average annual increase of 125% per year. As the record shows, Ricardo's unusual methods of management have been extremely successful. The data speaks for itself.

Next, the following four chapters will describe the five parts of the new Information-Age Purpose-Driven Business Model that will replace the currently used Industrial-Age Profit-Driven Business Model.

Chapter 10
Information Age Business
Model – Leadership

A leader is best when people barely know he exists; when his work is done, his aim fulfilled, they will say: we did it ourselves.

–Lao Tzu

As the Semco story illustrated, there is more than one way to run a business and there is more than one way to organize a business to be successful. One of those new ways of running a business is the Information-Age Purpose-Driven Business Model, which has five distinct parts that will be described in this and the next four chapters. The five elements are:

1. Level 5 Leadership
2. The Teleocratic Management System
3. A Statistic-Based Measurement System
4. A New Methodology for Performance Evaluation
5. A Productivity-Based Compensation System

This chapter will begin with the first element, a description of the characteristics of a Level-5 Executive, and then the following question will be addressed: Why do the companies that utilize the Information-Age Purpose-Driven Business Model also happen to have Level-5 Executives instead of Level-4 Effective Leaders?

During the research project that led to the writing of Jim Collins' book, *Good to Great*, Jim gave the researchers "explicit instructions to downplay the role of the top executives" while doing their research so they "could avoid the simplistic 'credit the leader' or 'blame the leader' thinking that is so common today."[209] The research was aimed at discovering why some companies that had lingered in mediocrity for years, suddenly transitioned into companies that outperformed the average public companies by a factor of over eight to one.[210] However, after they would interview the selected companies and spend time with the CEOs, they could not ignore the fact that all of the CEOs were different than what they expected, and they were all alike! "The good-to-great executives were all cut from the same cloth. It didn't matter whether the company was consumer or industrial, in crisis or steady state, offered services or products. It didn't matter when the transition took place or how big the company (was). All the good-to-great companies had Level-5 leadership."[211] During the research for his book on the most productive companies in the world, Jason Jennings made a very similar observation regarding the CEOs of those companies. He said, "There's an observation that applies across the board—an observation that stands in stark contrast to what most people witness while moving about the upper echelons of business: there's simply no bullshit and bluster, no sense of self-importance, about any of these people."[212] Jason Jennings was observing Level–5 Executives.

The description that Jim Collins and the staff created for Level-5 Leadership is as follows: He "builds enduring greatness through a paradoxical blend of personal humility and professional will."[213]

Level-5 Leaders have the following characteristics:

1. **Humility with a strong professional will;**
2. **Modesty;**
3. **Credits luck or others for success;**
4. **Looks to themselves when things are not going well;**
5. **Has ambition for the company.**

1. Humility With a Strong Professional Will

"Being humble does not mean being weak, reticent, or self-effacing. It means recognizing principle and putting it ahead of self."[214] Perhaps the best way to communicate the humility and the professional will of true Level-5 Leaders is by an example. Ken Iverson, the CEO of Nucor, the only company that was selected as one of the good-to-great companies and also as one of the most productive companies in the world, is an example of this humility. Ken took Nucor from near bankruptcy to being one of the most successful companies in the world. Nucor board member, Jim Hlavacek, had this to say about Ken Iverson:

> Ken is a very modest and humble man. I've never known a person as successful in doing what he's done that's as modest. And, I work for a lot of CEOs of large companies. And that's true in his private life as well. The simplicity of him. I mean little things, like he always gets his dogs at the local pound. He has a simple house that he's lived in for ages. He only has a carport, and he complained to me one day about how he had to use his credit card to scrape the frost off his windows, and he broke the credit card. "You know, Ken, there's a solution for it; enclose your carport." And he said, "Ah, heck, it isn't that big of a deal...." He's that humble and simple.[215]

In addition to the high levels of humility, the Level 5 Leaders also have an extremely strong professional will and ambition for the companies they lead. An example of this is Coleman Mockler, the CEO of Gillette from 1975 to 1991. During his tenure, Mockler turned back two hostile takeover bids by Revlon and a third attack from Coniston Partners. Rather than giving in and pocketing millions of dollars personally, Mockler chose to fight. "A quiet and reserved man, always courteous, Mockler had the reputation of a gracious, almost patrician gentleman. Yet those who mistook Mockler's reserved nature for weakness found themselves beaten in the end. In the proxy fight, senior Gillette executives reached out to thousands of individual investors—person by person, phone call by phone call—and won the battle."[216] Why did Mockler fight the takeover bids even though he personally could have made a quick fortune by giving in? Mockler knew that Gillette had new products in development (later to be known as Sensor and Mach3) the value of which was not reflected in the current stock price. Mockler's ambition was also for the company, the stock holders and the employees, not himself. As it turned out, because of Mocklers professional will to protect Gillette, the company thrived, the employees kept their jobs and the stockholders were three times better off in the long run.[217]

Another example of this strong professional will is Darwin E. Smith, the CEO of Kimberly-Clark, a CEO that most people have never heard of. In 1971, Darwin E. Smith, the company's quiet, easy-going lawyer, became the CEO of Kimberly-Clark, which at that time was a below-average-performing company. In the twenty years prior to Smith becoming the CEO, the stock of Kimberly-Clark had underperformed the market by 36 percent. Two months after becoming CEO, doctors diagnosed Smith as having nose and throat cancer, and predicted that he only had about a year to live. Mr. Smith informed the board of his condition and let the board know that he was alive and that he had no plans to die in the near future. As it turned out, Darwin Smith kept his busy schedule as CEO and commuted to Houston for weekly treatments and lived another twenty-five years.

Just as his strong will served him well in his personal life, Darwin Smith applied the same strong will in his professional life. Like all Level-5 Leaders, Darwin Smith's ambition was to make Kimberly-Clark a great company. To accomplish this, he made some bold and dramatic moves. Kimberly-Clark had for years thought of itself as a paper company. Its roots were with the paper mills that it owned, and in particular the paper mill in Kimberly, Wisconsin. The core business of Kimberly-Clark at that time was the production of coated paper. However, Mr. Smith understood that the economics of the coated-paper business were poor and were not going to improve. So what did Darwin Smith do? Did he blame the competition and then start cutting expenses so he could inflate the short-term profits to then sell the company with a big profit for himself? No, his purpose was to build a great company. So Darwin Smith made some bold (and some people thought stupid) decisions. Darwin Smith decided to get out of the coated-paper business, sell the plants and commit to becoming the leading paper-based consumer-products company in the world; that became his and the company's purpose. Many observers felt that this was a risky, gutsy move, and the business media called the move stupid and downgraded the stock. Darwin Smith did not blink. He sold the paper mills, even the one in Kimberly, Wisconsin, and put all of the proceeds into the paper products business with such products as Huggies and Kleenex.

Under the leadership of Darwin Smith, in the next twenty years, Kimberly-Clark went from under-performing the market by 36 percent to exceeding the market by 410 percent! The company easily beat rivals such as Scott Paper and Procter & Gamble, and in the next twenty years outperformed such companies as Coca-Cola and General Electric. Twenty-five years later, Kimberly-Clark owned Scott Paper and beat Proctor & Gamble in six of eight product categories. After he retired, Darwin Smith reflected on his exceptional performance and said, "I never stopped trying to become qualified for the job."[218] Level 5 Executives, just like great companies, all have a purpose that is beyond the maximization of profits. Their purpose is the building of great companies.

2. Modesty

David Packard, one of the founders of Hewlett–Packard, was also a true Level-5 Leader. Here is what Jim Collins had to say about Mr. Packard: "Shortly before his death, I had the opportunity to meet David Packard. Despite being one of Silicon Valley's first self-made billionaires, he lived in the same small house that he and his wife built for themselves in 1957, overlooking a simple orchard. The tiny kitchen, with its dated linoleum, and the simply furnished living room bespoke a man who needed no material symbols to proclaim 'I'm a billionaire. I'm important. I'm successful.'[219] Bill Terry, who worked for Mr. Packard for thirty-six years, says that Mr. Packard's idea of a good time was to 'get some of his friends together to string some barbed wire.' Upon his death, the family created a eulogy pamphlet with a picture of David Packard sitting on a tractor in farming clothes. It read very simply: David Packard, 1912 – 1996, Rancher, etc."[220] More words are not necessary.

3 & 4. Credits luck or others for success; looks to themselves when things do not go well.

Joseph F. Cullman was the CEO that presided over the transition of Philip Morris from a company with just average performance to a company with sustained great performance. However, when asked about the company's success, he "flat-out refused to take credit for his company's success." Instead he attributed the company success to "having great colleagues, successors, and predecessors."[221] Alan Wurtzel, the CEO of Circuit City, when asked to list the top five factors in his company's transformation from average to great performance, in order of priority, gave this answer: "The number one factor was *luck*. 'We were in a great industry, with the wind at our backs.'"[222] Perhaps the best example of these characteristics is the difference between the executives of Bethlehem Steel and Nucor. Both companies were in the steel business, competitors, and facing the same competition from low–priced, foreign steel imports. In 1983, Bethlehem Steels CEO blamed the company's problems on imported steel. "Our first, second, and third problems are imports." But Ken Iverson, the Level-5 CEO of Nucor, had a different perspective. He saw "the first, second, and third problems facing the American steel industry not to be imports, but *management*." He went on to say, "The real problems facing the American steel industry lay in the fact that management had failed to keep pace with innovation." Mr. Iverson saw the imports, not as a problem, but as a blessing. "Aren't we lucky; steel is heavy, and they have to ship it all the way across the ocean, giving us a huge advantage!"[223] What a difference between a Level-4 Effective Leader and a Level-5 Executive! It is like night and day. Level 4 Effective Leaders look to blame others or outside forces when things are not going well, but take all of the credit when things do go well. Level-5 Executives are just the opposite. They refuse to take the credit for successes and look to themselves to take action when things are not going well rather them blaming others or outside forces.

5. Have Ambition for the Company

For Level-5 Leaders, their greatest satisfaction and fulfillment is the company that they helped to build and what that company stands for. That is because the Level-5 Leaders see the company as a means to a greater end (the company purpose) and not an end of its own. It is not about them and their legacy or their ego. They sincerely and truly, deep down inside, gain self-fulfillment and gratification by serving others and pursuing the company's greater purpose. Their tool for serving others just happens to be building great companies that benefit all of the company's constituencies and at the same time fulfilling the company purpose. Great companies benefit their customers with great products and services, the employees with well paying jobs and respect, and stockholders with great returns on their investment; they are also an asset to the communities in which they do business. The essence of this is captured in the words of perhaps the most famous Level-5 Executive ever—Sam Walton, the founder of Wal-Mart. Mr. Walton said:

> "I have concentrated all along on building the finest retailing company that we possibly could. Period. Creating a huge personal fortune was never a particular goal of mine."[224]

Sam Walton's ambition was to build the best retailing company that he could, and his company was to stand for great customer service while providing products of great value. He said, "I always had confidence that as long as we did our work well and were good to our customers, there would be no limit to us."[225]

A part of the ambition that Level-5 Executives have for the companies that they lead is a desire to see the company have even greater success after they retire. To quote one Level-5 Executive, "I want to look out from my porch at one of the great companies in the world someday and be able to say, 'I used to work there.'"[226] In contrast, Level-4 Effective Leaders are so consumed with their image, their ego, their earnings, etc., that they are not concerned about the future of the company after they leave. In the research that Jim Collins and his staff did for the book, *Good to Great*, they identified not only the companies that transitioned from good performance to great performance, but they also selected an equivalent set of companies that were in the same business and had the same opportunity to succeed, but did not. They called these companies, "the comparison companies." Their research showed that "in over three-quarters of the comparison companies, we found executives who set their successors up for failure or chose weak successors, or both."[227] This explains why so many companies suffer a significant decline after the larger-than-life Level-4 Leader leaves the company. Before their departure, these Level 4 Leaders have taken actions to improve short-term results at the expense of the long-term future of the company.

Question: Why do the companies that utilize the Information-Age Purpose-Driven Business Model also happen to have Level-5 Executives instead of Level-4 Effective Leaders?

A simpler way to ask the question is, why do profit-driven companies consistently have Level-4 Leaders while purpose-driven companies have Level-5 Executives? The answer lies in the relationship between the purpose of a company and the priorities and company culture that the purpose will generate. When a company has no purpose other than the pursuit of profit, or the maximization of profit for the owners or stockholders, then the focus is only on the benefit that the company can provide to the owners/stockholders, period. In this case, the company is the end objective. The interests of everyone else—all the other constituencies—will be sacrificed, if necessary, in the name of increased profits. There is no moral imperative, no values that must be upheld; there is only the pursuit of profit. In this environment or company culture, it is every person for themselves. The environment where everyone is out for themselves fits very well with the characteristics of the Level-4 Leader. As we now know, for the Level-4 Leader, it is all about them being in the spotlight and how much money they can make. For them, the more money they make, the more the ego is fed. In the profit-driven environment, it can all be about them. They can be the center of attention throughout the company. These executives also compare themselves to their peers by how much each earns. Therefore, as long as another executive is receiving more compensation then they are, that hurts their ego so they are not satisfied and want more. There is no limit. The amount of money is not really the point for these executives. The point for them is whether or not they are making more money than their peers. The boards of directors of these companies also operate under the false assumption that to maximize the profits of the company, a hard-driving, egocentric, Level-4 Leader is what they need. The end result is simply that it is the company purpose of pursuing profit that leads the board to seek out a Level-4 Leader.

However, when the company purpose is something beyond profit, then the focus is on that company purpose, not the CEO. The pursuit of the company's greater purpose becomes the focal point of everyone in the company, including the CEO. Therefore, the job of CEO requires a person who, through their humility, can let their personal ambitions become secondary to those of the company and its purpose. That requires a CEO with the characteristics of a Level 5, not a Level 4. So, as it turns out, **it is the purpose of the company that dictates what type of CEO will be hired.** Profit-driven companies will seek out Level-4 Leaders while purpose-driven companies will seek out Level-5 Executives. That is what the data shows time after time, company after company.

Chapter 11
Information Age Business Model
– Management System

The second part of the Information-Age Purpose-Driven Business Model is a new management system which is named the Teleocratic Management System (TMS). TMS is a management-by-purpose management system that is designed for the information age. At the same time, the new TMS enables empowerment, trust, teamwork, and the pursuit of the company's purpose by all the employees. The difference between the old BMS and the new TMS is like night and day. For example, the BMS is a *fear-driven* system and the TMS is a *trust-based* system. This is a key point, because as the level of trust in an organization increases, so does the productivity. Just as there has been almost a 180-degree shift from the industrial-age business environment to the information-age business environment, the shift from the BMS to the TMS is also almost a 180-degree shift. The Teleocratic Management System derived its name from the Greek word *Teleos* which means "purpose." It was Lou Mobley and Kate McKeown in their book, *Beyond IBM*, who popularized the term "teleocratic" and the concept of management-by-purpose. Thus, the teleocratic management system (management-by-purpose) received its most recognition up to that time.[228]

The teleocratic management system is tightly coupled and integrated with the other four elements of the Information-Age Purpose-Driven Business Model. All five elements of the new business model work in harmony and complement each other. This linkage and alignment is very important as it is the key to the high levels of performance as documented by the companies highlighted in chapter 4. Because all five elements of both the Industrial-Age Business-Model and the Information-Age Business-Model are so tightly coupled and dependent upon each other, it is almost impossible to change one of them without changing all of them. However, when a company changes from being profit driven to being purpose driven, the other changes flow rather naturally. Additionally, the teleocratic management system and its new organizational structure eliminate many problems associated with old multilevel hierarchical business structure.

The Teleocratic Management System

The foundation or bedrock of a TMS is the organizational statements upon which it is built. These organizational statements define three things about a company: the company's purpose, values and vision. The first statement is the purpose statement. The purpose statement explains the "why" about a company—why the company exists; why it does what it does. It explains what the company stands for and what its greater purpose is.

Second, and extremely important, is the values statement. This statement defines the core values, which provide the principles upon which the organization will operate its ongoing business functions. The company values provide the guidelines and ethics for day-to-day operational decision-making within the context of the purpose and vision of the company.

The final element is the organization's vision statement. The vision statement provides a mental image of a future desired state. This statement also explains the "what" about a company—what the company wants to become in the future; what it is trying to accomplish through its efforts. The vision statement provides a guiding light for the company.

These three organizational statements combine to form the "full purpose" of the organization. This "full purpose" must be documented and communicated to all employees and stakeholders of the organization. Again, the company's "full purpose" is composed of these three elements:

1. Organizational Purpose Statement

2. Organizational Values Statement
3. Organizational Vision Statement

With these three statements in place, the company has defined in rather specific terms why it exists, what it wants to accomplish and the kind of company it wants to be. These are very powerful statements because they provide the leadership and all of the employees an instrument through which they can all participate in the creation of something greater than themselves. When these three statements communicate an ennobling future and are embraced by all of the employees, it is a very powerful force.

The First Element: The Organizational Purpose Statement

The first element that must be documented is the company purpose statement. A statement must be created that defines with clarity what the company's fundamental reason for existing is. Why is the company in business? Why does the company do what it does? What does the company stand for? For example, hanging over the main gate at the Newport News ship-building yards for many years was a sign that read:

> We shall build great ships.
> At a profit if we can, at a loss if we must.
> But we will build great ships.[229]

Clearly, the reason why Newport News is in business is to build great ships. Not average ships or good ships, but great ships. Furthermore, they are willing to do so at the expense of profits, if necessary. Another example of an organizational purpose statement comes from the Walt Disney Company. They are in the business to "bring happiness to millions, especially children."[230] That is why they do what they do. Some more examples:

- 3M   To solve unsolved problems innovatively.
- Mary Kay   To give unlimited opportunity to women.

- Fannie Mae   To strengthen the social fabric by continually democratizing home ownership.[231]

When a company discovers its purpose and then the leadership commits the company to the pursuit of the company purpose, that one key decision changes everything within the company. These changes will be described throughout the rest of the book, but by having a documented and communicated company purpose, some key changes are that it provides direction to the company and gives meaning and purpose to all of the employees and all of the work that they do. It simplifies decision making, because now everyone knows what to do and what not to do. The purpose provides a clear foundation upon which the employees can make decisions and determine which activities are essential and which are not. It becomes clear to everyone which business the company is in and which businesses it is not in. The purpose also focuses the company's efforts and energy on what is important and allows the company to become effective by being selective in its endeavors based on the company's purpose. It provides alignment throughout the company because now, everyone within the company shares the same focus and purpose. They are all following the same guiding light. This focus and alignment throughout the entire company based on the company purpose are one source of the phenomenal levels of productivity and financial performance that the purpose-driven companies have demonstrated. One example of the power and galvanizing capability of a common purpose is the story of the Springfield ReManufacturing Company (SRC) of Springfield, Missouri, and their CEO Jack Stack. SRC is in the business of rebuilding old, worn-out engines. In the early 1980s, SRC was a division of International Harvester which was experiencing hard times. In an effort to reduce the corporate debt, International Harvester decided to sell some of its assets. So, in 1983, Jack Stack and twelve fellow managers scraped together $100,000 and then borrowed $8,900,000 to buy SRC from International Harvester. Prior to the purchase, business volumes were very bad. They were so bad that all of the employees had gotten together and decided to work only four days a week instead of five just to avoid layoffs. After the purchase, everyone still had their jobs, but they also had a company that had a debt-to-equity ratio of 89 to 1, which meant that for all practical purposes, the company might as well have been out of business. So the challenge, the goal, or the common purpose was for Jack and all of the employees to turn that ratio around. Needless to say, they did turn it around and they have been highlighted in Jason Jennings' book, *Less is More* as *one of the eight most productive companies in the world,* based on metrics such as revenue per employee, return on equity and return on assets. They have been called a "management Mecca" by *Business Week* and have hosted more than 4,600 people from over 1,600 companies that have come to Missouri to see how they manage their business. Jack's business experiences led him to make the following statement. *"There's a lesson here, and it's the foundation of everything I know and believe about business.* **People can accomplish almost anything if they have a common purpose, a higher goal, and they all know what it is, and they're going after it together.** *Everybody needs to be going somewhere. People need a destination, or they get lost. If they have one, however, and if it's really their own, there's no telling what they can do. They can survive the darkest hours, beat the longest odds, (and) scale the greatest heights."*[232] As has been demonstrated by SRC and other companies, the power of a common purpose that is supported by all of the employees is an extremely powerful force. After a clear statement of the company's purpose has been created, the next step is to clarify what the company values are.

The Second Element: The Organizational Values Statement

The second element of the company purpose is the company's statement of core values. The company's core value statements are the source of the company's principles and beliefs. They explain to everyone how business will be conducted and how people (employees, customers and other constituencies) will be treated. They describe the beliefs that the company holds to be true. The values statement is also the company's source of ethics and must be supported by the everyday actions of management. If the actions of management are not in alignment with the stated values, then the management will lose all credibility and the value statements will become worthless.

The examples of management's actions in such companies as Global Crossing, Tyco and Enron provide clear evidence as to the importance of the values statements. These statements are also particularly important when a company is attempting to attract Generations X and Y because these generations have a natural distrust of business.

The first example of values statements comes from IBM. IBM has documented its values and called the values their "basic beliefs." The IBM values (basic beliefs) are as follows:

1. Respect for the individual
2. Service to the customer
3. Excellence must be a way of life

Thomas J. Watson Jr. (past Chairman of IBM), in his book *A Business and its Beliefs*, makes the following statement:

I firmly believe that any organization, in order to survive and achieve success, must have a sound set of beliefs on which it premises all its policies and actions.

Next, I believe that the most important single factor in corporate success is faithful adherence to those beliefs.

And finally, I believe that if an organization is to meet the challenges of a changing world, it must be prepared to change everything about itself except those beliefs as it moves through corporate life.

In other words, the basic philosophy, spirit, and drive of an organization have far more to do with its relative achievements than do technological or economic resources, organizational structure, innovation, and timing. All these things weigh heavily in success. But they are, I think, transcended by how strongly the people in the organization believe in its precepts and how faithfully they carry them out.[233]

Sam Walton captured Wal-Mart's number one value when he said, "[We put] the customer ahead of everything else. If you're not serving the customer, or supporting those who do, then we don't need you." James Gamble of Proctor and Gamble stated the company's core value of product quality as "When you cannot make pure goods of full weight, go to something that is honest, even if it is breaking stone."[234] Each of these value statements is piercing in its simplicity, but provides a huge amount of guidance for everyone and increases the speed at which decisions can be made within a company. As Roy Disney, the former Vice Chairman of the Walt Disney Company, noted, "It's not hard to make decisions when you know what your values are."[235]

Each company must document the values (beliefs and principles) that it holds to be true. However, there are three values that are extremely important for any company that plans to implement the new teleocratic management system. These three values are:

1. Democracy (All employees have input into decision-making.)
2. Transparency—All information is shared truthfully.
3. Profit sharing (Ownership and equity)

The values work in concert with each other and with the organizational purpose and vision statements. The values provide the glue that makes everything stick together and work together. While each organization must create their values statement for themselves, the omission of democracy, information sharing or profit sharing as a value will make it more difficult to achieve the full potential of a teleocratic management system. CEO Jack Stack made this observation. "Without education, you don't have democracy. The better educated people are, the more democratic you can be, and the better it will work."[236] Relative to the concept of sharing the company information with the employees, Jack Stack also says, "The more people know about the company, the better that company will perform. This is an ironclad rule. You will *always* be more successful in business by sharing information with the people you work with than by keeping them in the dark."[237] "Don't use information to intimidate, control, or manipulate people. Use it to teach people how to work together to achieve common goals and thereby gain control over their lives."[238]

The value of profit sharing must be used in its broadest sense. It must be used in a way that not only makes the employees *feel like* they are owners, but it must *make* them owners. This can be accomplished through a combination of education and profit sharing. Business education will give the employees the knowledge required to understand the linkage between their daily activities and the business results. Sharing of the company information in the form of the income statement and balance sheet on a monthly basis allows all employees to see how they influence the business results and the resulting increase in the value of their equity in the company. When this linkage is established and understood by all of the employees, it is an extremely powerful force.

The Third Element: The Organizational Vision Statement

The third element of the company purpose that must be documented is the company's vision statement. The vision statement should communicate where the company is going and what it will look like or what it wants to accomplish in the future. The vision statement should be uplifting and show the pursuit of higher order values. Stephen Covey, in his book *The 8ᵗʰ Habit*, says, "Vision is seeing a future state with the mind's eye. Vision is applied imagination. All things are created twice: first, a mental creation; second, a physical creation."[239]

Thomas J. Watson, when he became president of the Computing-Tabulating-Recording Company (CTR), had a vision of what the company should look like in the future. His vision was "World peace through world commerce." In his vision, he saw a company that spanned the world, a company that did business in all the major economies and by doing so brought understanding and peace around the world. Now that you know what Thomas J. Watson's vision was for the company, it becomes easy to understand why he renamed the company and called it the International Business Machines

Corporation. In 1924 when CTR was renamed IBM, IBM was hardly a dominant worldwide company. But Thomas J. Watson had a vision, he documented and communicated the vision, and it came to be. It took several decades for Watson's vision to become a reality, but without the vision, it probably would never have happened.

In August 1945, Masaru Ibuka started his company, Tokyo Tsushin Kogyo with $1,600 and seven employees in a bombed and burned-out old department store in downtown Tokyo. On May 7, 1946, less then a year after starting the company, Mr. Ibuka codified a prospectus for his company and in that prospectus was the company's purpose and vision. The document is a rather long one and the purpose and vision have been translated and condensed. However, in the prospectus is listed these three purposes for his company:

1. To establish a place of work where engineers can feel the joy of technological innovation, be aware of their mission to society, and work to their heart's content.
2. To pursue dynamic activities in technology and production for the reconstruction of Japan and the elevation of the nation's culture.
3. To apply advanced technology to the life of the general public.[240]

The vision for the company was captured in the following statement:

> "Become the company most known for changing the worldwide image of Japanese products as being of poor quality."[241]

Ten years after the company was formed, and against the wishes of their bank, Masaru Ibuka and Akio Morita (one of the first employees and future CEO) changed the name of the company from Tokyo Tsushin Kogyo to the Sony Corporation. When he was asked why they changed the name, Akio Morita gave the following response:

"Although our company was still small and we saw Japan as quite a large and potentially active market, it became obvious to me that if we did not set our sights on marketing abroad, we would not grow into the kind of company Ibuka and I had envisioned. We wanted to change the image [around the world] of Japanese products as poor in quality." He went on to say that the new name would allow the company to expand worldwide whereas the prior name was hard to pronounce in foreign countries.[242]

The similarities in the histories of IBM and Sony are striking. Both companies had a worldwide vision of themselves. Both companies changed their names to reflect that vision. Both companies had leaders who codified and communicated their visions. Both companies became known worldwide. As Stephen Covey noted, things are created twice. First is the mental creation, second is the physical creation. That is the power of a shared purpose and vision. Jack Stack of SRC uses the word dream rather than vision. He said, "I've come to realize that dreaming is an essential business activity. It may be the most important thing that people do. Why? Because a dream is ultimately the expression of your values. It shows what really matters to you. It defines who you are. And it will stay with you. You'll come back to it again and again as the years pass and ask yourself whether you've been true to your dream." Then he goes on to say, "When you're struggling with the hard facts of life, you need a dream to guide you—to remind yourself where you're going and why, (and) to help you figure out what you need to do next."[243]

Mobley and McKeown, in their book, *Beyond IBM*, define the purpose of business as follows: "Purpose is the business of the business. Corporate purpose defines the relation of a company to its larger environment, and therefore gives meaning to everything that goes on inside the company."[244] While Mobley and McKeown's view of a purpose statement is a good start, it is not sufficient for today's environment. In today's environment, the purpose statement must be more clearly defined with the addition of the vision and values statements and then communicated to all employees. With the completion of these three statements, the purpose statement, the vision statement, and the values statement, the full purpose of the organization has been defined. These three statements must be clear, in alignment with each other, and positive/uplifting in tone. As an example, following is the purpose, vision and values statements for Merck.

Purpose: To preserve and improve human life.

Vision: To transform this company from a chemical manufacturer into one of the preeminent drug-making companies in the world, with research capability that rivals any major university.

Values: Corporate social responsibility
Unequivocal excellence in all aspects of the company
Science-based innovation
Honesty and integrity
Profit, but profit from work that benefits humanity[245]

It was in the late 1920s that George W. Merck codified the purpose, vision and values for Merck. He envisioned Merck as "a world-class company that benefits humanity through innovative contributions to medicine—a company that makes superb profits not as the primary goal, but as a residual result of succeeding at that task."[246] In support of the company vision, in 1933 at the opening of the new Merck Research Laboratory, he said: "We believe that research work carried on with patience and persistence will bring to industry and commerce new life; and we have faith that in this new laboratory, with the tools we have supplied, science will be advanced, knowledge increased, and human life win even greater freedom from suffering and disease…. *We pledge our every aid that this enterprise shall merit the faith we have in it. Let your light so shine – that those who seek the Truth, that those who toil that this world may be a better place to live in, that those who hold aloft that torch of Science and Knowledge through these social and economic dark ages, shall take new courage and feel their hands supported* [emphasis his].[247] So began a quest to fulfill Merck's vision of over sixty years ago. The pursuit of that company purpose and vision and doing business within the guidelines of the company values has made Merck one of the leading pharmaceutical companies in the world today.

When a company has an inspiring and codified company purpose such as in the Merck example, those organizational statements provide all employees and prospective employees a basis upon which to decide if they want to participate as a member of the company. They can decide for themselves if the company's purpose is one that they want to be involved in. They can decide for themselves if the vision statement provides a future that they want to help achieve. They can decide for themselves if the values statement is in alignment with their own personal values. If the employee or prospective employee does not agree with each of the three statements, does not believe in each of the three statements, or does not feel that management is living the statements, then that employee should (and probably will) leave the company and go elsewhere.

When a company has stated values that are then reinforced through company policies and the actions of the executive management, it is an extremely powerful force. This is especially true for Generations X and Y as they are attracted to a company whose values are in alignment with their own. An example of this is Ben and Jerry's Homemade, Inc. of Burlington, Vermont. "The ideas of the company—social responsibility, giving back to the community—are what attract people to Ben & Jerry's."[248]

The mission[purpose] avows that the company is dedicated to making the best products it can, profiting economically from these products, and doing so in a socially responsible way. Ben & Jerry's is committed to initiating innovative ways to improve the quality of life of a broad community outside its doors.

To that end, the company gives away 7.5 percent of its pretax earnings in three ways: the Ben & Jerry's Foundation, employee Community Action Teams at five Vermont sites, and corporate grants made by the director of social mission development.[249]

Even though the employees at Ben & Jerry's put in long hours of hard work for relatively low pay, people are literally lining up to work at Ben & Jerry's.[250] "We recently opened a new manufacturing plant near our headquarters. We had less than fifteen positions open. We got something like one thousand resumes."[251] Ben and Jerry's is an excellent example of the dedication, commitment, and loyalty that the values of a company can elicit from the employees when they are supported by the visible actions of the company.

The thought process of evaluating a company's values and the decision process as to which company a new employee will go to work for is critically important for those companies that want to hire and retain Generations X and Y. During the industrial age, management, through the use of fear, combined with the ease at which an employee could be replaced, could command and control the employees. The employees were there at the pleasure of the manager. But today, that is no longer the case. Because of the knowledge powerbase shift, many employees are vital to the business and are not easily replaced. Because of their knowledge, they are in demand by other companies. Loyalty can no longer be mandated through fear. It must be earned with the company purpose (purpose, vision, and values statements) and living up to those statements by management. When this occurs, the employees will be loyal to the company because they believe in the company's purpose. The purpose then becomes a shared purpose, a shared vision, and shared values within the company. When these three elements are shared, then company loyalty is just the natural byproduct. When the employees identify with the company's purpose, when they experience a shared vision, and when their personal values are in alignment with the company's values, then they feel more like they are doing their life's work, not just doing time in a job. This is quite an uplifting and gratifying experience for all the employees. When these statements are in place and are supported by management's day-to-day actions, then an environment of mutual trust and respect can be achieved.

Perhaps you have noticed that no mention has been made of a mission statement. Mission statements and their use will be addressed later. Many people confuse and combine vision statements and mission statements, and the result is that neither one is created or used in an effective manner. The mission statement has its place and use but now is not the time for it.

The New View of the Company

The practitioners of the Teleocratic Management System must have a new view of the organization/corporation. The new view says that the organization/corporation consists of the employees and the knowledge they possess. That is what makes the company, and that is where the value comes from. In the industrial age, the organization/corporation was viewed as being the physical assets that it owned. One of these physical assets was the labor force (people). People were viewed as "labor things." In the early decades of the industrial age, this view was valid and accurate. It was accurate because in that time, the employees could be replaced in a single day because the employees were providing unskilled manual labor only. When this was the case, it was easy and fast to replace an employee. It was not easy and fast to replace the plant or other physical assets that the company owned. Therefore, to view the company as being the physical assets that it owned made good sense during the early days of the Industrial Revolution. Today, however, that has all changed. Now it is much easier and faster to replace the physical facilities than it is to replace the knowledge and skills possessed by all the employees. It is the information and skills that the employees possess today that define and make today's information-based company what it is.

A computer software company is just one example of why the company must be viewed as being the employees and the knowledge that they possess. In many businesses, from hospitals to oil exploration to manufacturing, it is the employees who possess the knowledge necessary for the company to operate. Studies of companies' organizational knowledge show that only 4% of the organizational knowledge is stored in a structured form. This structured knowledge storage is the information captured in formal company documents and computer storage as an example. Another 16% of the companies' organizational knowledge is in an unstructured state. It is kept in the employees' personal notes, files, etc. The remaining 80% of a company's organizational knowledge is personal. Personal information is all the information stored in the brains of the employees. It is the information that a person gains by lessons learned, from understanding a process flow, from one-on-one conversations, etc. So, if all the employees should leave on the same day, almost 96% of the information and knowledge needed to run the business would be gone! Again, the building and facilities in which the employees work (if they even work in them) can be easily replaced. However, to replace the knowledge the employees possess would take years to accomplish. If all of the employees decided to quit on the same day, the company would cease to exist. There would be no one left that knew anything. The company is in fact information in the form of knowledge, and that information is possessed by the employees. This characteristic is true of all companies today to varying degrees depending upon the industry. However, it is becoming truer of all companies as each day passes. Every day, knowledge and information become a larger part of every employee's job. Remember the statistic **"90 percent of all the information we have today, in the recorded history of mankind, has been created in the last fifteen years. That information is expected to double again in the next five years."** In fact, some companies are being bought today for other than the traditional reasons such as acquiring market share, earnings or cash flow. As Jack Stack, the CEO of SRC Holdings, notes, "I know of businesses that have been bought, not for the traditional reasons, but because the acquirers want the company's 'human capital'— that is, its people."[252] Clearly some of the more astute leaders of business today have already transitioned to the new view of the company.

However, it is this information explosion that is driving the knowledge/information content up for all employees. Every company, every day, is becoming more of an information-age company and less of an industrial-age company. Whether they like it or not, it is happening, and it cannot be stopped. Stephen R. Covey, in his book *The 8th Habit*, makes the following observation: "In the Industrial Age, people are an expense, and things, like equipment and technology, are an investment. Just think about this again! People—an expense;

things—an investment! This is the bottom-line information system. It is sick bloodletting."[253] Stephen has clearly pointed out another example of where the old Industrial-Age Business Model and its BMS is 180 degrees out of sync with the information age and the new view of the company.

With this new view of the company, the stockholders are considered to be the silent partners of the employees. The stockholders can no longer "own" an information-based organization. The stockholders cannot "buy" the employees. The stockholders must participate in the future of the company as the silent partners who provide financial support and little more. The new role of the stockholders is reflected in a new sequence of priorities that the management in the new business model will assign to the different constituencies. This sequence of priorities also recognizes that in today's business environment, the customer holds the marketplace power, not the producer. Therefore, the customers hold the number one position in the sequence of priorities. A great example of a new company that has capitalized on recognizing this is Google. The following is directly from the Google web site and list the first of ten things that Google has found to be true:

1. Focus on the user and all else will follow.

"From its inception, Google has focused on providing the best user experience possible. While many companies claim to put their customers first, few are able to resist the temptation to make small sacrifices to increase shareholder value. Google has steadfastly refused to make any change that does not offer a benefit to the users who come to the site:

- The interface is clear and simple.
- Pages load instantly.
- Placement in search results is never sold to anyone.
- Advertising on the site must offer relevant content and not be a distraction.

By always placing the interest of the user first, Google has built the most loyal audience on the web. And that growth has come not through TV ad campaigns, but through word of mouth from one satisfied user to another."

By focusing on the customer as their number one priority, Google has been able to create more wealth in a shorter period of time than any other company in business history. Therefore, the priority sequence of the constituencies within the Information-Age Purpose-Driven Business Model is as follows:

1. Customers
2. Employees
3. Management (my addition)
4. Business Partners (my addition)
5. Public/Community
6. Environment (my addition)
7. Stockholders/Owners[254]

Within the new model, the customers assume their rightful position as the number one constituency. Since they hold the marketplace power in the information age, they should be number one and they are number one. Second are the employees. The employees are second because they are the company; they serve the customers; and the Level-5 Leadership understands that the employees are the company's most valuable asset. The customers are number one over the employees, because without the customers, there would be no need for any employees. Third is the management. Management's job in the new model is to provide leadership and support of the employees. Then in fourth place are the business partners. They are called partners for an important reason. They are not suppliers and they are not vendors. They are business partners. Firms formerly called suppliers or vendors in the industrial-age model are now called business partners because the information-age companies understand that it is in their best interest to establish close mutually beneficial partnerships with the firms they do business with. These close mutually beneficial partnerships help the information-age model companies become more productive and financially successful. Fifth is the community or communities in which the company operates. Sixth is the environment (the only constituency that cannot speak for itself). Seventh and last is the silent partner, the stockholders. The stockholders are last not because they are unimportant, but because when the first six constituencies are well taken care of, the company will be more successful, and there will be more financial reward for the stockholders.

The new view also says that the value contributed by the employees is determined by the difference between all the goods and services sold minus all the goods and services bought. This difference, or value, is to be shared by all the stakeholders. As an example:

> 1/2 reinvested in the company for future growth
> 1/4 distributed to the stockholders
> 1/4 distributed to the employees[255]

The amounts will vary by company; however, the key point is that some substantial percentage must be reinvested in the company and distributed to the employees as profit sharing and stock options. The stockholders may forego their share and plan to receive their "share" through stock price appreciation. The important point is that all three stakeholder groups share in the profits.

The New Organizational Structure

A new organizational structure is needed that recognizes the new realities of the information age. It must recognize that all employees must be treated with the respect that they deserve and as responsible adults who share the power with management. No longer does top management hold all the power. This was evidenced by the knowledge-base power shift from management to the employees. It must recognize that the customer now holds the marketplace power. Almost all companies will have to make the transition from the old hierarchical pyramid structure to the new structure. In fact, transition has already started in many companies even though they may not be aware of it. See Figure 11.1.

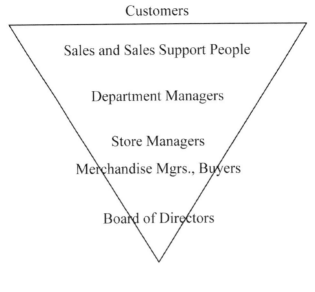

Fig. 11.1[256]

Figure 11.1 is the "company structure" of a real company that is renowned for company service. This company obviously recognizes that the marketplace power base has shifted and that the customer now wields the marketplace power, and therefore the customers are shown in their rightful position. To reflect the importance of the customer, they have inverted the pyramid and put the customer at the top. Who is this company? The answer is Nordstrom.

Another company has also inverted their pyramid. That company is PETCO. Brian Devine, the CEO, says, "We don't have a home office—home offices are places filled with people who get in the way of innovation and always cause more trouble than they're worth. Instead we have a national support center."[257]

Tom Peters in two of his books, *A Passion for Excellence* and *Thriving on Chaos,* highlighted a dairy turned grocery store in Norwalk, Connecticut, by the name of Stew Leonard's. Stew Leonard, the owner, proclaimed to the employees AND to the customers, that the customer was number one. On a large three-ton granite rock in front of every store are the following words:

Rule #1 The customer is always right.

Rule #2 If the customer is ever wrong, Re-Read Rule #1.

Stew Leonard's approach is unique, but it is also very powerful. Customers like being number one and they like always being right. These companies, by making the customer the number one constituency, have demonstrated that they are well into the transition from an industrial-age business-model company to an information-age business-model company.

However, when it comes to the transition and organizational structures, an upside-down pyramid is probably not the graphical representation of the business structure that is needed. But inverting the pyramid does show, in a powerful way, that the customer is number one in the marketplace.

To make the transition from the industrial-age business model to the information-age business model will require the changing of the organizational structure to a new structure that is compatible with the business environment of the information age. To make the transition will require four phases, which are shown in the following series of graphics.

Figure 11.2 shows the beginning point, the traditional BMS hierarchical pyramid structure from the front view.

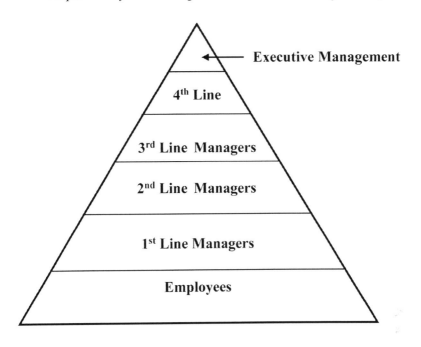

Fig. 11.2

To graphically show the transition, the first thing that must be done is to rotate Figure 11.2 and show the old pyramid structure from the top view. See figure 11.3.

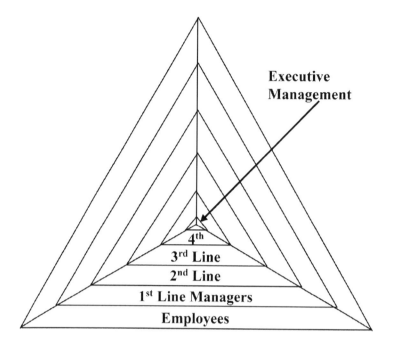

Fig. 11.3.

From this perspective, all of the levels of the organization can be seen, and at the very top in the smallest triangle is the executive management. The first phase in the transition is to make the de-layering or flattening step. Many companies began this process in the late 1980s. This step is shown in Figure 11.4 where three layers of management have been removed from the organizational structure.

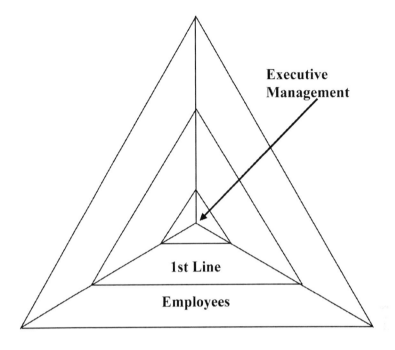

Fig. 11.4

Now that the de-layering step has been completed, it is time for the next phase, which is the flattening of the organizational structure. Imagine now, that a huge press will apply pressure from the top and force the top triangle down inside the second triangle, and then both triangles will be pushed down inside the third triangle. The result is a flat organizational structure with three concentric triangles. See Figure 11.5

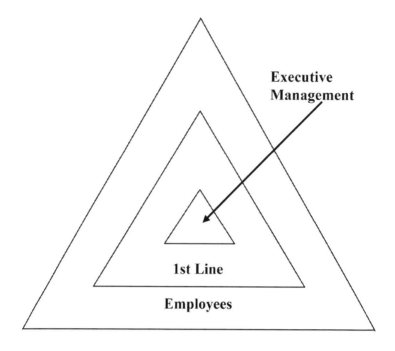

Fig. 11.5.

Now, the organizational structure is flat, with three concentric pyramids. The next phase is to start rounding the corners of the triangles until the triangles are transformed into three concentric circles. See Figure 11.6.

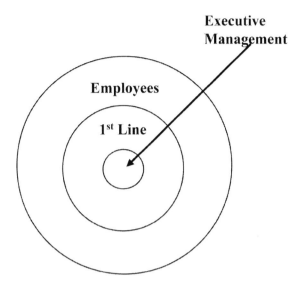

Fig. 11.6.

The final phase of the transition is to add the constituencies to the graphic (customers, business partners, etc). The final form from the top-view perspective is shown graphically in figure 11.7.

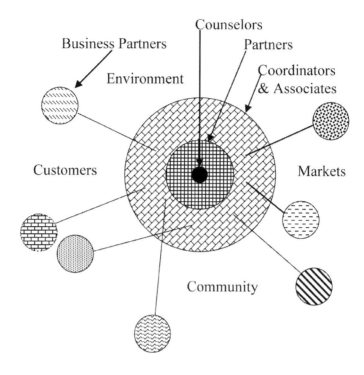

Fig. 11.7. New Information-Age Purpose-
Driven Business Model Structure

Another part of the transition is the renaming of groups within the organization to send a very clear signal that indeed things are different now. The solid black circle in the center labeled "Counselors" represents the group of managers formerly known as the executive management. The next larger circle labeled "partners" is the group of managers formerly known as divisional managers. The third crosshatched circle labeled "Coordinators/Associates" represents the group formerly known as middle management, first-line managers, and employees. Outside of the Coordinator/Associate circle resides the customers, markets, the community and the environment. The interface to the customer is at the edge of the Coordinator/Associate circle. There are other groups that cannot be seen from the top view; they are staff groups such as accounting, human resources, information technology, security, etc. The small circles (one of which is labeled "business partners") represent both suppliers and business partners who are closely coupled/linked with the organization. For example, these circles could represent an outside company that processes payroll, a major computer-software provider, outside security services, other major suppliers, etc. The relationship between the company and these outside organizations can be so close that on a personal level, they almost seem as one.

An example of this is the relationship between Toshiba and United Parcel Service (UPS). "Toshiba had developed an image problem several years ago, with some customers concluding that its repair process for broken machines took too long."[258] So Toshiba went to UPS and asked them to design a better system. The UPS response was to say, "Look, instead of us picking up the machine from your customers, bringing it to our hub, then flying it from our hub to your repair facility and then flying it back to our hub and then from our hub to your customer's house, let's cut out all the middle steps. We, UPS, will pick it up, repair it ourselves, and send it right back to your customer."[259] This type of collaboration between companies Thomas L. Friedman calls "insourcing—a whole new form of collaboration and creating value horizontally."[260]

As the information age and its new technologies continue to make their presence felt in the business environment, these types of collaboration between companies will become a necessity more and more often. As the information age makes every aspect of a company's operation more complex, companies will be forced to "insource" expertise (such as the UPS logistics expertise) to stay competitive. Companies in the future will have many close and intimate collaborations with other companies such as the Toshiba/UPS example. Toshiba, as large a company as it is, cannot economically create a logistics system comparable to a UPS or a Wal-Mart. Call it whatever you want, collaboration, outsourcing, or insourcing, in any case, the line of distinction between where Toshiba ends and UPS begins has become quite blurred for the customers of Toshiba and for the employees of both Toshiba and UPS. This intimate level of deep collaboration requires a huge amount of trust and intimacy between UPS and its clients.[261] The key word here is "trust." *In today's information-age business environment, it is necessary to operate from a position of trust and collaboration rather than from the old industrial-age position of fear and competition.* Trust is the lubrication that allows the Teleocratic Management System to operate with such speed and efficiency, and this is just one example of it.

Now that the new organizational structure is completed from the top- view perspective, it is necessary to look at it from a front view in order to see the rest of the structure. To accomplish this, Figure 11.7 is cut in half and shown from a front view in Figure 11.8.

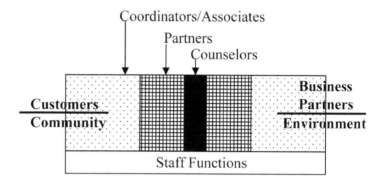

Fig. 11.8.

From the top view, the concentric circles can be seen, but from the front view, the organization is shown as if it has been cut in half, exposing each circle or layer and also showing the supporting staff functions that assist and interface to all groups within the organization. Information flows horizontally in this organization as needed. Also, the horizontal nature of the structure implies that everyone is equal in that they possess the power in their area of responsibility. That is to say that everyone is treated as an adult and with respect that reflects the power that they possess. Everyone has an important role to play. Everyone and every group must trust the other person or group to do its part. Power is spread out throughout the organization. Power is no longer concentrated at the top of a pyramid structure. The vertical-pyramid power structure is gone. Every circle has its own unique type of power in the new horizontal and collaborative business structure. The customer has the marketplace power, the associates and coordinators have the knowledge (job knowledge) power base, the partners and counselors have the leadership power base, and the "insourced" business partners have specific business-process knowledge power. Each group is important and dependent upon the other groups. They all work in harmony in an interdependent relationship for the same set of objectives as defined by the company's purpose statements. The straight lines at both sides represent the links from the company to the outside organizations such as suppliers and business partners. Thomas Friedman in his book, *The world is Flat,* points out that "when the world starts to move from a primarily vertical (command and control) value-creation model to an increasingly horizontal (connect and collaborate) model, it doesn't affect just how business gets done. It affects everything—how communities and companies define themselves, where companies and communities stop and start, how individuals balance their different identities as consumers, employees, shareholders, and citizens, and what the role government has to play."[262]

The next element of the organizational structure is the foundation of the company. The foundation upon which the organization is built is defined by its three organizational statements—the purpose, values, and vision statements—which are then added to the organizational structure as shown in Figure 11.9.

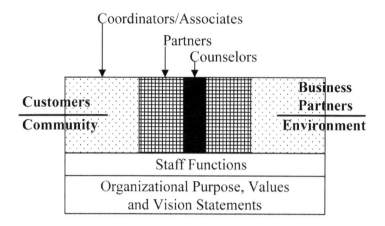

Fig. 11.9

After the company's purpose statements have been added to the structure as shown in Figure 11.9, the next step is to define the company's targets. For purposes of clarity, the targets have been separated into three categories: employee and business partner targets, customer and market targets, and financial targets. These targets must be in alignment and consistent with the organizational purpose statements. This alignment is vitally important. There must be a direct linkage between the company purpose and the targets. The targets for many items can be sourced from the annual business plan or budgets. For example, if the vision statement for a company is to become the largest supplier in their market, then there should be a market share target within the customer and market targets. These targets will then have a measure implemented to track the progress toward each target. See Figure 11.10.

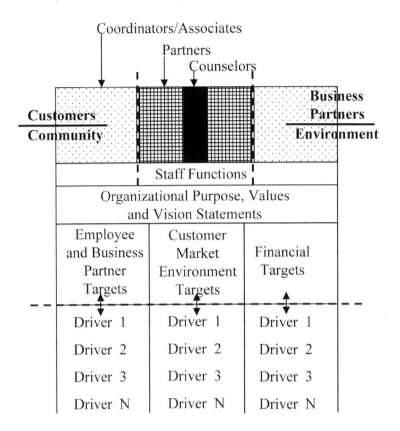

Fig. 11.10.

It is the measures (labeled as drivers) that provide the linkage and alignment between the company's direction and goals and all the employees within the company. Drivers are the measurements of the activities of the employees, that when accomplished, will achieve the targets. The driver measurements are derivatives of the targets, which are derivatives of the purpose statements. As an example, a driver measurement might be the number of new account sales for the month or the average days outstanding for accounts receivable. These numbers may not show on the income statement, but the results from focusing on these numbers will show up in the form of revenue and cash. It is this structure then that provides the alignment between the company's purpose and the associated measures of the activities at the employee level. Also, it is these measures that allow the groups of employees to know if they are doing the right things or not. It is quite simple. If the measures show that the target is being met or that progress is being made toward reaching the target, then they are doing the right thing. If the target is not being met and progress is not being made toward the target, then most likely, the group responsible needs to review their current activities. It is the measures at the department/team level that provide a crystal-clear picture for the employees of their success. There is no ambiguity as to what the goals are and if they are making progress toward achieving them.

In some cases, it is the responsibility of the counselors and partners to define the targets and the associated measures. It is then left up to the coordinators and associates to determine how to achieve the targets. However, when the new business model is completely implemented, the employees (self-directed teams) will be in a position to set their own targets and budgets. On the graphic in figure 11.10, between the partners and the coordinators/associates is a heavy dotted line. This line represents the separation of strategic decision-making from tactical decision-making. In this business model, the strategic direction and decision-making is the responsibility of the two inner circles. The tactical decision-making and operating budgets with profit-and-loss responsibility are delegated to, and are the responsibility of the outer circle, the coordinators and associates. Each department/team will have its own targets and associated measures.

The measures for each department or team must be in alignment with two things: first, the company objectives and budget; then secondly, the department/team's mission statement. For each department or team, a mission statement must be created. The mission statement defines with clarity what the group will improve, increase, or enhance as a result of their activities. If the group's activities do not improve, increase, or enhance anything, then the group provides no value to the company and should be disbanded. However, if it does improve, increase, or enhance specific things, then those things can be measured. The mission therefore defines what the department, group, or self-directed team is responsible and accountable to do. The group's responsibilities are then translated into activities or drivers to improve, increase, or enhance those things. Those drivers can then be measured to determine the level of success. It is these measures that must be in alignment with and be a subset of the overall company targets and measures. It is this structure that ensures the alignment of all the efforts within the organization toward the company's goals. This separation and delegation of the strategic versus tactical responsibility and decision-making were stated this way by Jack Stack, CEO of SRC Holdings, "We were the ones who focused on strategy and innovation. The managers of the subsidiaries focused on operations and optimization."[263]

Once the mission statements are in place for all the self-directed teams and each team has its own measures that are in alignment with the overall company targets, then the coordinators and associates can be given responsibility for achieving the team's targets. They have the measures and they have the knowledge. The measures will tell them if they are doing the right things or not. It is up to them to act like adults with common sense. **They will no longer need a "manager"; they can "manage" themselves.** It is up to the coordinators and associates on the team to work as a team to achieve the team's targets and be rewarded accordingly. With this structure, **the environment has been created that will allow the groups of employees to work as self-directed teams.** Everyone on the team shares in the responsibility to achieve the team's objectives. With everyone on the team striving to achieve the same team objectives, they are free to organize as they see fit. It is up to them to figure out how to reach the targets. They are adults; they can do it by themselves. With profit-sharing as one of the company values, everyone on the team will share in the gains as they innovate and become more successful.

Earlier, it was pointed out that one of the values that was necessary in order to realize the full potential of the new information-age purpose-driven business model was "Transparency—All information is shared, truthfully." With the old industrial-age business model, the power and financial information was reserved for management only, and in many companies this is still the case. In most companies, the financial statements, the income statement, the balance sheet and other documents such as the cash-flow statement are seen only by the upper levels of management. When this is the situation, it causes a number of things to happen. First of all, as a whole, the company is business illiterate. That is to say that the mid and lower levels of management and the employees would not know how to read and understand the basic financial statements of the company even if they had them. They do not understand how the company makes money and how it achieves success. They confuse revenue and profits. They may think that profits are the same as the money in the bank. They cannot explain the difference between generating a profit and generating cash. They don't know if borrowed money is an asset or a liability, or what the impact of depreciation is on net profit. When it comes to understanding the cost of acquiring new machinery and how the financing of that machinery affects the net profit of the company, their eyes glaze over. They have no real concept or understanding of the impact of their decisions on the overall financial performance of the company in the short-term or long-term. During the industrial age when the upper management made all of the decisions, this was not an issue. However, with the arrival of the information age, and the shift of the operational-knowledge power base from the management to the employees, it has become a very big issue.

We have seen with the examples of the military and Wal-Mart how the information age is flattening the hierarchy structure of companies today and, at the same time, it is driving the tactical and operational decision-making process down to lower and lower levels of the organization. In the new business model as shown in figure 11.10, the strategic and tactical decision-making responsibility has been separated. The strategic decisions are made by the management in the inner two circles, and the tactical decisions are made by those employees in the outer circle. Therefore, ALL employees need to be able to read and understand the financial documents of the company so that they can make informed decisions by taking the financial aspects of the decision into consideration. In other words, they need to be able to see and understand the big picture, just like an owner does, if they are to think and act like an owner when they are making the tactical decisions that have been delegated to them. They must be able to understand the financial impact of their decisions and be able to balance the short-term versus the long-term considerations of their decisions just like an owner would.

When the lower levels of management and employees do not have the knowledge that allows them to read and understand the company's financial statements, and they do not have access to those statements, they think like an average employee and they worry about their job, not the company. They assume that it is somebody else's responsibility to worry about the company's success, not theirs. Many employees have heard their manager say, "You aren't paid to think, you are paid to work!" In this environment, it is left up to the upper management to TELL everyone else what to do. Only upper management has responsibility for the profit and loss (P&L) of the company, and they are attempting to make all of the decisions. In this situation, many managers believe that it is their responsibility to do all of the thinking, fix all of the problems and, in the process, tell everyone else what to do, and even sometimes, how to do it. When management operates under this belief, the employees are forced to wait until they are told what to do. They are prohibited by management from taking the initiative and acting on their own because they have not been empowered and they do not have the information required to do so. When employees are managed in this fashion and are told things like, "All we ask you to do is to do your job, and nothing more," the employees do not have a challenge, nothing to get excited about, no shared purpose, vision or values. When this is the case, as CEO Jack Stack says, "What you wind up with are workers who think a job is just a job. I call them the living dead."[264]

This type of approach to managing employees is very inefficient and clearly will not work well in today's business environment, and it will be especially bothersome to the Generation X and Y employees.

The solution to this issue is the approach used by Semco and SRC Holdings which some call "open-book management." John Case in his book on this subject, *Open-Book Management,* cites more than twenty companies who have very successfully implemented some variation of the concept to achieve exceptional results. The open-book management element of the new business model consists of the following elements:

1. Sharing of the company financial statements
2. Business education for all employees
3. Establishing direct links between driver measurements and company targets
4. Opportunity to earn equity for all employees
5. Employee empowerment so they can then think and act like owners

The first element is the open sharing of the company's financial statements with all of the employees on a monthly basis. The second element is business education for all of the employees so that they can read and understand all of the company's financial statements. They can interpret the balance sheet, income statement, the cash flow statements and any other statement that may be important to their segment of the business. When the first two elements are in place, then direct links between the driver measurements of the self-directed teams and the company's targets must be established. This allows the employees to see how their day-to-day activities translate into the financial performance of the company. The next element is equity. The employees must be treated like, and become, "partners/owners" in the business, and then begin to think and act like owners. To accomplish this, they participate in profit sharing and stock options, which give them equity in the company just like the upper management. The equity element gives all employees equality and a reason to be concerned and care about the company's future financial success.

When the open-book management element of the new business model has been implemented, a dramatic change takes place. When all of the employees have the *ability* to read and understand the company's financial statements coupled with the *empowerment* of the self-directed teams and the *guidance* provided by the team's mission statement and driver measurements, the employees are now in a position to make a huge contribution to the future success of the company that they were never in a position to do before. When the employees can read and understand the financial statements, they begin to understand the business, not just their jobs. They understand where the money comes from, how it is spent, and how profits are, or are not, generated. For the first time they can see and understand at the financial-statement line-item level, where the money comes from and where it goes. They know whether they are making money or not. Further, they know how much money they are making, they know why they are making it, and they also have a good idea of what the future will be, because they see all of the numbers, every month. The employees can now see and understand the big picture. With this new-found knowledge and understanding, the employees start to consider what the financial impact of their decisions will be. That is because they now know how to start with sales and income at the top of the income statement and finally arrive at net profit at the bottom of the income statement. They can see how much the overhead is, how much salaries cost, how much the benefits such as medical insurance cost, how much the taxes are and so on.

When the employees do not understand the financial impact of their decisions, they cannot make decisions like a business person. With their understanding of the financials, and when the books are shared each month, the employees can now participate in the running of the business. This combined with equity in the company leads the employees to then think and act like owners. They no longer have to wait to be told what to do. The employees are now in the best position to manage their part of the business. The employees in this environment naturally take ownership of the driver measurements (the numbers) because they can now link the driver attainment to a specific line in the income statement, and they can see for the first time how it contributes to the company's bottom-line profit, profit-sharing and their financial future. When the employees can see and understand this linkage, and they have equity in the company, they no longer view themselves as employees, they view themselves as partners and owners in the business. Everybody is in the same boat, and they all sink or swim together. For the first time, EVERYONE is focused on BOTH making money AND pursuing the company's purpose. To make money, provide job security and enable the pursuit of the company purpose, the employees understand that it is up to them to make the numbers go in the right direction.

When the open-book element of the new business model has been effectively implemented, and the employees can see and understand the direct linkage between their activities and the impact that those activities have on the individual line items of the income statement and balance sheet, there are no longer any excuses. Everybody knows who or what group is responsible for which line items. If a group's line item is not up to expectations, there is no one to blame, they are responsible. Period. Jack Stack, the CEO of SRC Holdings, which is no doubt the leader in the United States in open-book management, says, "You have to take the excuses away. You have to create an environment where people can't blame anyone else for the situation they're in—where they see they make a real difference, where there's no gray area. It's very easy for people to think they don't make a difference. That's one of the biggest problems in business today. The bigger the company, the bigger the problem is. And then we compound the problem by not asking people to make a difference, by not insisting that they make a difference, by not creating environments in which they *can* make a difference."[265]

Nobody knows more about the employee's job then the employees do. Therefore no one is in a better position to figure out how to improve things than they are. This is where Level-5 leadership and a trust-based management system become very important. The Level-5 Leaders with their egalitarian and trusting nature combined with the trust-based Teleocratic Management System are in perfect alignment with the open-book management element of the new business model. It takes a Level-5 Leader to delegate the power and control to the lower levels of the business and, without a trust-based system, it would be impossible to effectively empower the self-directed teams. With all of these elements in place, the employees can see and understand that THEY are in control of their own destiny. They have the power to make the numbers improve or not. Since the numbers determine the profit, which enables them to pursue the shared company purpose, and it adds to the equity that they hold in the company, the employees naturally take ownership of the numbers and do all that they can to make sure that they continually improve. That is to the benefit of everyone. The difference between a company that utilizes open-book management versus one that does not, is like night and day.

An example of the difference comes from Sandstrom Products. Sandstrom Products is a small specialty-coating company that received a large new contract from a customer. However, Jim Sandstrom, the owner, determined that to fulfill the large order would require that the company purchase $500,000 in new equipment. Jim took the employees through the numbers and told them that he would like to have the business, but could not see how they should spend the $500,000 since he was not sure if the demand would be permanent or temporary. Then he asked the employees if they had any ideas. "The workers got together and came up with the idea of dividing up into three shifts rather than two, thereby maximizing production from the company's existing equipment. They negotiated who would work which shifts. They agreed there would be no shift differential and that they didn't need any extra people. *They put the plan into effect immediately.*"[266] Jim Sandstrom was amazed. "If management had come down and said, "There's only one answer, we're gonna work three shifts!", there'd have been pandemonium. Everybody would have been screaming. I'm not working another shift! I want differential pay!"[267] The results were that the entire contract was fulfilled in thirteen weeks using the current equipment. Productivity for the quarter was up 86 percent and Sandstrom Products recorded record profits.[268]

To use a couple of parables from John Case's book, not having open-book management is like empowering a truck driver to drive a truck but not telling the driver where to drive it, or having a marching band where only the drum major has sheet music. With open-book management, the truck driver knows at all times where he is and where he is going, and every member of the band has sheet music. The difference is huge. Another benefit is that communications from the top to the bottom of the organization are crystal clear. Everyone is communicating with the same language and the same numbers.

There is no ambiguity. The financial statements are the same every month, only the results (numbers) change. As Jack Stack points out, "When you communicate with people through the financial statements, knowledge gets to them quickly, without being distorted by internal rivalries."[269]

Once a company has the open-book element of the new business model fully implemented, the self-directed teams can take over the responsibility for their part of the business. As Steve Wilson, the founder of Mid-States Technical, points out, "They do all the work. I truly don't have to be responsible for everything anymore."[270] In the case of Semco, Ricardo Semler, in speaking of decision–making, says, "Success means not making them myself." The management within the inner two circles of the organizational structure is now free to focus on the long-term strategic direction of the company without having to worry about or being distracted by the day-to-day operations of the business. That has been delegated to those that can do a better job of it than management can. As Tom Corbo, the president of Manco, puts it, "Power is in the information, and the guy doing the job has the information. He has more power than you do because he knows more. 'So you better trust that guy, and you better let him know you depend on each other to get the job done and done right, or the whole ship sinks.'"[271] Now, everyone in the company can focus their knowledge and energies on the parts of the business where they have the knowledge power base and where they can be most effective. That is one of the great strengths and secrets of the new business model.

After these elements have been implemented and the employees can look forward to profit sharing and an increase in their equity, there will be anxious anticipation each month to see the numbers. The monthly sharing of the numbers then can become an opportunity for teambuilding, celebration and a big morale boost for everyone. This monthly report, however, should not be limited to the company's financial reports only. Any other numbers that are of company-wide interest should be included, such as new sales, customer satisfaction or progress in a particular problem area that is being addressed. By using the company's financial statements as a communication vehicle between the senior management and the rest of the employees in the company, the communications are dramatically improved. As mentioned earlier, everyone is talking the same language and using the same terms. The breakage and translation that occurs in the old BMS hierarchical pyramid structure has been eliminated. As Jack Stack noted, "The payoff comes from getting the people who create the numbers to understand the numbers. When that happens, the communication between the bottom and the top of the organization is just phenomenal."[272]

The new structure also addresses many issues associated with the mobile worker of today that works from their house and rarely makes an appearance at the "home office." With this new structure, it is very easy to provide mobile workers with the direction and guidance that they need electronically. All that is required is an email with the latest numbers. If a change in direction is needed, an email can be sent with the new driver measurement and an explanation of the new driver number. The employee is self-directed just as teams at the main location are. All of the same rules apply. The drivers are reported on monthly or whatever the case may be. With the timely electronic reporting and sharing of the driver performance, all parties can know how things are going and if any unusual action is required. The monthly sharing of the company performance can be delivered to the mobile workers electronically if necessary, but if that is the case, then a quarterly meeting where the executives deliver their message in person would be a good idea.

The potential for increased productivity and job satisfaction that the new teleocratic management structure provides for the self-directed teams is enormous. In today's businesses, there is a large disconnect between the company's goals and objectives and the goals and objectives of the employees at the bottom of the pyramid. The disconnect leaves the employees unclear about where the organization is headed and what its highest priorities are. With this disconnect, the employees are frustrated, bogged down, and distracted. Most of all, they don't think there is anything they can do about it, and they are right.

Under the teleocratic management structure, the employees know that the organization has the right purpose, that their job is worthwhile, and that what they do makes a difference. With the barriers removed, the employees are free to be creative, innovative, responsive, and to work as a team for the good of themselves, the organization, and the community. It may appear that with the self-directed teams, control has been lost, but it has not. It has merely been transformed from control to self-control. The self-directed teams control themselves. The responsibility for achieving the company's objectives has shifted from the managers to the self-directed teams. The teams are now responsible for most of the items that were the responsibilities of the middle and first-line management.

To implement self-directed teams requires trust on the part of management. This is an important point. The BMS was a fear-driven system in direct conflict with trust, which is required for the creation of empowered self-directed teams. Only under the trust-based TMS can truly empowered, self-directed teams be created and a corresponding dramatic increase in productivity achieved. When empowered self-directed teams are combined with a profit-sharing system where the employees can see a direct relationship between their efforts and the profit (open-book management), the results are amazing. The bottom-line result of all of these elements of the new business model is ***superior operational execution!*** The companies utilizing these techniques simply out-execute their competition. Period. One key aspect of this execution is the monthly meeting to review the performance of the company in the open-book management element. Monthly, companies such as SRC Holdings meet with the employees to review the performance of all key measures (drivers and targets) and thereby can identify issues much more quickly and take corrective action before their competition even knows that there is a problem coming.

In addition, the new work environment that is created by the TMS and self-directed teams unleashes the human potential. When the self-directed teams are created, empowered, and given responsibility, a tremendous increase in productivity is the result. It is the creation of the self-directed teams along with the guidance provided by the team measurements and their direct linkage to the organization's purpose and profits that create the environment which allows all employees, especially Generation X and Y employees, to become self-motivated and work as part of a cohesive team toward a common set of objectives. This is highly important for Generations X and Y because they are quite different from the prior generations. They are quite independent-minded, and they have a distrust of business and government. It is these and other characteristics that make managing them much like trying to herd a group of cats. However, these generations find the self-motivated, self-directed aspects of the self-directed teams to their liking, and this allows management to "herd the cats" in the direction they want them to go. This is accomplished through the team drivers, the team mission statements and the aligned structure of the new business model. The combination of the drivers, mission statements, and the freedom of the self-directed teams allows Generations X and Y to "manage" themselves while pursuing the company targets and purpose by their own free will. That is because the goals and values of the Generations X and Y and the company are in alignment. The reality is that management has created an environment that allows the cats (Generations X and Y) to herd (manage) themselves. The "cats" are happy, and management is happy.

In his book, *The 8th Habit: From Effectiveness to Greatness*, Stephen R. Covey speaks to the roles of the company leadership and says, "The next two roles of leadership, aligning and empowering, represent the execution. This means creating structures, systems, and processes that intentionally enable individuals and teams to translate the organization's larger 'line-of-sight' strategic goals or critical priorities into their actual day-to-day work and team goals. In short, people are *empowered* to get the job done." It is interesting to note that the types of structures, systems, and processes that Mr. Covey is asking for are the ones that are delivered by the information-age business model and its Teleocratic Management System. However, it is management's responsibility to lead the transition from the current structures and systems (industrial-age business model) to the new structures and systems (information-age business model). The transition will result in a company that is very different from the company that exists today.

The differences between a company that operates under the old industrial-age profit-driven business model and a company that operates under the new information-age purpose-driven business model are enormous. For example, when a company is profit-driven, and the maximization of profit is the number one objective, then the company will be very, and in some cases extremely, internally focused on the numbers and profits. This strong internal focus then significantly reduces management's cares or concerns about anything else. There is only one concern, and that is about the pyramid and what goes on inside it. The result is poor treatment of the company's constituencies: the customers, employees, suppliers, etc., which in time will lead to negative feedback loops being created. That in turn will then lead to average or below-average performance. However, when the company discovers its core purpose, values and vision, everything changes. The company will then become energized and outwardly focused. The management and employees will be focused on the company purpose and their customers, and will view the entire business world differently. They will operate with different vision, values, priorities and ethics. The company will be totally different. In almost every aspect, the purpose-driven company will be 180 degrees different from the profit-driven company. As a case in point, profit-driven companies are internally focused while purpose-driven companies are outwardly focused. That is a difference of 180 degrees in direction and perspective. The view of the business world by the outward–focused, purpose-driven company is graphically represented in Figure 11.11.

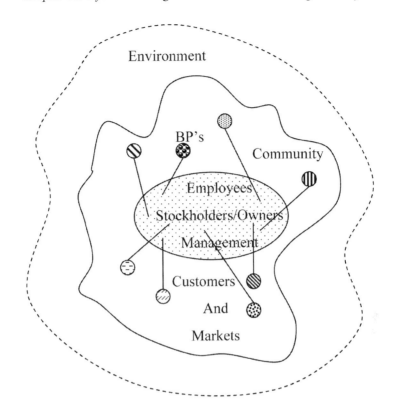

Fig. 11.11.

The oval in the center of figure 11.11 represents the company, all of the employees, and the silent partners, the stockholders. The small circles with lines leading inside the oval represent the business partners of the company and are intended to represent a flat and networked structure. This networked structure operates within the markets and communities that the company is there to serve as defined by the company's purpose, and this is shown by the solid black line. Finally, the company, its customers, markets and communities all reside within the larger context of the environment as represented by the dotted line surrounding everything else. While the old industrial-age business model operates from the mechanistic paradigm, the new business model operates from the eco-system paradigm. The rules of the eco-system paradigm say that every element of the system is dependent upon every other element of the system so they are interdependent and all either win together or they lose together. When the eco-system paradigm is applied to a business, then the business will be outwardly focused and will seek win/win solutions for all of its interactions, both internally and externally. The company understands that they can be healthy only when the other elements are healthy. However, a company operating under the industrial-age paradigm will seek to dominate every transaction for their gain at the expense of every other party. They will seek to complete win/lose transactions. To be successful in the future, companies must transition to the new business model and seek win/win transactions.

Chapter 12
Information Age Business Model
– Measurement System

"Complex systems cannot be understood without statistics."

– W. Edwards Deming

The Information Age Business Model — Measurement System

A new measurement system is needed to address the negative impact of the industrial-age accounting-based measurement system that invokes the perversity principle and all of the inefficiencies that result. As was shown in Chapter 7, when the world is viewed through the old bureaucratic measurement system, the viewer gets a distorted view of the real world. The view of the real world is distorted because the accounting-based measurement system does not handle the normal variation that the real world presents. With the old system, some goal is set by some questionable process and then goodness or badness is determined relative to the arbitrary goal that was set. If the output is above the goal, then that is good. If the output is below the goal, then that is bad. The industrial-age measurement system is quite clear on this point.

The new measurement system is designed to deal with the variability of the real world and to give the viewer a clear picture of reality. For the purposes of business and management, the real world consists of a large number of interrelated systems that comprise what is known as a business. If you went to any business, you would find a number of systems in place. These systems are somewhat interrelated and achieve all the functions necessary for the company to operate. There will be the accounting system, the payroll system, the production system, the sales system, etc. The word "system" is used here because it has a broader context than does the word "process"; however, in many cases, either word could be used.

When measurements of any of these business systems are taken, the measurements will vary from measurement to measurement. That is the real world. The measurements will vary year to year, month to month, day to day, and hour to hour. The new measurement system will analyze the measurements and their variation and make sense out of them. The first challenge of the new measurement system will be to determine whether or not the variation of the measurements is showing *normal* variation or *abnormal* variation. This is a critical distinction, because the action to be taken is totally different depending upon the type of variation being observed.

When the variation is normal, that means that the system is doing the best that it can in its current configuration. If the measurement is not acceptable, then the system must be changed in some way in order for the measurements to improve. As long as the observed variation is normal and the system is not changed, then the measurements on the average will not improve. When the observed variation is *abnormal*, then it is up to the observer to find out what is causing the abnormal variation and then remove that cause from the system so that the system can return to its normal level of performance. So the question is, how can a person determine if the observed variation is normal or abnormal?

To determine if an observed data point (measurement) is either a normal or abnormal variation requires the use of a statistical chart. Through the use of statistical analysis, an analysis chart can be constructed to show when variation is normal and when variation is abnormal. This is accomplished by determining the average of the measurements taken, which becomes the centerline on the system analysis chart, and then determining the standard deviation of the data. On the system analysis chart, there are three important lines: the centerline, which represents the average of all the data points; the upper control limit (UCL); and a lower control limit (LCL), which are three standard deviations from the centerline. The upper control limit is three standard deviations above the centerline while the lower control limit is three standard deviations below the center (average) line as shown in Figure 12.1.

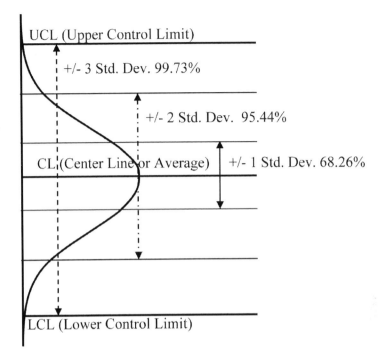

UCL (Upper Control Limit)

+/- 3 Std. Dev. 99.73%

+/- 2 Std. Dev. 95.44%

CL (Center Line or Average)   +/- 1 Std. Dev. 68.26%

LCL (Lower Control Limit)

Fig. 12.1. System Analysis Chart

On the systems analysis chart (assuming a normal distribution of the data), 68.26% of the data points will fall between +/- 1 standard deviation from the centerline or the average of the data; 95.44% of the data points will fall within +/- 2 standard deviations from the center; and 99.73% of the data points will fall within +/- 3 standard deviations from the center as shown in Figure 12.1. All data points that fall between the UCL and the LCL (or +/- 3 standard deviations from the centerline) represent normal variation. When a data point falls outside of the UCL or LCL, then that is abnormal variation. Figure 12.1 shows that 99.7% of all the data points will fall between the two control lines. That is true assuming that the data would show a normal distribution curve when plotted, which is usually (but not always) the case. For the purposes of this book, it is only the concept of the analysis chart that is of importance. When system analysis charts are constructed for actual use, a statistician must be consulted to ensure that the correct data collection techniques have been used and that the correct formulas have been applied to determine the standard deviations. There are five different formulas depending upon the type of data collected and the characteristics of the samples. Perhaps an example will help to make these concepts clearer. Figure 12.2 shows a system analysis chart with all the basic elements.

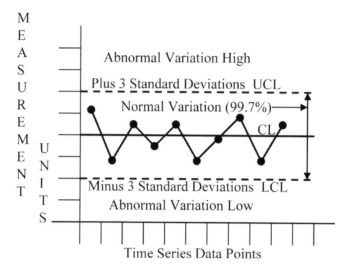

Fig. 12.2. System Analysis Chart.

It is important to note that the centerline and the upper and lower control lines are determined by the data. The control lines are not set by people in some arbitrary fashion. The lines come from the data. They are determined by the system from which the data was taken. The data points between the control limits will comprise 99.7% of the data points, assuming a normal distribution curve. That means that when a data point is outside of the control lines, it is a rare occurrence of only three per thousand chances, and there is some special reason for it. That reason, whatever it is, needs to be identified and removed from the system. Dr. W. Edwards Deming, in his book *Out of the Crisis*, calls the abnormal variation, "Special Cause Variation," because it is the result of some special cause.

If all of the data points are within the normal range of variation, then it is up to the owner(s) of the system to determine if the performance of the system is acceptable or if it needs to be improved. If the owners of the system determine that improvement is needed, then they can apply standard quality improvement techniques to achieve that objective. That decision is left up to the owners of the system. If the system is delivering acceptable performance, then no action is required.

To make the concept of abnormal or special variation clearer, the following example will be used. Since most readers work for a living and most readers probably drive to work, the driving-to-work system will be the example used. The driving-to-work system has a number of elements: the driver, the car, the roads traveled, the traffic control lights, the weather, etc. All of these elements are part of the drive-to-work system.

The first step in analyzing any system is to take a number of measurements (gather the data) and then analyze the data. The drive time to work for Joe, the salesman, is shown in the table below. The data was collected for two weeks but was only collected on the way to work. The drive time (the data) was recorded to the nearest whole minute. Since Joe is a salesperson, his drive home could begin from anywhere in his sales territory and therefore could not be used for comparison purposes. The data collected for Joe's drive to work is shown in Table 12.1.

Day	Drive Time
Monday	27
Tuesday	31
Wednesday	30
Thursday	29
Friday	36
Monday	28
Tuesday	46
Wednesday	30
Thursday	29
Friday	27

Table 12.1. Daily Drive Times for Joe Salesman.

After the data has been collected, the first step is to calculate the average of all of the data. The average determines where the centerline will be placed on the analysis chart.

Next, a few simple calculations reveal that the standard deviation for the data in Table 2 is 3.34. To find the upper and lower control limits (plus or minus three standard deviations), we must multiply the standard deviation of 3.34 times 3, which results in 10.02 minutes.[273] The average of the ten days of data is 30 minutes. Therefore, the system analysis chart will have a centerline at 30 minutes, an upper control line (UCL) at 40 minutes, and a lower control line at 20 minutes as shown in Figure 12.3.

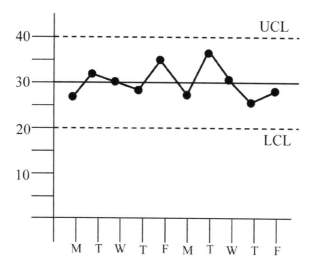

Fig. 12.3. Joe's Drive-to-Work System Analysis Chart

Now that we know what the normal range of time variation is for Joe's drive-to-work system, we are now in a position to be able to analyze further data. Suppose that one day, it takes Joe 39 minutes to drive to work. Does that mean that Joe should panic and possibly look for a new route to work? No, it does not. A time of 39 minutes is in the expected range of normal variation, so no action is required.

However, the next week on Tuesday, it took Joe 55 minutes to drive to work, making him quite late. His manager was not happy. In this case, the 55 minutes is outside the normal range of variation (a clear case of abnormal variation) and needs to be investigated to find the cause so that the cause can be removed from the system. When Joe's manager asked Joe why he was late for work, Joe said that he had a tire blowout on the way to work, and he had to change the tire. This is an example of abnormal variation, or as Dr. Deming would say, special-cause variation. Joe's manager asked Joe how many miles he had on the tires. Joe said that he had about 65,000 miles on the tires and that the tread was getting pretty worn. Joe's manager recommended that Joe get some new tires so that he would not have this problem again in the near future. Joe replaced the tires and probably eliminated this particular type of abnormal variation from his drive-to-work system for some time.

For the benefit of any readers who have a background in quality concepts, the system analysis charts and statistical control charts are the same. They are created using the same formulas. Only the names are different here. The names are different, because the charts are being used for management purposes only and not for process control or process improvement.

System analysis charts, once implemented, will provide the users with a great deal of useful information. For instance, if seven data points in a row show a downward trend, that is statistically significant. That means that something has changed in the system, and the downward trend will most likely continue. When this trend is spotted, it must be investigated immediately, even though all seven points may still be within the normal range of variation as shown on the system analysis control chart. One of the primary reasons for using the system analysis charts is that the chart can tell the user when the performance of an employee is within the normal range and when it is not. See Figure 12.4.

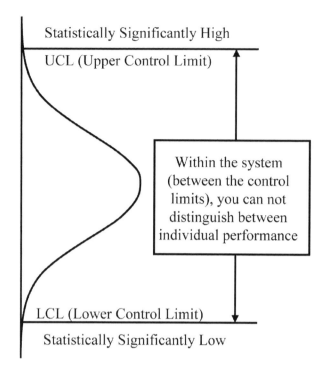

Statistically Significantly High

UCL (Upper Control Limit)

Within the system (between the control limits), you can not distinguish between individual performance

LCL (Lower Control Limit)

Statistically Significantly Low

Fig. 12.4.

When system analysis charts are used for the purpose of evaluating an employee's performance, there are three possible results. First, the employee's performance data point falls outside the control limits on the high side. When that is the case, it can be said that the employee's performance is statistically significantly high, and that it is due to the employee, not the system. Second, if the employee's data points fall between the control limits, then it can be said that the employee is performing within the system and is achieving expected results. Further, all employees whose data points fall between the control limits are achieving expected results, and there can be no distinguishable differences between any of the employees' performances. Based on this data, all of these employees are performing at the same level. When each employee's data points fall between the control limits, those data points are determined by the normal random variation of the system. **It is the normal variation of the system that is moving the employee's data points up one measurement period and down the next. Therefore, all of these employees are considered to be performing at the same level, based on the data.** Third, if the employee's data point falls outside the control limit on the low side, then it can be said that the employee's performance is statistically significantly low, and that the performance is due to the employee, not the system. When this occurs, it is up to the employee and the manager to investigate the cause of the low performance and to take the appropriate action.

When a company has a number of people doing the same job, say twenty or more, it is possible to statistically determine if the performances of the employees fall within the normal range of the system within which they work or not. If an employee's performance falls outside of the normal range of the system, it is probably due to something unique to that employee. Dr. Deming, in his book *Out of the Crisis*, beginning on page 380, has an example of this. In this example, the company was making stockings. In the making of the stocking, there is an operation called "looping" which is the closing of the toe of the stocking. Looping is done by the looping machine operators called "loopers." Once the stockings have completed the manufacturing process, they are inspected and graded as firsts, irregulars, seconds, thirds, or rags. The company only made money on the stockings that were graded as firsts. Stockings graded at the other levels were sold at a loss. After the data was collected and the system analysis charts were put in place, it was determined that 4.8% of the stockings were graded as something other than first. The next step was to have each of the forty-seven loopers keep their own individual data. The individual data revealed that looper number 75 was an excellent looper. The company was able to incorporate many of her techniques into the general department routine to the benefit of all. The data for looper number 22 was showing abnormally high error rates. Her supervisor studied her work habits and recommended that her eyes be examined. The physician found her to be blind in the left eye and with vision 6/20 in the right eye. He was able to correct her right eye to 20/20. Her work improved at once.

This incident caused management to examine their policy with respect to eye examinations. The new policy was to examine all loopers' eyesight and to establish a regular pattern of reexamination. The initial examination discovered a dozen operators who had difficulty trying to see what they were doing. Operator 27 was perhaps the poorest of all the loopers. When the supervisor reviewed her data with her, her response was, "I have been here five years, and this is the first time that anybody ever told me that care mattered. I could do a much better job, if it makes any difference." Her record thereafter showed great improvement. Another looper who had many points beyond the control limits explained that she had been on the job five years and that no one as yet had ever explained to her what looping meant. She had observed other workers, and they had tried to help her, but she had learned a lot of bad habits, still not understanding what the job should have been.[274]

There are many reasons why the system analysis charts are important for any company. But for the purposes of the Teleocratic Management System, these charts provide a statistical basis for determining two things. First, is the observed level of performance normal or abnormal? With this information known, the appropriate actions can be taken to address the situation. Secondly, when the performance is abnormal, is it due to the employee or something else? This can be determined by using the system analysis charts at the individual level as opposed to the system level. The charts will then let the employee know for the first time if their performance is in the normal or abnormal range. When abnormal performance is identified, it can be investigated and addressed appropriately as in the case of the loopers. It is in the best interest of all employees to know which level of performance they are at.

It is important to understand the magnitude of the difference between the two measurement-system approaches. To make this point, an example of sales attainment will be used.

ABC Company

At the ABC Company, the vice president of Sales and Marketing, with the aid of his staff, devotes many man-months to the setting of sales quotas for each new calendar year. During the month of January, the new sales quota is passed down from manager to manager and finally to each individual salesperson. All is well at ABC Company until May when management finds out that less than half of the salespeople are making their monthly objectives. The sales management is alarmed at the bad performance of the salespeople and suspects that the salespeople could do better if only they cared more about the company and worked a little harder. In an attempt to get the salespeople to work a little harder, management decided to implement a sales contest. The management thought that would get the salespeople's attention and drive up sales. So, the sales contest was announced. Several months later, sales have not improved. The sales management now thinks that possibly they should fire some of the lower producers and hire some new people that are "hungrier." Management thinks that will get everyone's attention and improve sales.

The above example is typical of industrial-age management today. Management today operates from the paradigm that all mistakes are made by people, so they blame people for all the problems. When sales attainment does not live up to expectations, it is normal for them to blame the salespeople and to devise ways to get them to work harder. The next example is the ABC Company after system analysis charts have been put in place.

In May, the sales-system owner (the owner may or may not be management) notices that the sales attainment is not up to expectations. The sales-system owner then reviews the sales-system analysis charts and determines that all of the salespeople are performing within the normal range of variation (normal performance), and therefore, the problem is not the salespeople. This company has a system view of the world rather than the old industrial-age mechanistic view. They understand that if the sales system is not producing the desired result, then the only way to change the output of the system is to change the *system.* The search is started to find out what needs to be changed in the sales system to improve sales. The research discovers two items of interest. One, many salespeople report that two competitors have announced much better financing arrangements than those offered by ABC Company. Two, a new competitor has entered their market. In addition, the new competitor's product has two features that the customers really like. In response to the newly discovered information, ABC Company announces new financing options that are competitive. ABC also began working on adding the two new features that the customers liked to their own products. What a difference in the two approaches! The old approach, when sales are not meeting expectations, is to try approaches to get the salespeople to work harder. The new approach, when sales are not meeting expectations, is to find the cause of the problem using the system analysis chart as an aid and then fix the problem when it is found.

Three natural byproducts of implementing the system analysis charts are as follows. First, when the employees have the charts, and when they construct the charts, their natural desire is to improve the output of the system. If the system analysis chart shows abnormal variance, they will want to eliminate that variance. Once the system has been stabilized and is consistently performing within the normal range of variance, then the only way improvement can occur is if the system is improved. If the decision is made by the system owners that improvement is desired, then the tools of the quality community can be utilized to accomplish that task.

Secondly, the employees will soon discover that it makes no sense to set a goal for the system to achieve. The system will only produce what it is capable of producing in its current state, which is the normal range of variance (performance) as shown on the system analysis chart. Setting a goal outside the normal range of variance of the system just means that the goal will not be achieved. The employees can work as hard as possible, but the goal will remain out of reach. The system cannot reach a higher level of performance unless something is changed within the system. Setting a goal within the normal range of performance only means that the goal will be reached sometimes. In either case, it will not change the ability of the system to produce more output. Only a change to the system will accomplish that. Only the improvement of the system will result in a higher level of performance. The setting of goals will only drive up the cost of operation. This is because it takes time to determine what the goal is to be, then it takes time to track the performance relative to the goal, then meetings will be held to discuss why the goal is not being achieved. All of these efforts are simply a waste of time and achieve nothing.

The third and most important natural byproduct of using the systems analysis charts is that it creates an environment within which **the truth can be told without penalty!** With the use of the system analysis charts, the discussions are about systems and the measurements of systems. The discussions are not about who made the mistakes and who is going to take the blame. Because the discussions are about data rather than opinions and because the resulting focus is on finding the problem rather than finding someone to blame, the employees are then free to tell the truth. The fear has been removed from the environment. An environment of trust has been created. The data is what it is. It is neither good nor bad; it is just data. Another reason that the fear has been removed is that the team no longer has management "overseeing them" or "looking down their throats." The self-directed teams are their own managers. When management demonstrates their trust of the self-directed teams by empowering the teams and then listening to and acting on their recommendations, truth is the result. **For the first time, top management is in a position to know what the truth really is!**

Chapter 13
Information Age Business Model –
Evaluation and Compensation Systems

The New Performance Evaluation System

To correct the many deficiencies of the industrial-age methods of performance evaluation will require a new approach. As companies make the transition from the industrial-age business model to the information-age model, the methods of employee performance evaluation will also change. The goal of these changes is to eventually eliminate the annual performance evaluation as we know it. In time, this can be accomplished as the self-directed teams establish themselves and gain experience in self-management. When the transition is complete, the teams themselves can take over the major responsibilities for determining who the team members are and what a fair compensation is for each team member. Between now and that time, a new approach for a performance-evaluation system can be used that utilizes three categories of items:

1. Numerical items that can be measured
2. Items over which the employee has complete control
3. Intangible items

1. Evaluation of Items That Can Be Measured Numerically

The first category of items to be discussed is numerical data that is collected on the items that are being measured. When numerical data is used for the purpose of employee performance evaluation, the data must be statistically analyzed using the statistical analysis charts. This bears repeating: *statistical analysis charts must be applied to all numerically based items that are used as a basis for conducting an employee's annual performance evaluation.*

The new performance-evaluation system assumes that the system analysis chart has been put in place and is being used for all numerical items that will be used in the employee performance-evaluation system. The system analysis chart is in fact a prerequisite to the implementation of the new performance-evaluation system.

The first group is those items that are part of an employee's performance plan and that are also part of a measurement system. One example of this might be something like sales attainment. The individual employee's sales attainment can be tracked, and the system analysis chart can be constructed for the sales system as a whole. With this data at hand, it is easy to determine the level of performance of the individual. See Figure 13.1.

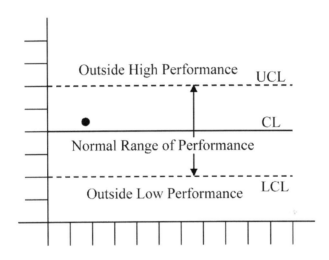

Fig. 13.1. Sales System Analysis Chart.

With the aid of the system analysis chart, it is easy to see where the employee's level of performance falls.

a. In this case, the employee's performance number (represented by the black dot) falls between the upper and lower control lines, which is within the normal range of performance. Any point that falls between the upper and lower control lines is considered to be normal performance. So, the employee is meeting the requirements of the job. Their performance falls within the expected normal range.

b.   If the employee's number had been above the upper control limit, then it may be possible to say that this employee's performance is clearly superior. That would be true if there were no exceptional or unusual items in the sales attainment number. For example, perhaps a large company moved into the salesperson's territory and placed a large one-time order that caused that employee's attainment number to be unusually high. A situation like that would be called a special cause of variation. The special-cause transactions must be removed from the attainment number before a clear picture of the employee's real performance can be seen. If, however, there are no special situations and the employee's attainment number remains outside the control limits on the high side, then that would be clearly superior performance on the part of the employee.

c.   If the employee's sales attainment number falls below the lower control line, and there were no special causes of variation, then that would clearly be performance that does not meet requirements. That employee's performance must be analyzed to determine the cause of such low performance. The low performance could be caused by any number of things:

- Lack of education or training
- Improper tools
- Poor sales territory
- Etc.

A thorough investigation must be made to determine the cause of the low performance. The investigation will determine if it is due to the employee or other causes, and the appropriate action can then be taken. Regardless, the performance level is rated as "Does not meet requirements." It is then management's or the self-directed team's responsibility to find out why the performance is abnormal and take the appropriate action.

Summary

There are only three performance levels for numerically measured items:

a. Superior performance (above the UCL with no special causes)
b. Meets requirements (between the control limits)
c. Does not meet requirements (below the lower control limit with no special causes)

With this performance-evaluation methodology, it is no longer up to the whims of a manager to determine the level of performance of the employee. The performance level is determined by the measurements and the system analysis chart. The performance analysis comes from the data. The employees can now know from measurement period to measurement period where their performance falls.

Special Situations

If an employee's attainment number is in the upper or lower one-third of the normal range of variation for seven or more measurements in a row, then that is most likely attributable to the employee. The services of a qualified statistician are required to implement and use the system analysis charts and to educate all users on how to interpret them. The statistician's assistance will also be required to identify and analyze non-typical charts and to ensure that the charts have been constructed correctly.

2. Evaluation of Items Over Which the Employee Has Total Control

The second group of items that are to be included in the employee's performance evaluation is those items over which the employee has complete control. If the employee does not have complete control over the item, then it should not be included as a part of the performance plan or evaluation. The items in this group should be things that the employee would expect to do as a normal part of the job. This group of items will help facilitate a common understanding between the employee and the evaluator as to what the work content of the job should be. For example, if the employee is a new account sales person, their performance plan might call for the salesperson to make a minimum of X prospecting calls per workweek. This minimum requirement, along with all the other items, is to be discussed and agreed to by the employee and evaluator when the performance plan is put into place. Another example might be to complete some job-related education. The important point is that the employee and evaluator must agree that these items are under the employee's complete control and that the employee can accomplish the tasks at will.

3. Evaluation of Intangible Items

The third group of items to be included in the employee's performance evaluation is the items known as intangibles. Intangibles are such things as teamwork, attitude, level of competency, integrity, working well with others, etc. This area should also link back to the company's values statement. While this is a difficult area to include in the performance plan because finding the appropriate verbiage can be a challenge, the intangibles are important and must be included. The intangibles of teamwork, integrity, and competency are especially important. The requirement for employees to work as a team is a necessity within the Teleocratic Management System. To be a good team member, the employees must be competent at their assigned responsibilities. These are just two examples of intangible items, but all major intangibles that relate to teamwork should be included in the employee evaluation. These intangibles are the most important element of the employee's evaluation and should be treated as such.

Evaluation of the Three Groups of Items

1. The first category of items which are plotted on a systems analysis chart are self-evaluating in that there can be no argument

as to which area the performance falls into. The performance is in one of the three categories, and the chart shows which one it is. The only other requirement is for the evaluator to determine if there were any special causes of variation that affected the results. The employee will usually know if special causes were present. All that is required is that the employee be asked.

2. The second category of items requires that these items in the plan be tracked so that verification of attainment can be made. The purpose of these items is to guide the employee by showing the employee the types of activities that are necessary to be successful in the job position. The rating for these items is either satisfactory or unsatisfactory.

3. Intangibles. The evaluation of the intangible items in a performance plan should be completed by conducting a survey of the employee's peers and customers (internal or external customers or both, depending upon the job). It is important that peers and customers be involved in the evaluation process because they know what the truth really is. They work with the employee every day, on good days and on not-so-good days. The evaluator should have no more than one-fourth of the weight as far as determining the evaluation of the intangibles. A reasonable guideline would be for the evaluator to be weighted 25%, the evaluation by the peers 50%, and evaluation by "customers" 25%. These weightings certainly could and should be modified depending upon the individual job and the availability of feedback from peers and customers.

Levels of Performance Evaluation

No more that five categories of performance should be used:

1. Far exceeds requirements in most areas
2. Far exceeds requirements in some areas
3. Exceeds requirements in most areas
4. Meets requirements in most areas, exceeds in some areas

    5.   Does not meet requirements in some or most areas

In fact, a system with only four levels of performance is preferable. In a system with five levels, a rating of 1 to 4 is satisfactory and a rating of 5 is unsatisfactory.

The evaluator of performance has much less power in determining the overall evaluation than in the past with traditional evaluation systems. That is by design. The evaluation of the first two categories of items is almost automatic. There is little for the evaluator to do beyond the collecting and recording of the data. In the third category of intangibles, the people doing most of the evaluation are the employees' peers and customers. These are the people who know what the truth really is. The peers work with the employee every day; they know the good from the not-so-good employees. They know who is a team player and who is not. They know who is competent and who is not. They should carry the most weight when an evaluation of the intangibles is to be made, not the evaluator.

Weighting of the Three Groups

Every employee should meet or exceed the requirements of the first two groups of items. That is assuming that the employees have received the necessary training and equipment for the job. It is the third group of items, the intangibles, that becomes the real differentiator in the evaluation process. Items such as teamwork, integrity, and competency are quite important for employees working in self-directed teams. For this reason, a guideline of twenty-five percent for each of the first two groups and fifty percent for the last group of items is a reasonable weighting.

This new method of performance evaluation will be viewed as much more fair and balanced by the employee than the current performance-evaluation system. One of the primary reasons for this is that the evaluation under the old system was determined primarily by the employee's immediate manager. It is clear to all employees that most managers have their favorite employees, and these "favorite" employees naturally receive the best evaluations and rewards. As the old saying goes, "It is not what you know, but who you know." With the new performance-evaluation system as outlined here, the impact on the overall evaluation by the immediate manager has been drastically reduced, thereby making the evaluation more balanced and fair.

This new performance-evaluation structure will be much more appealing to Generations X and Y. For Generation X, it will allow them to have a higher degree of trust in the outcome of the evaluation because a much smaller percentage of the overall evaluation is coming from management, which they naturally distrust. It also appeals to their need for equality and to be treated as a peer by management. For Generation Y, the new structure appeals to their socially conscious nature and their desire to participate in all aspects of the self-directed teams. By participating in the performance-evaluation process, they can satisfy the need to be socially conscious, to ensure that discrimination does not occur, and also satisfy their concerns regarding morality and fairness.

The New Compensation System

The new compensation system has three components, depending upon whether or not the company is privately held or publicly held. For the companies that are privately held, the compensation for the employees will consist of three elements:

1. Salary
2. Variable compensation tied to productivity
3. Profit and Equity Sharing

For the employees of companies that are publicly held, the compensation will consist of four elements.

1. Salary
2. Variable compensation tied to productivity
3. Profit Sharing

4. Stock grants and/or stock options

The salary for each individual can be determined by traditional means such as salary surveys. Once the salary for a particular position has been determined, then some percentage of that amount will be paid as salary. For example, the salary might be 80% of the industry rate. Then the variable compensation, which is tied to the performance of the team driver measurements, would be added to the base salary. The combination of the base salary and the variable compensation should be structured such that the employee's total compensation is more than the industry rate. For the employees who have staff positions or other positions where any direct measurement is not clear, then the variable compensation should be tied to the performance of the group or segment of the business of which they are a part. Stock options or stock grants must be available to all employees. They are no longer the domain of only the top management.

With the new performance evaluation and compensation systems in place, the company is now on a new business spiral as shown in figure 13.2.

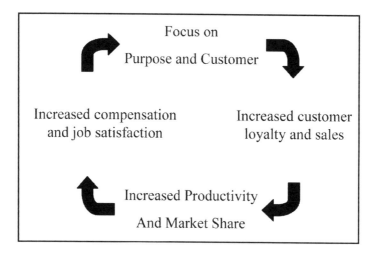

Fig. 13.2. Upward Business Spiral

As the company focuses on the company purpose and satisfying the customers, the sales then increase, as does customer loyalty. The increased sales then lead to increased productivity and market share. Since the employees are now paid on productivity, the increased productivity leads to increased compensation and job satisfaction for the employees. This in turn leads the employees to continue their focus on the purpose and on satisfying the customers, but at the same time, the employees are now constantly trying to improve things. The employees will work to improve the products, decrease the costs, and find new and better ways of doing things. They do this because now they can see the linkage between their actions and the financial results of the company, which means profit sharing and increasing their equity in the business. They also are constantly improving things because the self-directed teams are empowered to make the decisions regarding their part of the business. It is a self-reinforcing spiral in which everyone wins. The more the employees improve the efficiency and product design, everyone wins—the customer, the company, the employees and the stockholders. It is a win, win, win, win system!

The objective of the compensation is to ensure that all of the employees have some ownership in the company. It is this ownership or equity in the company that gives them a reason to care, a reason to be excited about going to work in the morning. In concert with the rest of the information-age purpose-driven business model, the equity that the employees have in the company allows them to be, think and act like owners. Providing the employees with equity in the company is about much more than just providing another employee benefit. As CEO Jack Stack says, "First and foremost, it's a vehicle for change. The goal is not just to reward people for the work they do, or to maximize profits for their own sake, or to enhance shareholder value, improve cash flow, or whatever. Rather, equity is used to involve people in the process of making a difference in the world. Why? Because business is not an end in itself. It's a means to an end. It's a tool that allows us to accomplish the things that matter most to us, and those things must transcend business to have real meaning and value. The precise nature of those loftier goals will vary from company to company, and even from person to person, but you must have them. They are what makes ownership worth caring about."[275]

"It's about what one person can do for another person. It's not just a set of rewards; it's a reward system. People come together, struggle together, build something together, and enjoy the benefits together. Yes, there are hardships along the way. Life is full of hardships. But when people are working toward a common goal, they can rise above the hardships. They can put aside the petty issues and think at a higher level. They can realize how important they are to one another, and come together as a team, and create something better than existed before. Because people have hope. They have something to look forward to in their lives."[276]

When the employees have equity in the company, whether it is in the form of equity in a privately held company or stock in a publicly held company, and they are able to see and understand the linkage between their day-to-day efforts and the increasing value of that equity, "there's a sense of pride, identity, direction, and purpose. People know they're part of something bigger than what they do on a day-to-day basis. They belong to something, and it belongs to them. They have ownership, and it's a two-way street."[277] It is the sense of ownership, thinking and acting like owners that helps the employees and the company make it through the tough times much better than other companies. As Jack Stack observed, "Whenever the going has gotten tough, we've been able to draw together as a family, figure out what has to be done, and then go out and take care of business. I doubt that would have happened if a few of us had kept all the stock to ourselves. The other people would have felt (correctly) that they were working for someone else. By sharing equity, we put everybody in the same boat, and so we could make sure we all were pulling together when the seas grew rough. As a result, we learned we could handle adversity. It tested our mettle and made us stronger."[278]

Once all of the elements of the new business model are in place, the level 5 leadership, the new organizational structure, the new measurement, performance evaluation and compensation systems;

the role of management and the relationship of management with the employees has changed dramatically. There is now a relationship of mutual respect, trust and partnership in determining the future success of the company. "Management" has been transformed from the role of "command and control" to a role of support and enablement. As one CEO observed, "managing" employees who think and act like owners is different. "You can't manage owners, and most people don't want to be managed anyway. You challenge people. You encourage them. You tell them the truth. You try to help them understand reality. But you don't manage them, at least not in the traditional sense."[279]

Chapter 14
The Power of Purpose, Overcoming Bureaucracy

The previous chapters have provided a description of the elements of the new information-age purpose-driven business model. The Semco story is one example of a company that has implemented many of the elements of the new information-age business model including the circular, flat organizational structure that produced impressive levels of productivity increase. This chapter will provide examples from the companies highlighted in Chapter four and show how these companies have utilized the elements of the information-age purpose-driven business model to achieve their extraordinary levels of performance.

Overcoming bureaucracy

In Chapter four, forty-three companies were listed that represented the following four categories:

- Companies that transitioned from average to great performance
- The most productive companies in the world
- The best financially performing companies
- The premier companies that have stood the test of time

The question is, what exactly does this group of companies do, that allows their stock to outperform the stock of their peers by a factor of about six times? What common traits of the information-age purpose-driven business model are these forty-three companies using that explains this outstanding performance? By examining the common traits of these companies, we can gain an understanding of the elements that have led to such high levels of performance. Those common traits are:

1. They are purpose-driven.
2. They translate the company purpose into practice.
3. They live by their company values.
4. They select Level-5 Leaders.
5. They think long-term.
6. They utilize trust, truth and transparency.
7. They operate from the win/win, cooperative eco-system paradigm.
8. They constantly strive to improve.
9. They get the people part.
10. They relate compensation to productivity.
11. They create strong, unique company cultures.

1. They are purpose-driven

All of these companies are purpose-driven companies. That is to say that their number-one objective is something other than the pursuit or the maximization of profits. Purpose explains what the company stands for: the company's fundamental reason for existence beyond just making money. These companies stand for something greater than profits, something that is good and noble. They understand that the company is not an end itself, but rather a means to an end. They view their purpose in one way or another to improve the human condition and also the condition of all of their constituencies. Their purpose is to provide great products and services to their customers, provide exceptional returns to the stockholders, provide an energizing place to work for the employees, and improve the communities and the environment in which they operate. They believe that their purpose is to do all of these things. When a company goes through the process of discovering its core purpose, the core purpose will almost always involve some form of improving the human condition. The exact wording may be different, but in each case the end result is the same. A good example is Cargill's purpose: *To improve the standard of living around the world.*[280] The first key aspect of a company purpose is that it gives meaning to all work for all the employees. No longer is the job just a McJob, the job takes on a whole new context. When a company has a stated purpose that is supported by the actions of management, many times the employees feel like "they are as much volunteering for a cause as showing up to work for a paycheck."[281] In the case of the employees at Cargill, their efforts are helping to lift the standard of living of people throughout the whole world. The employees feel good about what they do and take pride in all of their successes because their successes help improve the wellbeing of all humanity. That is the power of a noble company purpose that is stated. Words are not sufficient to capture the enthusiasm, dedication, loyalty, energy and passion that an ennobling company purpose engenders. However, *a noble company purpose is the single key feature that sets these forty-three companies apart from their peers.* One example of the importance of employee passion for the company purpose is Starbucks. Howard Schultz, the CEO of Starbucks, when speaking of their employees says, "Their passion and devotion is our number-one competitive advantage. Lose it, and we've lost the game. In business, that passion comes from ownership, trust, and loyalty. If you undermine any of those, employees will view their work as just another job."[282]

The executives of these companies spend a great deal of time communicating and then re- communicating the company purpose. As one example, while speaking to a group of HP managers, David Packard described the company and its relationship to its purpose as follows:

> I want to discuss *why* [emphasis his] a company exists in the first place. In other words, why are we here? I think many people assume wrongly, that a company exists simply to make money. While this is an important result of a company's existence, we have to go deeper and find the real reason for our being. As we investigate this, we inevitably come to the conclusion that a group of people get together and exist as an institution to accomplish something collectively that they could not accomplish separately

– they make a contribution to society, a phrase which sounds trite but is fundamental…You can look around [in the general business world] and still see people who are interested in money and nothing else – to make a product – to give a service – generally to do something which is of value. So with that in mind, let us discuss why the Hewlett-Packard Company exists – the real reason for our existence is that we provide something which is unique [that makes a contribution].[283]

It is abundantly clear from David Packard's comments that the company he helped to create and grow was founded on a purpose that was beyond just the pursuit of money.

Mr. Packard also made the following statement: "[In 1949], I attended a meeting of business leaders. I suggested at the meeting that management people had a responsibility beyond that of making a profit for their stockholders. I said that we had a responsibility to our employees to recognize their dignity as human beings, and to assure that they should share in the success, which their work made possible. I pointed out, also, that we had a responsibility to our customers, and to the community at large, as well. I was surprised and shocked that not a single person at that meeting agreed with me. While they were reasonably polite in their disagreement, it was quite evident they firmly believed I was not one of *them*, and obviously not qualified to manage an important enterprise."[284] In 1949 and still today, Level-5 Executives such as David Packard are still in the minority. The two primary reasons for this are that most companies have yet to discover their core purpose, and most boards of directors are misguided.

A recent example of what can happen to a company that rather than moving toward a purpose-driven management system decides to move to an even more rigid form of the industrial-age bureaucratic command-and-control profit-driven system is the Home Depot story. The following quote is taken from the book, *Firms of Endearment*. "Under CEO Bob Nardelli, Home Depot has moved aggressively in recent years to adopt an overtly militaristic culture that puts it squarely at odds with the social, cultural, and managerial trends we highlight in *Firms of Endearment.*

"According to a cover story in *Business Week*, Nardelli is a devotee of the aggressive approach to business espoused in George Stalk's *Hardball: Are you playing to Play or Playing to Win?*. Nardelli, a former officer in the ROTC who just barely missed getting into West Point, has a military fixation that borders on the obsessive. As of March 2006, nearly half of the 1,142 people hired into Home Depot's store leadership program were former junior military officers. To develop a motivational message for its 317,000 'store troops,' the company relied heavily on the Marine Corps Doctrinal Publication 1 on 'War Fighting' which includes a chapter on 'developing subordinate leaders.'

"Rather than building morale and motivation among rank-and-file employees, these moves have had the opposite effect. According to many former executives, Nardelli has created a 'culture of fear' in which managers are so 'paralyzed with fear' that they worry about *when* they will be fired, not if. The numbers bear this out; an astonishing 98 percent of the company's top 170 executives were replaced between 2001 and 2005. Nardelli is no believer in work-life balance; 'he treats Saturdays and Sundays as ordinary working days and often expects those around him to do the same.'

"Companies are not like the military, whose culture has to be defined by a 'command and control' ethos. Companies must earn the loyalty of customers, employees, and suppliers every day. Successful companies today treat all their stakeholders like customers, because the best employees and suppliers can always choose who they want to do business with.

"Though Nardelli has voiced support for a stakeholder view of the world in the past, today's Home Depot appears not to treat even *customers* like customers. Since Nardelli became CEO in 2000, Home Depot's customer satisfaction ratings have fallen precipitously; 2005 data from the University of Michigan's respected American Customer Satisfaction Index show that Home Depot ranks dead last among all major U.S. retailers, trailing even Kmart. A quote from store manager Don Ray in the *Business Week* story illustrates the mindset that has contributed to this decline: 'In the military, we win battles and conquer the enemy – at [Home Depot], we do that with customers.' Instead of inspiring employees to deliver better customer service, the company focuses primarily on measurement. As one former executive anonymously commented, 'My perception is that the mechanics are there. The soul isn't.'[285]

"With employees terrified and customers turned off, who is benefiting from Nardelli's regime? Nardelli, for one. For the year ended January 30, 2005, his pay package came to $28.5 million. He is the only employee guaranteed with a bonus, which rose to $5.8 million in 2004 from $4.5 million in 2003 – even though the company's stock price was below where it was in 2000, when Nardelli took over.

"In fact, Home Depot's stock performance under Nardelli contrasts sharply with that of Lowe's, its more 'touchy feely' competitor. While Lowe's stock rose nearly 210 percent between December 2000 and March 2006, Home Depot's was down approximately 7 percent. This despite the fact that revenues grew at 12 percent annually and margins improved from 30 to 33.5 percent. But Lowe's has grown revenues 19 percent per year, and its margins are close to Home Depot's."[286]

The forty-three elite companies spotlighted in Chapter 4, because they are purpose-driven companies, avoid this type of negative change in corporate direction. For these companies, a key aspect of the company purpose is that it can never be achieved. Because of this, these companies never stop changing and progressing in order that they can live more fully in their purpose. In the example of Cargill, there is no end to the effort of improving the standard of living around the world. No matter how much it is improved, it can always be made better. This causes a tension to exist between the company in its present state and the pursuit of the company purpose, which causes the company to constantly strive to improve over its past performance. GE captured the essence of their company purpose in the slogan "GE – we bring good things to life." As one employee expressed it, "Most wouldn't admit it, but everyone at GE gets chills when they hear that jingle. The simple, corny phrase captures how they feel about the company — it means jobs and growth for the company, quality and service for the customer, benefits and training for the employee, and challenge and satisfaction for the individual. It means integrity, honesty, and loyalty at all levels."[287] As in the case of GE, the purpose of these companies serves to bind all of the employees, management included, in the common goal of fulfilling the purpose and vision. Jim Collins, the author of two well-known business books, discusses the relentless drive for progress that the core purpose generates. He says, "The drive for progress is not a sterile, intellectual recognition that 'progress is healthy in a changing world' or that 'healthy organizations should change to improve' or that 'we should have goals'; rather, it's a deep, inner, compulsive – almost primal – *drive*."[288] The combination of the company purpose, which gives meaning to all work for the employees, and the drive to continually improve, energizes these companies. In the words of a Hewlett-Packard manager: "We're proud of our successes, and we celebrate them. But the real excitement comes in figuring out how we can do even better in the future. It's a never-ending process of seeing how far we can go. There's no ultimate finish line where we can say 'we've arrived.' I never want us to be satisfied with our success, for that's when we'll begin to decline."[289]

Another characteristic that sets these companies apart from other companies is that they are not fooled by the profit paradox. The paradox, or as it is sometimes called, the profit myth, is thinking that by focusing on profit and making it the number-one objective, you maximize profit. The truth is, that by focusing on profit and making profit the number-one objective of a company at the expense of the other constituencies, profit is then sub-optimized.

Howard Schultz, the CEO of Starbucks, explains the profit paradox this way: "A company that is managed only for the benefit of shareholders treats its employees as a line item, a cost to be contained. Executives who cut jobs aggressively are often rewarded with a temporary run-up in their stock price. But in the long run, they are not only undermining morale but sacrificing the innovation, the entrepreneurial spirit, and the heartfelt commitment of the very people who could elevate the company to greater heights.

"What many in business don't realize is that it's not a zero-sum game. Treating employees benevolently shouldn't be viewed as an added cost that cuts into profits, but as a powerful energizer that can grow the enterprise into something far greater than one leader could envision. With pride in their work, Starbucks people are less likely to leave. Our turnover rate is less than half the industry average, which not only saves money but strengthens our bond with customers. But the benefits run deeper. If people relate to the company they work for, if they form an emotional tie to it and buy into its dreams, they will pour their heart into making it better. When employees have self-esteem and self-respect, they can contribute so much more: to their company, to their family, to the world."[290] Howard went on to say that the Starbucks mission statement (read "purpose statement") "puts people first and profits last."[291]

Focusing on profit and making it the number-one objective is what Bob Nardelli did at Home Depot, and we saw what the results were in today's business environment. That is not what the forty-three purpose-driven companies did. To optimize profits, companies must make long-term decisions, focus on the customer, their purpose, and the employees. Focusing on profits as the number-one objective, to use a sports analogy, is like focusing on the score rather than how you are playing the game. These companies focus on how they are playing the game and let the score (profits) take care of itself.

George Merck II of Merck explained the profit paradox this way: "I want to express the principles which we in our company have endeavored to live up to — here is how it sums up. We try to remember that medicine is for the patient. We try never to forget that medicine is for the people. It is not for profits. The profits will follow, and if we remembered that, they never failed to appear. The better we have remembered it, the larger they have been."[292]

2. These companies put the company purpose into practice

It is one thing for the executives of a company to go on a retreat, meet, discuss and come back with a purpose, vision and values statements. It is a whole different ballgame when the executives believe in the company purpose at a bone-deep level and put it into practice. The executives of many profit-driven companies have gone offsite and returned with a mission or vision or perhaps even a purpose statement that they have crafted and committed to paper. This usually happens because a consultant has convinced them that, "this is the thing to do." The sad part is that most consultants are incompetent and do not clearly understand the difference between vision and mission statements. As a result, the new mission or vision or a combination of the two is published with great fanfare, but then nothing changes. It is business as usual. That is because the executives do not really believe at a bone-deep level in the vision or mission they created, and their number-one objective (purpose) is still to maximize profits.

For the forty-three purpose-driven companies, it is a totally different story. In his book *Built to Last,* Jim Collins makes the following statement: "The essence of a visionary [purpose-driven] company comes in the translation of its core ideology [purpose and values] and its own unique drive for progress into the very fabric of the organization – into goals, strategies, tactics, policies, processes, accounting systems, job design – into everything that the company does."[293] I inserted the words "purpose-driven" and "purpose and values" into the statement by Mr. Collins to make it clearer. In his book, Mr. Collins defines a core ideology as a company's core purpose and core values, then he refers to these companies as visionary companies, which in the terminology of this book are purpose-driven companies. Terminology aside, the one thing that separates these forty-three elite companies from their peers is that these companies do in fact ingrain the company purpose into every aspect of the company just as Jim points out.

When a company puts the company purpose into practice, one natural outflow of that process is the creation and documentation of the company values. It is the company values that provide the operational guidelines for the company purpose. When purpose-driven companies codify their company values, they do not always use that terminology. They may call the company values something else. For example, when IBM codified their company values, they called them the IBM Basic Beliefs. HP is another example. Dave Packard wrote: "Our main task is to design, develop, and manufacture the finest [electronic equipment] for the advancement of science and the welfare of humanity." Notice the wording, "for the advancement of science *and the welfare of humanity.*" When HP put the company purpose into practice, they created what they called the four "musts." HP *must*:

- make its profit through technological contribution;
- recognize and respect the personal worth of employees and allow them to share in the success of the company;
- operate as a responsible citizen of the general community;
- attain profitable growth.[294]

These four "musts" are really the HP core values, they just are not labeled as such. However, it is the core values that are required when the company purpose is put into practice. The core purpose and core values then provide the guidelines for day-to-day decision-making for all of the employees. The employees no longer need or require any management review or approval. The employees in this environment can be totally empowered. They know what the company purpose and values are and they can apply them to their decision-making.

An example of this is HP and the HP Way. One element of the HP core purpose is that new products must provide "for the advancement of science" or the operational term used at HP was technical contribution. If a new product could not demonstrate enough technical contribution to "the advancement of science" then the product would not be brought to market, no matter what the market potential might be. In the words of Bill Hewlett, "If you had the opportunity to listen in on one of our management sessions, you would find that many approaches are rejected because people feel there is not enough of a technical contribution to justify bringing a particular product to market."[295] This self-imposed standard led HP to pass up many high-volume markets because their products did not provide enough "technical contribution."

An example of this was the IBM-compatible PC market. Following is a 1984 discussion between a seasoned lab manager and a younger product manager regarding a PC product.

Product Manager
   "We've got to introduce an IBM-compatible personal computer *now*. That's where the market is going. That's where the volume is. That's what customers primarily want."

Lab Manager
   "But where's the technological contribution? Until we figure out a way to make an IBM-compatible personal computer with a clear technological advantage, then we just can't do it – no matter how big the market."

Product Manager
   "But what if that's not what customers want? What if they just want to run their software and don't really care about technical contribution? And what if the market window will close unless we act now?"

Lab Manager
   "Then we shouldn't be in that business. That's not who we are. We simply shouldn't be in markets that don't value technical contribution. That's just not what the Hewlett-Packard Company is all about."[296]

Eventually HP would bring a PC to market, but not until it met the requirements of the company purpose and core values.

These forty-three elite purpose-driven companies ensure that the company purpose is ingrained in all that they do. It permeates every aspect of the company. They indoctrinate the employees in the company purpose and the unique company culture that in many cases is so strong that it almost has a cult-like feeling about it. They carefully grow future managers within the company and instill them with the purpose and culture. The result is that they achieve alignment between the company purpose and all aspects of the company such as goals, strategies, policies, tactics, personnel practices and even organizational design.

Jeffrey L. Sturchio, the director of science and technology policy at Merck summed it up this way: "I used to work at another major American corporation before coming to Merck. The basic difference I see between the two companies is rhetoric versus reality. The other company touted values and vision and all the rest, but there was a big difference between rhetoric and reality. At Merck, there is no difference."[297]

3. These companies live by their company values

In the process of living and being true to the company purpose, these leading companies codify and then live by their core values. The core values for these companies stand on their own merit. They require no further explanation or justification. They are simply an extension of the definition of the company purpose and they provide guidance for day-to-day decision-making. It is important that a company codify the company core values, but it is more important that they live by them. That is the difference between these companies and their peers. They live, eat and breathe the company purpose and values daily. It is clear to everyone by the actions of the company and management that the purpose and values are not just some piece of meaningless paper, but the purpose and values are alive, well and are defended at all cost. These companies are willing to change everything about themselves *but* their core purpose and values. They express this commitment in everything they do. As Thomas J. Watson Jr., the former CEO of IBM, said of IBM's Basic Beliefs (values), "I believe the single most important factor in corporate success is faithful adherence to those beliefs — beliefs must always come before policies, practices, and goals. The latter must always be altered if they are seen to violate fundamental beliefs." He went on to say as far as he was concerned, "those values were the rules of life — to be preserved at all costs, to be commended to others, and to be followed conscientiously in one's business life."[298]

The process of discovering the core purpose and values within a company is a very energizing experience for the employees. During this process, one executive vice president of a large bank said, "I've worked at this company my entire life, and I'd begun to lose hope. But once we became clear in our own minds about what we really stand for and began to change the organization to fit with that, well, the release of human energy has been amazing. People all the way down to the individual branch level feel that their work has more meaning than it used to. And now that we know what is core and should remain fixed, we've felt liberated to change everything else – to slay sacred cows that had really been getting in our way. It's like awakening a sleeping giant."[299]

<u>Clarity and Focus</u>

The prior quote highlights another key characteristic of these companies. That is the fact that these companies have clarity of purpose, which allows them to focus and thereby identify anything that is not directly related to fulfilling the company purpose. These companies do not change direction year to year nor do they lose focus on the objective, which is the company purpose. Day after day, month after month, year after year, they are focused and disciplined. They don't get distracted by the "priority of the day" or "what the competition is doing." They actually pay very little attention to the competition. They believe in just staying focused on their company and their purpose, and letting the rest take care of itself. The clarity provided by the company purpose allows them to identify items or parts of the business that are not directly related to the core purpose, and when identified, they can be eliminated.

When a company does not have a stated purpose, that leads to a lack of clarity and focus which eventually leads to "an inability to move quickly, hidden agendas, unhappy workers, turf wars, finger pointing, a constant need for phalanxes of outside consultants to try and sort things out, palace intrigue and eventually a CYA mentality. It's tough to be productive when there's a swamp full of superfluous man-made issues to wade through each day."[300]   One of the things that these companies consistently identify as being unnecessary, distracting, costly and that must be destroyed is bureaucracy. In these companies, the level 5 CEOs lead the way. For example, Dan DiMicco answers his own phone, Michael O'Leary sends his own faxes, Bill Zollars answers his own emails and Pat Lancaster has personally flown out to fix a customer's problem.[301] Ken Nordin of IKEA says, "We still have what's called 'Anti-Bureaucracy Week.' For at *least* one week every year, everyone has to work in a store. And that can be anything from pushing carts to serving as a cashier, or in sales, whatever you can do." And Nordin adds, "All of the executives must be there on weekends, when the stores are the busiest, teeming with shoppers of all kinds, crying babies and arguing couples. It's not enough to check in on a Monday and out on a Thursday afternoon. You have to be there when the heat is on." Ingvar Kamprad, the founder and CEO of IKEA, created the program because "he is dead scared of bureaucracy. He is very afraid about the people making decisions becoming out of touch."[302] These companies stick to their knitting and eject everything that is not in alignment with their purpose and values.

For these companies, it is the company's core values that lead to integrity, honesty and trust. One example of this is Marion and Herb Sandler, the husband-and-wife team who run the publicly traded Golden West Financial, the parent of World Savings. The five values of Golden West Financial are the source of what Herb Sandler calls the company's moral fiber. Shortly after Herb and Marion had purchased Golden West, the following happened. In Herb's own words, "In 1966 the United States faced its first serious liquidation problem since World War Two. And when I say things were tight, I mean there was simply no money in the system. Like all other financial institutions we had all kinds of loan commitments for money we'd agreed to lend and there was no money to honor our commitments. Savings were going out but there were no new savings coming in. All the other banks and S&Ls were canceling their commitments to borrowers but we made a promise to ourselves to not cancel a single commitment. Every day we'd count the dollars coming in from loan repayments, and whenever we had enough, we'd fund another one. Ultimately we funded every loan, even though we were losing money. To the best of our knowledge, we were the only company to honor every single commitment." Marion Sandler finished the story: "You might wonder why we did that. The reason is simple. **A great business is built on trust – doing what you promise to do. You can lose your reputation in a single day and you can never get it back. Trust is something you build over your life**."[303] That is the power of a value like trust in a purpose-driven company. No wonder these companies have such loyal customers!

Just like Golden West Financial, Southwest Airlines has a large amount of tolerance in many areas, but when it comes to the company values, the tolerance stops. In the words of CEO Herb Kelleher, "One area where there's no compromise is values. An employee who compromises on those is out." These companies also understand the relationship between values, passion and productivity. Charles Koch, the CEO of Koch Industries, says, "People are most productive and have passion for their work when they agree with the values of the company. Those who don't may still be good people, but would be happier somewhere else."[304]

When companies have no company purpose and therefore no company values, the company has no compass and lacks the moral fiber of the companies that do. Unfortunately, there have been too many examples of these companies recently. Tyco, WorldCom, Adelphia Cable and Enron, to name a few.

4. Purpose-driven companies select Level 5 Leaders

It is not an accident that these forty-three most elite of the elite companies all have Level-5 Leaders. The reason they all have Level-5 or Level-5-like Leaders is that they are all purpose-driven companies. Purpose-driven companies are looking for an executive that has the humility and modesty to put their ambitions second to that of the company and its purpose. However, they also are looking for an executive that also has a strong professional drive. When the priority is the company, its purpose, its customers and its employees, that leaves little focus, attention or priority for the CEO. In this environment, the ego-centric Level-4 Effective Leader is just not a good fit. The Level-4 Leaders want all of the focus to be on them, and their agenda is to satisfy their own personal ambitions, not the company's. In addition, an executive team that consists of Level-4 Effective Leaders is an enormous financial drain for any company in two main areas. First is their spending habit on personal perks and second is their propensity to make decisions that hurt the company in the long run but help their personal compensation in the short run. A classic comparison of the two types of executives is the difference between the executives at Bethlehem Steel and Nucor. These two companies are in the same industry, steel, and they are competitors.

Perks and Spending Habits

The executives at Bethlehem Steel for some reason felt that their executive parking spaces, corporate jets, employment contracts, company cars, hunting lodges and so on were not enough. So, they decided that they should have among all their other perks, an executive golf course. Then, they built one at company expense. Shortly after the course was completed, the middle managers complained because they were not allowed to use the golf course. So what was the response of the executive team? Rather than share their golf course with the other managers or the employees, the executive team decided to build two more golf courses at company expense. One for the other managers and one for the employees![305] After all, when you already have a large expensive headquarters with an executive dining room, executive washrooms and executive parking, you must have an executive golf course just like your peers in other companies. Your ego would not settle for anything less. To remain consistent with the status that an executive receives with all of these perks, they must also have a compensation package that is commensurate with such a position and status. As a result, these Level-4 executives somehow feel that they have "earned" all the compensation that they receive. For example, the average CEO of the S&P 500 companies received $11.75 million in compensation in 2005.[306] In addition to the CEO compensation of about $12 million per year, when the cost of all the additional perks such as the corporate fleet of jets, lavish headquarters at expensive locations, golf courses and so on are added to the direct compensation, the cost of the CEO to the company can easily be double the amount of direct compensation. To put this in perspective, if a company makes 10% net profit after taxes on sales, that would mean that the profit from sales of $240 million dollars would be required just to pay for the CEO's compensation package and perks! That does not include the other top executives, just the CEO. When the other top executives are included, *it could easily require the profits from over five hundred million to one billion in sales just to pay for the compensation and perks of the executive team.* That is a huge drain on any company.

Contrast that with Level-5 Leaders. In 2005, Jim Sinegal, the Level-5 Leader of Costco, received a total of $550,000: $350,000 in salary and a $200,000 bonus even though he was the CEO of a $57-billion company.[307] Ken Iverson, the CEO of Nucor, a $3.6-billion company, the third largest steel company in America, was paid a salary of $450,000. In 1982, when the steel industry was in a severe slump, his salary dropped to about $110,000.[308] Speaking of his $110,000 salary in 1982, Ken said, "When a friend showed me an article, later that year, that listed me as the lowest-paid Fortune 500 CEO, I wasn't ashamed. The company was not performing. I'd have been ashamed to earn more."[309] Furthermore, he said, "Managers don't need or deserve special treatment. We're not more important than other employees. And we aren't better than anyone else. We just have a different job to do."[310]   He went on to say, "Our executives get the same group insurance, same holidays, and same vacations as everybody else. They eat lunch in the same cafeterias. They fly economy class on regular commercial flights. We have no executive suites and no executive cars. At headquarters, our 'corporate dining room' is the deli across the street. Our executives wouldn't have it any other way. They see our egalitarian culture serving their interest as much as the interests of our employees. For one thing, our managers don't have to waste time fretting over their chances to get the fancy corner office or arguing over who gets to use the company plane. We don't have those perks, and we imagine they would cause a lot more stress than fulfillment. What a bunch of nonsense! Chasing meaningless status symbols and tokens of power. When you look back on your career, will those things seem important?"[311]   Here is what Ken has to say about a headquarters building: "What makes Nucor's headquarters so impressive, I think, is that it is so *un*impressive — twelve thousand feet of rented office space in a Charlotte office park. We never got around to building an elaborate temple to ourselves, like those you see sprawled across swanky suburban enclaves. *We're too busy building our business.* Besides, our entire headquarters staff, including the clerical personnel, numbers just twenty-two. I take pride in Nucor's little headquarters. To me a big headquarters isn't grand. It is a waste of money — a gross tribute to some executive's ego."[312] Think about what Ken just said. A company of $3.6 billion in size has an entire corporate staff of only twenty-two people, and they were too focused on building the business to worry about a headquarters building! That says a lot about Level-5 Leaders versus Level-4 Effective Executives.

There is another huge difference between a Level-4 Executive and a Level-5 Leader that should not go unnoticed. That difference is the way they view employees. The typical Level-4 Executive views the employees primarily as just another expense line item to be controlled and minimized. The Level-5 Leader, however, understands that in the information age, the employees are the company, and are the company's most valuable asset. The employees hold the knowledge power base and they are the engines of innovation and productivity increase, and, most importantly, the Level-5 Executives understand that loyal, passionate, knowledgeable, happy employees deliver superior service to the company's number-one constituency, the customer. Level-5 Leaders understand this relationship and, as David O'Reilly, the CEO of O'Reilly Automotive, told his managers, "If we take care of our own people first and value them above everything else, that superlative customer service happens naturally."[313] Starbucks is famous for the fact that it provides generous health benefits for its employees. Howard Schultz, the CEO of Starbucks, said of the decision to provide health benefits to the employees, "It turned out to be one of the best decisions we have ever made. It's true our health insurance program is costly. Over the years, we've added coverage far more generous than most companies our size, with coverage for preventive care, crisis counseling, mental health, chemical dependency, vision, and dental. Starbucks subsidizes 75 percent of coverage; each employee pays only 25 percent." "But Starbucks gets back plenty for its investment. The most obvious effect is lower attrition. Nationwide, most retailers and fast-food chains have a turnover rate ranging from 150 percent to as high as 400 percent. At Starbucks, turnover at the barista level averages 60 percent to 65 percent. For store managers, our turnover is only about 25 percent, while at other retailers, it's about 50 percent. Better benefits attract good people and keep them longer. More significantly, I found that the health plan made a huge difference in the attitudes of people. When a company shows generosity toward them, employees show a more positive outlook in everything they do."[314] "Many retailers encourage turnover, either consciously or unconsciously, in the belief that it keeps down wages and benefits. But high turnover also affects customer loyalty. Some of our customers are such regulars that the minute they walk into the store, a barista recalls their favorite drink. If that barista leaves, that strong connection is broken."[315] In company after purpose-driven company, you see the same thing. These companies value and take care of their employees and the employees in turn take care of the company and the customers.

<u>Modesty, Business Focus and Stewardship</u>

There are several characteristics that run through the Level-5 executives of the forty-three elite companies listed in Chapter 4. One, they are modest and humble people. This modesty is manifested in the way they live, the way they treat people (customers and employees) and the way they run the business. They consistently have modest compensation packages, their companies have modest headquarters and staff, and they are lean and mean. Two, they are extremely focused on the business and what is in the best interests of the business, the stockholders, the employees and the customers. Marion and Herb Sandler of World Savings provide a great example of this business focus. When World Savings is making a business decision, they ask one question of themselves. The question is as follows: "What's the good business reason for doing this?" When World Savings was ready to expand, they applied this concept and asked the question, "What is the purpose of a branch office?" Marion said, "At the time, most financial institutions were building branches of ten thousand to fifteen thousand square feet, but a little industrial engineering makes you wonder why you need all that space. The purpose of a branch office is to collect deposits from people. Why would you need fifteen thousand square feet to do that?" Herb said, "Our branches average about three thousand to four thousand square feet; imagine how much more economically you can run a branch that's one-quarter the size of the other guy's." Then Marion added, "It wasn't only the cost savings realized with a smaller branch but what was going on inside these big vast spaces. There was always a male branch manager sitting on a pedestal whose job it was to glad-hand people, while the real work was being done by a woman, the head teller/operations officer. We eliminated the position of male branch manager right away."[316] Here is a vivid example of the difference between Level-4 executive leadership and Level-5 leadership. The financial institutions with Level-4 ego-centric executive leadership builds the ten-to-fifteen-thousand–square-foot elaborate branch offices with a high-paid branch manager to oversee the operations, while World Savings with Level-5 leadership builds a modest three-to-four thousand-square-foot branch office with only the necessities, one of which is *not* a branch manager!

Ken Iverson of Nucor is another example of this. He said that "Our competitive strategy is to build manufacturing facilities economically, and to operate them efficiently. Period."[317] The difference in cost structures that these companies have when compared to their peers is enormous and is obviously a great benefit to the stockholders. These examples begin to give some insight into why the companies with Level-5 leadership perform so much better financially than the companies that have Level-4 executives. One reason, their costs are much lower, and now you can see *why* they are so much lower.

Level 5 leaders through their modest compensation not only save their companies a lot of money, but they also send a clear message that they are not exploiting the employees, customers or suppliers for the personal gain of top management. That is a powerful message and the third characteristic of Level-5 Executives. These level 5 executives view themselves as "stewards" of the stockholders' investment, the company and the employees' future. CEO Robert Silberman of Strayer Education said in his letter to the shareholders, "I would be remiss if I didn't express, on behalf of the entire Strayer management team, how fortunate we consider ourselves. We are truly grateful for the opportunity to be the stewards of your capital in an enterprise which creates so much value, opportunity, and un-alloyed joy for our students."[318] Strayer Education was one of the nine companies selected by Jason Jennings and his staff to be included in their book, *Think Big Act Small,* about the best-performing companies in America. After each interview with the CEOs of these companies, Jason and his staff would always end up discussing the same subject: "What was the magic that allowed these companies to be the top revenue performers in the nation? And we always ended up with the same conclusion: the unassuming nature of the people who head these companies is central to the enterprise's ability to consistently grow revenues. Egos are just not relevant at these companies. The people who lead the businesses get a strong psychic reward from the success of their enterprises and their contribution in guiding them in ways that less successful, less humble CEOs can only envy."[319] Mr.

Jennings went on to say, "The people who founded and/or now lead these nine companies want the same things everyone else wants: a nice home, a good living, financial security for their families, and the opportunity to be in charge of their own destinies and make the world a better place. In the truest sense, they are stewards."[320] They are also excellent examples of Level-5 leadership.

For all of these Level 5 CEOs, the story was about the company, not them. In fact when Mr. Jennings and his staff would attempt to discuss the CEOs' role in the success of the business with the CEOs, they would get noticeably uncomfortable. In the words of Mr. Jennings, "Nobody was anxious to share their personal story because no one believed there was a story to be told. They maintained that the real story was the company and that their personal contribution(s) in founding or leading it was of little importance."[321] What a difference! For the ego-centric, Level-4 CEOs, it is all about them, their status, their ambition, them, them, them. For the Level-5 modest and humble CEOs, it is all about the employees, the customers and the company, and never about them. Somehow it appears that there may be more than a 180-degree difference between the two, if that is possible.

5. They think long-term

The executive leaders of publicly held companies endure an intense amount of pressure from the stockholders and stock analysts to make the quarterly profit objectives. Interestingly enough, the quarterly profit objectives most often come from the executives themselves in the form of future guidance that they give to the stock-analyst community. Once the projections have been made, then the executives may be forced to apply a great deal of pressure on themselves and the employees to achieve the short-term objectives. As Jason Jennings describes it, "When all decisions are based on the short-term, the results are predictable: people become dispensable ('If he doesn't pull his thumb out, get someone else who can do it.'), vendors are ruthlessly pitted against one another ('I want a better price, I want it now, or you're dead meat!'), and the name of the game becomes getting today's job done ('I don't care how you do it, just get it done!')."[322]

In many cases, the executives of profit-driven companies will make decisions in the interest of short-term results even when they know that those decisions will hurt the company in the long-term. As was pointed out earlier, this pressure also causes the company to become very internally focused. A study by the National Bureau of Economic Research found that to protect short-term results, 80 percent of executives would cut market and R&D expenditures, *even if they truly believed that doing so would hurt the company in the long run.*[323] Those 80 percent of the executives are clearly Level-4 executives.

The true Level-5 executives take a different approach. They refuse to be intimidated by the stock analyst and some even refuse to give any future guidance. Herb Sandler of World Savings said, "We don't give guidance, we pay attention to measuring and improving those things that make us successful, and when we release our results everyone gets them at the same time."[324] Ken Iverson (the Level-5 former CEO of Nucor) said the following: "Managing with a long-term perspective is just common sense to us. But, I'll admit, not everybody sees things as we do. And, like managers of most large businesses, we must sometimes answer to those who froth at the mouth, pound on the tables, and yell at us to do whatever it takes to maximize earnings *right now*! I'm referring, of course, to stock analysts."

Following is the gist of Ken Iverson's opening comments to stock analysts in New York. "Many of you with your short-term view of corporations, remind me of a guy on drugs. You want that quick fix, that high you get from a big spike in earnings. So you push us to take on more debt, capitalize start-up costs and interest, and slow down depreciation and write-offs. All you're thinking about is the short-term. You don't want to think about the pain of withdrawal that our company will face later on if we do what you want. Well, Nucor isn't going to respond to that kind of thinking. We never have and we never will." Ken went on to talk about speculators versus investors. He said, "Speculators, of course, believe in the fast buck. They wave the capital in your face and expect you to abandon common sense. The amazing thing is, it works! Time and again, executives dance to their tune. We refuse to do it."

Another Ken Iverson quote, "I like to remind our managers: 'We're not dogs on a leash, doing tricks to manage the stock price or maximize dividends quarter-by-quarter. We're eagles. We *soar.* If investors want to soar, too, they'll invest in us. The speculators? We don't need them.'" Speaking of thinking long-term within the company, Ken said: "Every decision we make as managers is rooted in long-term perspective. You have to understand that in order to take in the true meaning of what I want to tell you about management. A focus on long-term survival over short-term considerations can change every aspect of your business, because it drives fundamentally different priorities. Most of all, it is a safeguard against management's tendency to make business decisions solely in response to the pressures of the moment."[325] In 2007, Nucor was ranked number 4 in the Business Week's 50 Best Performers with revenues of $14.8 billion and net income of $1.8 billion.[326]

Jason Jennings, while researching the most productive companies in the world, was searching for what was different about these companies. What made them so much more productive than the comparison companies? Regarding this point he said, "The difference, I discovered, is that these company chieftains solve short-term issues by taking a long-term view." In a special 2005 edition of *The McKinsey Quarterly*, Richard Dobbs noted, "The companies that created the most shareholder value over the past 15 years also created the most employment and invested the most in R&D." The McKinsey research also "examined the relationship between a company's short-term performance and its long-term health. Healthy companies are those that sustain superior performance over time. They are characterized by 'a robust strategy; well-maintained assets; innovative products and services; a good reputation with customers, regulators, governments, and other stakeholders; and the ability to attract, retain, and develop high-performing employees.' *Unfortunately, especially for investors, too many companies fail to realize that focusing on achieving exceptional short-term results can be highly damaging to their long-*

term health"[327] [emphasis mine]. In his research on the premier companies selected for the book, *Built to Last*, Jim Collins found that purpose-driven companies "invested for the future to a greater degree than the comparison companies." They "consistently invested more heavily in new property, plant, and equipment as a percentage of annual sales" and they "plowed a greater percentage of each year's earnings back into the company, paying out less in cash dividends to shareholders."[328] The managers of these forty-three elite companies make long-term decisions and focus on *managing their companies, not the stock price.*

6. Trust, Truth, Transparency and Speed

"You can't have success without trust. The word trust embodies almost everything you can strive for that will help you to succeed. You tell me any human relationship that works without trust, whether it is marriage or a friendship or a social interaction; in the long run, the same thing is true about business, especially businesses that deal with the public."[329]

– Jim Burke, former Chairman and CEO, Johnson & Johnson

Many companies, when they list the company core values, list items such as honesty, integrity, respect for the individual, and so on. These values are good, they are important and they enlist trust on the part of the employees in management. That is one level of trust, the trust of management by the employees, which is important. However, there is a second level of trust that is even more important. That is the trust of the employees by management. Without this second level of trust in an organization, the entire purpose-driven business model will fall apart. The company will fall apart. The two pillars that these forty-three companies stand on are number one, purpose, and number two, trust. Without either of these two pillars, the elite levels of performance that these forty-three companies demonstrate and the implementation of the new business model is not possible. When it comes to trust, management must take the first step. For 80+ percent of managers today, this will require a leap of faith. They will just have to believe that trusting their employees is the right thing and in the long run the most financially rewarding thing to do. The management teams of these companies do two things. They earn the trust of their employees by their actions, and they also trust their employees. They demonstrate their trust in their employees by empowering them, implementing personnel policies based on trust, and being transparent.

Trust is unique in that it can take days, weeks, months or years to establish, but only a few seconds to destroy. It can be intensely strong but fragile at the same time. It requires honesty, integrity and transparency all of the time, because the employees will be watching all of the time. As Dan DiMicco, CEO of Nucor, put it: "You have to live what you say. If you say it, you better do it. Not partway, not halfway, not three-quarters-way, but all the way, all the time."[330] Social cognition research shows that "individuals pick up on all the signals in their work environment — big and small." Also, "People want to believe in their company — but will be ever watchful for the tiny inconsistencies that allow them to say 'Aha! See, there you go. I knew management was just blowing smoke. They don't really believe their own rhetoric.'"[331]

The management of these companies is as honest as the day is long. They have no reason to be otherwise. They work for a purpose-driven company, they believe in the company purpose and its values and they are there for the long term. They have no reason not to be completely truthful and trusting.

In his book on the most productive companies in the world, Jason Jennings selected the company, Yellow Freight, to be included. For years, Yellow Freight had operated in a government-regulated industry, and then the government de-regulated the freight industry. Overnight Yellow Freight had to face new competitors and non-regulated pricing and, as a result, was facing bankruptcy. To address these issues, the board of directors turned to, and hired, Bill Zollars. To make a long story short, Bill turned the company around and turned it into one of the most productive companies in the U.S. During his research into the company, Mr. Jennings was in Kansas

City doing some interviews when Greg Reid, the Senior VP and chief marketing officer, pulled him aside to share a comment about the company's CEO. "Look, there's something you should know about Bill Zollars." He took Mr. Jennings behind a partition, lowered his voice and said, "I need to tell you this. Bill is the most honest man I've ever worked for in my life. He trusts people, gives them permission to do what they think is right and then guides them. That's why he's been so successful at turning Yellow Freight into such a productive company." Mr. Reid went on to say, "People only trust someone to lead them if *everything* they say is true."[332] The relationship between trust, truth and productivity is not unique to Yellow Freight. As Mr. Jennings and his staff interviewed other companies, they found the following: "The same scenarios played out over and over at almost every company. So many people — a receptionist, a VP, a supplier, a factory worker — would pull me aside to praise the truthfulness of their company's leaders. They explained and agreed that it was *truth* that made their company productive."[333] "Trust is one of the most powerful forms of motivation and inspiration. People want to be trusted. They respond to trust. They thrive on trust."[334]

In these forty-three elite companies, there is trust both ways. The employees trust the management and the management trusts the employees. In this environment, the management feels free to share the company information with the employees. We have already seen the example of Ricardo Semler at Semco and how they publish the financials each month and even taught classes to their employees so they could read and understand them. An example of the elite forty-three who also publishes the financials is SRC Holdings of Springfield, Missouri. SRC (Springfield Remanufacturing Corporation) was a division of International Harvester until Jack Stack and a dozen other managers scraped up enough money to buy the ailing division from International Harvester. When he and his co-owners bought SRC, they had $100,000 in equity and $8,900,000 in debt. A company with that much debt in relationship to its equity is essentially brain dead. (See the full story on pages 72-73 of Chapter 4) One of Jack's first actions was to call all of the three hundred employees into the lunchroom and explain to them that they still had a job, but that the company was in dire financial straits. Jack decided to do two things. First, trust his employees, and then to share with them the company's income statements and balance sheet. He promised to teach business to every worker in the company so they could see the big picture. Jack made good on his promise by calling the whole company together weekly for a detailed review of the company financials. Still today, a visit to any SRC facility starts in the lunchroom where an entire wall details the company financials including how much money they have in the bank.[335] Jack wanted all of his employees to be involved in the game of business, and he accomplished that by trusting them and sharing information with them, another sign of trust. The education on business and reading financial statements gave the employees a "psychic ownership" of the business and the financials. He explained it this way. "The salespeople own the sales line, and the discount line, the allowance line, and the receivable line." When you relate the business back to the fundamentals of a balance sheet, all of a sudden you realize that "the income statement is nothing more than people, and someone is responsible for each one of those lines."[336] Since Jack became CEO of SRC, the company has grown 15 percent per year in good times and bad. In addition, the company now has twenty-two plants with revenues of $200 million annually. Finally, SRC "handily beats their competitors on all the productivity metrics — revenue per employee, operating income per employee and return on invested capital."[337] The proof is in the pudding.

These companies have discovered the direct relationship between trusting the employees, engaging them in the business by sharing the financial information with them, empowering them to make operational decisions and then compensating them for increasing productivity. Ken Iverson the former CEO of Nucor said, "I think there are really just two ways to go on the question of information-sharing: *Tell employees everything or tell them nothing.* Otherwise, each time you choose to withhold information, they think you're up to something. We prefer to tell employees everything. We hold back nothing." John Correnti, the CEO of Nucor, said, "By sharing everything, we give our people the opportunity to do their jobs to the best of their ability. Employees need a lot of information to manage themselves and to keep our costs in line. Besides, our incentive pay is based on group productivity results." Ken also made the point that "Sharing information is another key to treating people as equals, building trust, and destroying the hierarchy."[338] Another observation from Mr. Iverson shows the impact that the information age and information explosion is having on the workplace. "Technology is advancing too quickly on too many fronts. No small group of executives can possibly keep fully informed. You have to let people decide for themselves which tools are best, then hold them accountable for their decisions."[339] The Container Store and New Balance are two privately held companies who also share their financials with their employees. For The Container Store, "This gives employees a stronger feeling of connection with management and management's objectives. It also is a sign that management trusts employees with information that in most private companies is top secret." Jim Davis, the CEO of New Balance, has said that he "is convinced that openness with information is a big reason why his U.S. factories are ten times more productive than the overseas factories."[340]

Productivity, trust and truth. They are all interrelated and it is hard to discuss one or have one without the other. Pat Lancaster, the Chairman of Lantech, put it this way: "When people lie, I think it means they have something to hide. Or else they don't respect the person or people they're lying to." "You can't build a productive company where trust isn't a guiding principle, and you can't have trust without truth."[341] Jason Jennings made the following observation: "Productive companies are open with all the numbers, and they score everything that's important." Substitute the word "drivers" for the words "everything that's important" and you gain a great deal of insight into the information-age business model and the Teleocratic Management System. The information-age, purpose-driven business model is based on trust. It is designed to empower the employees so that they can be innovative, creative and productive and realize their potential. Stephen M. R. Covey made this observation, "How you go about achieving results is as important as the results themselves, because when you establish trust, you increase your ability to get results the next time. And there's always a next time.

To get things done in ways that destroy trust is not only shortsighted and counterproductive; it is ultimately unsustainable."[342] How can you possibly build a highly productive company by utilizing the old, industrial-age, profit-driven, command-and-control, fear-based business model? How can the employees be highly productive when management does not allow them to use their brains and knowledge to make decisions that only they are qualified to make? How can you create a highly productive company with a fear-driven management system that does not trust and empower the employees? The answer is, you can't! In fact, Professor John Whitney of the Columbia Business School has said, "Mistrust doubles the cost of doing business."[343] So, according to Professor Whitney's data, there is at least a potential to double productivity by increasing trust in an organization.

"High-performance organizations are high-trust organizations. Trust is the lubricant that allows companies, employees, customers, and other stakeholders to work together with minimal friction and maximum harmony. Trust between rank-and-file employees and senior management enables companies to make short-term sacrifices for long-term prosperity. A high degree of trust goes hand-in-hand with an open, inclusive culture that does not waste energy on monitoring and policing people's behavior."[344]

Trust is also a prerequisite for implementing self-directed teams. Truly productive self-directed teams cannot be successfully implemented without complete trust on the part of management, and that is exactly what these companies have been able to accomplish. Companies such as Nucor and Semco have first trusted their employees, then empowered them as self-directed teams and achieved tremendous increases in productivity and financial performance. The financial impact that a high level of trust and self-directed teams generate within these types of companies was quantified in the following study: "A 2002 study by Watson Wyatt shows that total return to shareholders in high-trust organizations is almost three times higher than the return in low-trust organizations."[345] The trust-based self-directed team environment is also in alignment with the work environment criteria of Generations X and Y. These generations are motivated by a work environment that includes an informal work structure, flexible hours, and a low level of oversight. *"If you're ready to create a fun, flexible, educational, nonmicromanaged work atmosphere where Xers have a variety of projects to engage them, you'll have Generation X beating down the door to go to work for you."* [346]

It is clear that the work environment created under a bureaucratic management system is not the type of atmosphere that Generation X is looking for, but the work environment under the purpose-driven self-directed team environment is almost exactly what they dream about. Generations X and Y also have the skills to excel when working with self-directed teams. "The nice thing about Xers is they are virtually self-developing. Their early years gave them the ability to learn quickly and develop skills on their own." [347] The self-learning and skills-development abilities of the Gen Xers make them valuable employees on self-directed teams. The self-directed teams also give the Generation Xers the involvement and participation they are looking for. *"Most employees like to have the feeling that they have control over their work. It shows up on job-satisfaction surveys, employee morale charts, and incentive reports again and again. Give people more control of their work, and they will do better work, and more of it."* [348]

Generations X and Y will excel when they are allowed to participate in achieving the company vision, find new and innovative ways to get the work done, and be themselves in the process. The combination of the trust-based Teleocratic Management System and the self-directed teams with the driver measurements for direction create an environment that is not only attractive to Generations X and Y, but it creates a work environment where they can thrive.

"Gen Yers want to be part of a highly motivated team of committed people." [349] Gen Yers not only want to be part of a great team that consists of high-quality people, but they want to make a difference in the world. "The 'magic' for Gen Yers comes in making a difference — in producing something worthwhile — while working with a great team and getting rewards they feel they have earned." [350] Not only does this generation want to be part of a great team, their ability to work in a team environment is clearly superior to the generations before them. Both generations, and especially Generation Y with their innovative ways of doing things, have the potential to achieve increases in productivity the likes of which have never been seen.

7. They operate from the win/win, eco-system paradigm

These companies operate from a win/win paradigm and view themselves as being much more like a living organism rather than a machine. Machines are self-contained; they do not have brains and they do not feel. A living organism, however, does think, does feel and does relate to and react to its environment. The industrial-age profit-driven business-model companies operate from the win/lose paradigm, have the zero-sum view of the world and are not particularly concerned with the health of their vendors, employees, the community or the environment. They operate from the view that they are independent and rely upon no one but themselves. The profit-driven companies believe that their health is independent of the health of their constituencies. Therefore, they are concerned about no one but themselves. The inward focus that a profit-driven company naturally has, only adds to the opinion of the executives that everyone and everything can be replaced. No one and nothing is indispensable. Operating from the mechanistic paradigm, these companies view every transaction as a win/lose situation. Someone has to win and someone has to lose, and they are out to win. For example, the profit-driven companies will be very demanding of price concessions from their vendors. They view vendors as objects to be exploited for the benefit of the company. They will pit vendors against each other and demand that the vendors cut their prices, or they are "dead meat." They could care less if the vendor survives; their view is that there are a lot of vendors and their job is to get the best price. It is the vendor's job to look out for themselves, not the companies.

The companies operating within the information-age purpose-driven business model, however, have a completely different perspective of the company-vendor relationship. Since they are outward-focused purpose-driven companies operating with the win/win mentality, they operate with a cooperative ecosystem model. Their view is that the best way for a company to be healthy is to live in an ecosystem where all of the elements of the ecosystem are healthy. From a business perspective, this means that a company can be healthy only when the employees, the vendors, the stockholders, the community and the environment are all healthy. They also understand that all of these constituencies are interdependent. As compared to the industrial-age business-model companies, where the relationship between a company and its vendors is an independent and adversarial one where they don't look to vendors for support or help, the companies operating with the information-age business model view vendors as valued business partners that can help them be more successful. They view the company-to-vendor relationship as being an interdependent relationship where, when the company works with the vendor to communicate in intimate detail the needs of the company, that then allows the vendor to make recommendations to the company about the changes it can make to better meet the needs of the company. Within the information-age business model, this is a win/win relationship. These companies involve the vendors and look to them for support and help. As the two companies work together, they both benefit. As the company becomes more successful, it buys more from the vendor. As the company buys more from the vendor, then the vendor becomes more successful. It is an interdependent, mutually beneficial relationship.

One company has gone so far as to make the improvement of these relationships the company mission. There is a large sign that greets visitors at Dot Foods' home office informing everyone that the company's mission is: TO POSITIVELY AND SIGNIFICANTLY CONTRIBUTE TO THE SUCCESS OF OUR BUSINESS PARTNERS.[351] Dan Devine, the CEO of PETCO, has said, "When you try to run roughshod over your manufacturers, you're going to become the company they're talking about, and if they believe you're trying to screw them, they're going to look for a way to pay you back and screw you first." He went on to say that their job isn't to buy merchandise from vendors and just resell it in their stores; instead, it is to help lead manufacturers to the achievement of greater success. If that happens, they reason, they'll be more successful as well.[352] Cliff Hudson, the CEO of Sonic Drive-In, when speaking of their suppliers and vendors, has said this: "Our partners are always invited to company meetings and retreats. Their long-term interests are so allied with our own that it only makes sense to include them, make them full participants, and actively solicit their input." The vendors and suppliers view their relationship with Sonic Drive-In "with near reverential awe, wondering why other companies don't get it and work with their vendors and suppliers the same way."[353]

While doing his research on the most productive companies in the world, Jason Jennings made the following observation: "One of the misplaced macho holdovers in a lot of businesses is the adversarial relationship they maintain with vendors and suppliers. Many seem to think they're being savvy businesspeople when they beat up vendors and suppliers on every issue ranging from price to delivery of returns. That prehistoric approach isn't what we found in productive companies where vendors are treated with respect and encouraged to think of themselves as part of the team. That's not to suggest productive companies are touchy-feely places where the buyers roll over, play dead and pay any price. Instead, we observed complete openness with their suppliers where the mutually understood rule is, 'Here's the margin we're going to make when we sell a product to our customers. We'd like to do business with you. Let's work together to figure out how you can help us sell our product at the margin we need, while allowing you to make the margin you need.'"[354]

The win/win, cooperative ecosystem-interdependent relationship applies not only to vendors, but to all of the constituencies of a company. For example, companies like Costco, Wegmans Food Markets and Trader Joe's prove the point. "They offer outstanding wages to their employees and competitive prices to their customers — and make healthy profits to boot. The higher wages and benefits paid by these companies do not show up in the prices consumers pay. The greater productivity of higher-caliber employees and lower employee turnover in part explains this. Also, employee-generated process improvements continuously show up because employees care enough to continuously strive to make the company more profitable. Finally, the link between satisfied employees and customer loyalty is beyond question."[355]

Another example of this concept in action comes from Stephen M. R. Covey as he describes his experience with Shea Homes, a homebuilder. "Let me share with you the experience of Shea Homes. Shea Homes decided to create a different model. Among the many steps they took, they renamed their subs as 'true partners' and opened their financials to them on shared projects. They were transparent. Their operating premise was, 'We want to win, but we want you to win, too. And together, we can better help our customers win. So how can we make this work?'" The results that Shea Homes achieved when they switched from the traditional adversarial approach to a trust-based, partnership approach was enormous. "Nearly every measure: the number of days it took them to build homes went down, cost went down, quality errors decreased, customer satisfaction increased, and referrals from customers increased. They made more money. Their partners made more money. Their customers were happier. Everybody won."[356]

Some of the old-school analysts criticize the companies that utilize the new information-age purpose-driven model primarily because of the long-term focus at the expense of the quarterly earnings. One such analyst wrote, "Costco continues to be a company that is better at serving the club member and employees than the shareholder." However, Jim Sinegal, the CEO of Costco, responded, "We think when you take care of your customers and your employees, your shareholders are going to be rewarded in the long run. And I am one of the shareholders; I care about the stock price. But we are not going to do something for the sake of one quarter that is going to destroy the fabric of our company and what we stand for."[357] For the record, in the two years ending in July 2006, Wal-Mart stock declined 7 percent while Costco stock increased 40 percent.[358] Costco managed to produce this stock-price performance while paying its employees 65 percent more than Wal-Mart and 40 percent more than Sam's Club. In addition, the employee benefits are more generous than Wal-Mart. Costco achieves this performance by being very efficient (spends only 9.8% of sales on SG&A) and having a low employee-turnover rate. Costco's employee turnover is 6 percent compared to 21 percent at Sam's and 50 percent at Wal-Mart.[359] The better pay, better benefits and lower employee turnover "has paid off in significantly higher productivity per employee than Sam's Club experiences. It also translates into higher customer satisfaction scores and increased income per employee. It also keeps customer retention significantly higher than at Sam's Club. Costco's customer-satisfaction rating in 2004 according to the American Customer Satisfaction Index was 79 points in a 100-point system. Very few companies across all industries earn a rating higher than 80 points. The average among all companies is 73 points. Sam's Club was indexed at 75 points and Wal-Mart at 73 points in 2004. However, in the grocery category, Wal-Mart was pegged below average at a meager 70 points." The business result is that Costco averages $121 million per store while Sam's Club averages $70 million per store.[360] Costco is a clear example of how the impact of the win/win ecosystem view within the information-age purpose-driven business model delivers better results for all of the constituencies. Costco and the other purpose-driven companies consistently have happier customers, better-paid employees and higher-rewarded stockholders.

Time and time again, these forty-three elite companies prove that by operating with the win/win cooperative ecosystem view of the business environment they can achieve much higher levels of productivity, which results in higher pay for their employees, happier customers, better partnerships with their suppliers, and improvement of the communities and the environment in which they operate, *and they can still deliver much higher returns to the stockholders.* Indeed they continually prove that the company and its constituencies either all win together or all lose together. In reality there is no win/lose, there is really only win/win or lose/lose. The days of the win/lose or zero-sum thinking in the business world are numbered. The authors of the book, *Firms of Endearment,* made the following observation on this point. "A zero-sum view of business is becoming unsustainable. For a value-creation system to thrive, each participant must make a profit; that is, each must ultimately get back more value than they originally invested. If they consistently fail to make a reasonable profit, they will inevitably drop out of the system."[361]

With the fear–based, industrial-age, profit-driven business model, as the level of fear and control increase, the levels of innovation, productivity, morale, customer satisfaction, financial performance and creativity decrease. However, when a transition is made to the trust-based, information-age, purpose-driven business model, as the level of trust and empowerment increases, so does the level of innovation, productivity, morale, customer satisfaction, financial performance, creativity, employee loyalty, etc.

8. They constantly strive to improve

Continuous Improvement

For purpose-driven companies, there is always a tension between today and the purpose of the company. The purpose of the company, such as Merck's (to preserve and improve human life) can never be fulfilled. It can only be strived for. This causes the tension between today and the purpose of the company, which drives these companies to constantly get better. They are never satisfied with today's accomplishments. They always want to do better so that they can come closer to fulfilling the company purpose. There is no finish line where they can just coast and live off the fruits of their labor. The tension always exists which drives constant improvement within these companies. During his research for the book, *Built to Last*, Jim Collins made the following observations: "The concept has been commonplace for decades — over a century in some cases. William Proctor and James Gamble, for example, used the concept of continuous improvement as far back as the 1850s. William McKnight brought the concept to life at 3M in the 1910s. J. Willard Marriott embraced the concept soon after opening his first root beer stand in 1927. David Packard incessantly used the term 'continuous improvement' beginning in the 1940s." He went on to say, "Our research findings clearly support the concept of continuous improvement, but not as a program or management fad. It is an institutionalized habit — a disciplined way of life — ingrained into the fabric of the organization and reinforced by tangible mechanisms that create discontent with the status quo." Further he said that these companies "apply the concept of self-improvement in a much broader sense than just process improvement. It means long-term investments for the future; it means investment in the development of employees; it means adoption of new ideas and technologies. In short, it means doing everything possible to make the company stronger tomorrow than it is today."[362] This is exactly the focus one would expect from a Level-5 Executive. They are always striving to improve their company and make it great. Many companies today under-invest in the education of their employees for fear that the employees will leave and the educational investment will be lost. However, when one anonymous CEO was asked the question, "What if you train everyone and they all leave?," he responded, "What if we don't train them and they all stay?" These companies invest in their employees' education and reduce their exposure by having very low rates of turnover. The low rates of employee turnover at these companies represent a huge financial savings. "On average, it cost companies one-and-a-half to two times the annual salary to replace an existing worker."[363]

The methods used to achieve continuous improvement are as varied as the number of companies. All of the companies are different and their methods are different, but they are all focused on the same end result, continuous improvement. In the early days of Wal-Mart, Sam Walton used the "Beat Yesterday" ledger book where the sales figures were tracked on a daily basis and compared to the same day a year earlier. These ledgers were used to push the sales standard up and up, forever. Nordstrom used a different approach to create an environment to ensure constant improvement. They measured each sales person by "sales per hour." In this environment, there are no fixed standards that when achieved, the sales person can coast and be satisfied with the past performance. There is always motivation to do better. Boeing utilizes a unique technique called "eye of the enemy." "It assigns managers the task of developing (a) strategy as if they worked for a competing company with the aim of obliterating

Boeing. What weaknesses would they exploit? What strengths would they leverage? What markets could be easily invaded? Then, based on these responses, how should Boeing respond?"[364]

On the Google web site (another purpose-driven company), you can find the company philosophy, which is "Never settle for the best." Although Google has the most popular search engine, they are not satisfied. "'The perfect search engine,' says Google co-founder Larry Page, 'would understand exactly what you mean and give back exactly what you want.' Given the state of search technology today, that's a far-reaching vision requiring research, development and innovation to realize. Google is committed to blazing that trail. Though acknowledged as the world's leading search technology company, Google's goal is to provide a much higher level of service to all those who seek information, whether they're at a desk in Boston, driving through Bonn or strolling in Bangkok. To that end, Google has persistently pursued innovation and pushed the limits of existing technology to provide a fast, accurate and easy-to-use search service that can be accessed from anywhere. To fully understand Google, it's helpful to understand all the ways in which the company has helped to redefine how individuals, businesses and technologists view the Internet."

Another quote from the Google web site is: "From its inception, Google has focused on providing the best user experience possible. While many companies claim to put their customers first, few are able to resist the temptation to make small sacrifices to increase shareholder value. Google has steadfastly refused to make any change that does not offer a benefit to the users who come to the site:

- The interface is clear and simple.
- Pages load instantly.
- Placement in search results is never sold to anyone.
- Advertising on the site must offer relevant content and not be a distraction.

By always placing the interest of the user first, Google has built the most loyal audience on the web. And that growth has come not through TV ad campaigns, but through word of mouth from one satisfied user to another." Also on their web site, is listed the ten things that Google has found to be true. Number one is, "Focus on the customer and all else will follow." Number ten is, "Great just isn't good enough." "Always deliver more than is expected. Google does not accept being the best as an endpoint, but a starting point."[365]

These companies (like Google) place the customer as the number-one-priority constituency. Their mode of operation is simply "take care of the customer first and foremost, and all else will follow." One side benefit of this customer focus by these companies is the fact that they do not rely on traditional modes of marketing and competing for "market share." They rely on word-of-mouth recommendations by their loyal customers to generate sales. For these companies, "Delighted customers, employees, and suppliers tell others about these companies, reducing the need to advertise to create awareness. Consider that Google became one of the most valuable brands in the world — without any advertising. Starbucks became an international brand with virtually no advertising. Costco and Harley-Davidson built powerful brands with uncustomarily low levels of advertising."[366] These companies "do not rely on frequent sales and other dramatic promotions. This is a huge cost saver as well as a source of comfort for customers, who do not have to wait for a sale to buy what they need now."[367] One example of these cost savings is Jordan's Furniture, which was spotlighted in the book, *Firms of Endearment.* Most furniture companies rely on weekly or biweekly sales that are heavily advertised in the local newspaper and television to drive sales. Companies like Jordan's Furniture on the other hand rely much more heavily on reference sales. As a result, Jordan's spends only 2 percent of gross revenue on advertising where the average furniture company spends 7 percent of gross revenue on advertising. Yet, Jordan's manages to generate sales of almost $1,000 per square foot when the average furniture store sells between $150 and $200 per square foot.[368] Jordan's is a clear example of the financial advantage that a purpose-driven company, that is constantly improving to serve the customer better, has, when compared to the average profit-driven company.

By focusing on the customer and constant improvement, these companies are able to achieve extraordinary levels of productivity, which then translates into the high levels of financial performance as shown in chapter 4. For example, IKEA generates 25 times more profit per employee than the industry average.[369] They also achieve sales per employee that is 50 percent greater than the industry average.[370] The Warehouse, a New Zealand company, out-performs Wal-Mart by a factor of two. Where Wal-Mart puts 3.3 cents of every sales dollar to the bottom line, The Warehouse puts 6.6 cents to the bottom line.[371] While the average airline worker generates $190,000 in revenue, and the employees at Southwest produce $209,000, the employees at Ryanair produce an amazing $297,000 per employee.[372] The employees at Nucor's Darlington, South Carolina plant increased the steel production from thirty tons per day to one hundred tons of steel *per hour*![373] How was this amazing increase in productivity accomplished? An example from Ken Iverson's book, *Plain Talk,* will help give some insight. In his book he wrote, "We started a crew on a straightener machine — which straightens steel angles to meet customer requirements — at a production-bonus baseline of eight tons per hour. The rated capacity of the machine was ten tons per hour. Well, that crew kept tinkering and experimenting trying to make it produce more. They installed a larger motor, fed the angles into the machine in various ways and so on. Within a year, their production was up to twenty tons an hour — twice the machine's rated capacity."[374] Another example from Ken's book related that Tim Patterson, a 23-year-old engineer at their Nucor-Yamato Steel plant in Blytheville, Arkansas, made a large contribution to productivity and cost savings. "Tim calculated that we were spending about $1.5 million annually to lubricate and maintain a series of supporting screws under the Nucor-Yamato rolling line. He noted that shims (tapered pieces of metal) would require no lubrication, and that they might work even better than the screws designed into the equipment by the manufacturer. Turned out to be a pretty smart suggestion. It cut out downtime significantly and is saving us more than a million dollars a year in maintenance costs."[375] These are but a few examples of how Nucor has become one of the most productive companies in the world, and these examples show one key element of productivity improvement. That is that the improvements come from the employees, not from managers. The key to productivity increases through constant improvement in the information age, is primarily through the utilization of the brain power, creativity and the innovation of the employees. As Ken Iverson put it, "Employees — not managers — are the engines of progress."[376]

Making Mistakes to Succeed

A part of the culture of these companies is that they expect their employees to make mistakes. They expect them to try a lot of stuff and keep what works. That is how progress and innovation occurs. Greg Reid of Yellow Freight said of their CEO, Bill Zollars, "Bill expects us to make mistakes; it's the only way to learn how to not make more mistakes." Ingvar Kamprad, the CEO of IKEA, wrote in *A Furniture Dealer's Testament*, "Our objectives require us to constantly practice making decisions and taking responsibility, to constantly overcome our fear of making mistakes. Only while sleeping one makes no mistakes. Making mistakes is the privilege of the active — of those who can correct their mistakes and put them right." When it came to the relationship between making mistakes and innovation, William McKnight, the CEO of 3M, had an interesting way of expressing it. He said, "If you put fences around people, you get sheep. Give people the room they need." At 3M they understand that "mistakes will be made, but — the mistakes he or she makes are not as serious in the long run as the mistakes management will make if it is dictatorial and undertakes to tell those under its authority exactly how they must do their job. Management that is destructively critical when mistakes are made kills initiative, and it's essential that we have many people with initiative if we are to continue to grow."[377]

One of the more famous quotes regarding the making of mistakes comes from Thomas Edison: "I didn't fail ten thousand times. I successfully eliminated ten thousand materials and combinations that didn't work."[378] Warren Buffett said, "We all make mistakes. If you can't make mistakes, you can't make decisions. I've made a lot of bigger mistakes myself."[379] Warren Bennis and Burt Nanus recounted the following story about Tom Watson Sr., the former CEO of IBM. "A promising junior executive of IBM was involved in a risky venture for the company and managed to lose over $10 million in the gamble. It was a disaster! When Watson called the nervous executive into his office, the young man blurted out, 'I guess you want my resignation?' Watson said, 'You can't be serious! We've just spent $10 million educating you!'"[380] Tom Watson also said, "If you want to increase your success rate, double your failure rate."[381] Ken Iverson said, "None of the people I've seen do impressive things in life are perfect. They never settle for latching onto one approach or mastering one way of doing things. They experiment. And they often fail. But they gain something significant from every failure. That's what it takes to achieve, I think, in business as well as in life."[382]

Unending Pursuit of the Company Purpose

Finally, these companies understand and live day-to-day in the pursuit of the company purpose. This pursuit of the company purpose works hand-in-hand with the strong ongoing drive to get better. Being the best is not good enough for these companies. Being the best has not yet allowed them to fulfill the purpose and reach their vision, so there is always more to do. This drive capitalizes on the human need to explore, to discover, to create something new and to achieve a great deal of personal satisfaction in doing so. As Google stated so clearly, "Google does not accept the best as an endpoint, but a starting point." Also, because of the dramatically increasing rate of change brought on by the information age and its information explosion, the rate at which problems present themselves is also exploding. Because of this, it is imperative that companies utilize the brain power of all of the employees to address the unending parade of problems to be solved. No longer can companies afford to have the employees waiting around until the managers have solved the problems and then tell the employees what to do. The employees must be motivated and empowered with the authority and information to solve the problems without waiting for management's involvement. The employees must be empowered to solve the problems, because in today's environment, they are the only ones that have the information to do so. That is what these companies do a much better job of than their peer companies. They capitalize on the ability of the employees to solve problems, to constantly improve things and as a result, constantly improve productivity.

9. They get the people part

These forty-three elite companies put the same passion and effort into taking care of their employees as they do in pursuing the company purpose. They understand at a very deep level that the employees are their most important asset. In the information age when knowledge is the key resource, and the employees have most of the knowledge, it only makes good business sense to take care of the company's knowledge base, the employees. As was noted earlier with the new view of the company in the information age, the employees *are* the company. So, when management places a high priority on the care and feeding of the employees, they are in reality placing a high priority on the care and feeding of the company. Charles Handy, in a *Harvard Business Review* essay, made the following statement: "The greater component of value of most companies today lies in their people and their intellectual property, not in hard assets."[383] Companies are only extensions of people. That is what these companies understand, and the management of most other companies has not yet figured out.

With New Hires, Character Counts

With the understanding that the employees are the company's most valued asset, these companies are very selective when hiring additional personnel. During the hiring process, they evaluate candidates not so much on technical skill as much as they do on the candidates' perceived ability to fit into the company culture and their character traits. In selecting the "right people," these companies "placed greater weight on character attributes than on specific educational background, practical skills, specialized knowledge or work experience. Not that specific knowledge and skills are unimportant, but they viewed these traits as more teachable, whereas they believed dimensions like character, work ethic, basic intelligence, dedication to fulfilling commitments, and values are more ingrained."

As Dave Nassef of Pitney Bowes put it: "I used to be in the Marines, and the Marines get a lot of credit for building people's values. But that's not the way it really works. The Marine Corps recruits people who share the corps' values, then provides them with the training required to accomplish the organization's mission. We look at it the same way at Pitney Bowes. We have more people who want to do the right thing than most companies. We don't just look at experience. We want to know: Who are they? Why are they? We find out who they are by asking them why they made decisions in their life. The answers to these questions give us insight into their core values."[384]

Dan DiMicco, CEO of Nucor, said, "You have to hire the right people. So the hiring process is a very important part of our culture and our system. We've gotten better at applying tools to help us pick the right people. And it's a very involved process. 'First we go through an extensive screening process filled with criteria we've developed over the years. Then we do interviews fitting people to a psychological profile — even at the entry-level positions, not just management. What we end up with are people who fit and who will respond enthusiastically to our system. We take the time to make sure that we hire accurately.'" Stephen Tindall, CEO of The Warehouse, agrees with the extensive screening and interviewing. From his viewpoint, the most important characteristic of an employee is attitude. "When we're interviewing applicants," he says, "it's much more about, 'Do these people fit with this culture?' 'Are they the sort of people that subscribe to our values and fit our company?'"[385] Jason Jennings, while studying these companies, observed that the hiring of a new employee is "more like extending *membership* in an exclusive club than offering someone a job. Once membership in a very special organization has been offered and after a mutual decision has been made, you can expect that the new employee will fight fiercely for the well-being and success of the organization — including doing things that might not be part of an original job description."[386] The bottom line is that these companies believe that the "right person" has more to do with character traits and innate capabilities than it does with specific background, knowledge or skill that the person may possess.

Bill Zollars, CEO of Yellow Freight, argued that "until you get the 'people thing' right, no amount of technology can make you more productive."[387] The CEOs of these companies understand the linkage between employees and things like productivity, customer satisfaction, retention, innovation, responsiveness, adaptability and so on. All of these things are people driven. They come from people, not technology. As David O'Reilly, CEO of O'Reilly Auto Parts noted earlier, "if we take care of our own people first and value them above everything else, that superlative customer service happens naturally."[388]

Avoiding Attrition

Because these companies and their executives understand the importance of people to the success of the company, not only do they go to great expense to hire the "right people," but they also go to great measures not to lose the good people that they have. Brian Devine, CEO of PETCO, said, "Our number one secret at PETCO is that we never lose good people. When someone comes into my office to resign I simply tell them that I won't accept their resignation and then I go to work on them. 'I sit here and talk to them as long as it takes to have them rescind their decision.' He adds that 'sometimes it's taken as long as three days of talking to have them change their mind, but generally things are worked out within one or two days.'"[389] The bottom line is, that the management of these companies understands that it is the employees, the people, who give them the competitive advantage, not technology, and the management responds accordingly.

Equality and Respect

The leaders of these companies, as noted earlier, are Level-5 Leaders. As such, they possess the personal characteristics of modesty and humility, and they are egalitarian in nature. Because of this egalitarian nature (treats the employees as equals), it is natural for these leaders and their companies to treat the employees with respect, as equals, and to trust them with important decision-making for the company. The ability of these companies to completely trust the employees to make important business decisions without consulting management, which in turn drives tremendous improvements in productivity and speed, all starts with the egalitarian nature of the leadership. The egalitarian nature of these leaders is manifested in such statements as the one by Ken Iverson, former CEO of Nucor: "Managers don't need or deserve special treatment. We're not more important than other employees. And we aren't better than anyone else. We just have a different job to do. Mainly, that job is to help the people you manage to accomplish extraordinary things. That begins with remembering who does the real work of the business (something managers, with their outsized egos, often forget). It means relying on employees to make important decisions and take significant risks."[390] Speaking of these managers with outsized egos (Level 4 Executives), Ken went on to say, "Rarely will these managers stoop to solicit an employee's advice on an important issue, entrust employees to independently carry out crucial assignments, or challenge employees to do more than they, the managers themselves, have been able to do. If you worked for such managers, how important would you feel? Would you think management knew what you really could do? Would you believe that you have a chance to make a difference in the business? Most significantly, how long would you go on even *trying* to make a difference?"[391] Furthermore, Ken said, "I think some companies deserve unions. Their managers just don't treat employees right. They use the hierarchy to keep people down. But when a company's managers treat employees as equals, they earn trust. And the bond of trust enables managers to do things that would never fly in a company based on '*We* vs. *They*.'"[392] Ken's egalitarian nature, like the other Level-5 Leaders, led him to trust and empower the employees at Nucor. The employees at Nucor are treated as equals by the executive team and, as Ken said, "Pure equality brings out pure adrenaline and pure effort. It is a beautiful sight and, as our people will tell you, an exhilarating experience."[393]

<u>No Layoffs</u>

These companies not only show their respect for the employees by treating them as equals, but when times are hard, that is when these companies show their ultimate respect in the form of no layoffs. Most companies will address hard economic times by reducing the work force through layoffs. In fact, many managers will lay off a few employees just to make the quarterly or annual profit objectives even though the company is still making a lot of money. Not these companies. These companies do everything they can to avoid layoffs, and many have no layoff policies. Jack Stack, CEO of SRC Holdings, said, "There have been times when markets have collapsed and we've been devastated and we didn't lay anyone off. Sometimes it takes a long time to recover from those hits but you won't ever recover from them and move forward without your most important asset – good people." He went on to say, "Look, we have a tremendous passion for keeping and maintaining jobs. And so we put our money where our mouth is. We have a stock program where everyone earns stock based on the performance of the company. Then we have individual bonus programs tied to productivity and specific things we're trying to accomplish. Next you've got the earnings of the company itself." All of these come into play in a business downturn. "What we've built is a four-layer process to protect everyone here during tough economic times. The stock program would be affected before we'd ever cut a job. Next the bonus program would be hit and then a depletion of corporate earnings. These are the things we'd do before even considering laying someone off."[394]

At Nucor, there is a company promise that there will never be a company layoff. So how does Nucor handle the economic downturns that affect all companies? In the words of Dan DiMicco, the CEO, "In a bad economy, the first thing to go is every executive perk and bonus, followed by plant managers and supervisors giving up theirs. Only then are the steel workers affected and we start by reducing a work week from five days to four and if that's not sufficient we might even go to three days even if we use one of those days cleaning the plant and doing housekeeping."[395] Jason Jennings says this about layoffs. "Casual layoffs, which may have the seemingly happy side effect of momentarily nudging up the stock price, are in fact absolutely counterproductive in the long term. Layoffs create more problems than they solve. Frequently, the employees who remain end up more concerned with their personal financial well-being than the company's productivity and become preoccupied, wondering if they'll be next, which often results in valuable workers seeking a more stable environment elsewhere. Eventually, assuming revenues start to improve, the company finds itself facing the costs of recruiting and training to fill the same position they blew off during the reduction. The big whammy of course is the inability of an owner, manager or CEO to build any kind of productive culture in a business known for balancing its books by cavalierly offing people."[396]   Companies could get away with this type of behavior when there was a labor surplus, but with the coming labor shortage, the companies that continue to act in this fashion may find it very difficult to attract new employees. The forty-three elite companies and other companies like them understand that it is more efficient and economical in the long run to do everything possible to retain employees. This is also one of the classic differences between companies whose management thinks in the long term versus the short term. Profit–driven, short-term-thinking executives will utilize layoffs to achieve their own short-term objectives. Purpose–driven, long-term-thinking executives will not; that is a huge difference especially when things like employee loyalty, productivity and attitude are taken into consideration.

10. Compensation and Productivity

The differences between these forty-three elite companies and their peers in the area of compensation begins at the top. The typical Level-5 Executive will have an annual compensation package of under one million dollars while the average of the S&P 500 executives is almost twelve million. That is a difference of over twelve-to-one. This difference in compensation for the top executives obviously has a positive impact on earnings, but it also sends a clear message to all of the employees that the company is not out to exploit the suppliers, customers or employees for the personal gain of the executive management team. In addition to paying the executive team much less than the industry average, these companies pay their people more than industry standards. This just makes good business sense to the Level-5 Executives of these companies. Jim Sinegal, the CEO of Costco, has been criticized by many stock analysts for being overly generous to the customers and the employees of Costco. However, this is what Jim has to say about employee pay: "Paying your employees well is not only the right thing to do but it makes for good business. In the final analysis, you get what you pay for. Paying rock-bottom wages is wrong. It doesn't pay the right dividends. It doesn't keep employees happy. It keeps them looking for jobs. Plus, managers spend all their time hiring replacements rather than running our business. We would rather have our employees running our business. When employees are happy, they are your very best ambassadors... If we take care of the business and keep our eye on the goal line, the stock price will take care of itself."[397]

The problem with most companies today is that they focus on how much a person in a certain position earns. That is not the important issue. Ham Lott, a general manager for Nucor, made the following observation: "Most businesses focus on what a person makes. We think what matters is how much labor cost goes into the product. If we pay our people twice what a competitor does, but that opportunity to earn more motivates them to produce three times as many joists per hour, our joist cost less. Our employment cost in 1996 (including fringe benefits) was less then $40 per ton of steel produced, roughly half the total employment cost per ton produced by big steel companies. Our people earn more because they're more efficient and more productive. We didn't make them that way. We just structured compensation to give them a clear incentive and turned them loose. We've trusted in their ingenuity to keep us competitive. And they haven't let us down."[398] Notice the words "We've trusted"; once again, the relationship between trusting the employees and empowering them results in dramatically increased productivity.

The problem with most companies today is that first, the employees are not trusted, and then there is no linkage between productivity and compensation. In fact there is a negative incentive to be productive. In most companies, when an employee works hard or produces more through some form of innovation which increases the productivity of the group, they may get some kind of a reward or insignificant form of recognition, but then they are expected to continue the higher level of productivity *for the same pay*! So the employee's real reward is that they are expected to work harder to keep productivity up with no increase in compensation.

The preferred method of compensation of the information-age purpose-driven companies is to tie compensation to productivity. There are about as many different ways to link compensation to productivity as there are companies. Nucor pays about 66 to 75 percent of the industry average plus an "at risk" bonus that is tied to productivity.[399] The pay at Ryanair, one of the most productive companies in the world, is one-third base salary, one-third bonuses from team sales of refreshments and merchandise onboard and one-third bonuses for the number of flight segments they work.[400] Medline Industries pays their salespeople based on the gross margin of their sales with *no cap*. The average salesperson at Medline earns more than $100,000. Some make as much as $500,000, and the top sales representative earns over $800,000. Charlie Mills, the CEO of Medline, says "We have salespeople in the company earning more money than the CEO, and that's the way it should be. After all, the top executives also have stock that appreciates based on the work the salespeople perform in the field."[401] While Medline's competitors have been slashing their sales forces as a cost-cutting measure, to increase productivity at the sales rep level, Charlie Mills says, "We do the opposite and believe in maintaining and generously compensating a large sales force. We see it as an investment in the future."[402]

The forty-three elite companies are also different in the range and types of compensation that they give to their employees. In addition to the base salary that most companies pay their employees, these companies pay a base salary plus a bonus tied to group productivity, and on top of that the employees receive profit-sharing earnings and stock options. The compensation packages offered by these companies give the employees a stake in the company. Through profit-sharing and stock options, all of the employees become stakeholders or owners. The employees then feel more like owners than employees. When the employees can see a clear link between the productivity of their group or function and their compensation, then they are motivated to innovate and increase productivity, and they feel good about what they accomplish. They feel ownership. Nucor distributes 10 percent of the profits as profit-sharing.[403] Cabela's distributes 15 percent of their profits as profit-sharing.[404] But Semco distributes an even greater percent of the profits to the employees, 23 percent. Ricardo Semler, CEO of Semco, says "As a principal shareholder — and patron — of SemcoPar, I have to admit I initially thought 23 percent was awfully high. At other companies it runs between 8 and 12 percent. But I kept telling myself I stood to make at least as much money in partnership with a motivated workforce as I would as the sole beneficiary of the fruits of less-inspired workers. What would you rather have, the tail of an elephant or an entire ant?"[405] Ricardo was correct—by sharing 23 percent of the company profits with the employees, he gets the whole elephant tail, not just an ant.

"When everyone is made a stakeholder and there are clear responsibilities for each function, the employees working in those functions are happier and naturally become more productive because they are in charge. It becomes *their* line, *their* department, *their* bagel shop."[406]

11. They create strong, unique company cultures

In the process of pursuing the company purpose and living day-to-day by the company values, these companies just naturally develop a strong, unique company culture. The culture that is created is a product of the company purpose and values, and therefore it supports the company's purpose and goals. These companies institutionalize their purpose and values by such things as the initial indoctrination of new employees, company universities, company songs, the actions of management and company policies. Through all of these actions, the company purpose and values are ingrained in every aspect of the company and each employee's behavior. Joining one of these companies is similar to joining any tight-knit group that shares the same values such as an environmental, religious or political organization. If a person's own personal values are not in alignment with the values and purpose of the company, then that person will find the company an uncomfortable place to work. Many of these company cultures have been described as cult-like because of the dedication and loyalty that the employees show for the company and its purpose and values. In fact, a few companies consider their cultures cult-like and proclaim it so. Vernon Hill, the founder of Commerce Bank, tells his employees, "You are all cult members. And if you can't buy in, this isn't the place for you."[407]

Like everything else, the strength of the cultures varies by company, but as a group, these companies have company cultures that are considerably stronger and more unique than most companies. Some examples of the companies that have a long history of strong cultures are companies like IBM, Disney, Procter & Gamble, HP and Motorola. If a person wants to be happy and work for one of these companies, then their personal values must be in close alignment with the values of those companies. "If you are not willing to enthusiastically adopt the HP way, then you simply don't belong at HP. If you're not comfortable buying into Wal-Mart's fanatical dedication to its customers, then you don't belong at Wal-Mart. If you're not willing to be 'Procterized,' then you don't belong at Procter & Gamble. If you don't want to join in the crusade for quality (even if you happen to work in the cafeteria), then you don't belong at Motorola and you certainly can't become a true 'Motorolan.' If you question the right of individuals to make their own decisions about what to buy (such as cigarettes), then you don't belong at Phillip Morris. If you're not comfortable with the Mormon-influenced, clean-living, dedication-to-service atmosphere at Marriott, they you'd better stay away. If you can't embrace the idea of 'wholesomeness' and 'magic' and 'Pixie dist,' and make yourself into a 'clean-cut zealot,' then you'd probably hate working at Disneyland."[408]

These strong, unique company cultures also work as an employee-selection filter. People either seem to fit the company culture, or they do not. If they don't fit, they won't last long. The culture and the other employees will make it so uncomfortable for anyone who does not conform and buy into the culture that they will soon be gone. They will be ejected as if they were a virus. Dan DiMicco, the CEO of Nucor, noted that "some of the people the company hires don't fit the Nucor culture and quit, because they're unable to successfully work on a team."[409] Violations of the culture norms or the company values can bring immediate and decisive actions in these companies. If a sales person at Nordstrom's becomes irritated with a customer, for any reason, the response is immediate and direct. "Where's John?" He was "sent home for the day — penalized for getting irritated with a customer. He'll be back tomorrow, but they'll be watching him closely for a few weeks."[410] Part of the Disney culture is wholesomeness, which Walt Disney enforced with rigorous discipline. For example, it was forbidden to use four letter words in mixed company at Disney, and if someone did slip up in Walt's presence, "the result was immediate dismissal, no matter what type of professional inconvenience the firing caused."[411] When Tom Watson formed the culture at IBM, smoking was discouraged and alcohol was forbidden. A violation of the alcohol policy was a firing offense at IBM. In recent years, this policy has been relaxed and now beer and wine are offered at some IBM-sponsored functions, but not hard alcohol. This is just an example of how companies may adjust their policies over time, but the basic values, in this case IBM's three basic beliefs, do not change. It is only the purpose and values that are sacred, everything else is open for review, even IBM's alcohol policy.

During his research of the elite companies with respect to financial performance, Jason Jennings said this about these companies, their values and culture: "You either agree with and adhere to the values held by each of these enterprises and their leaders or you'll promptly be shown the door. Each of the people who lead them stands for something. There's nothing wishy-washy about the principles, beliefs, or code of conduct at any of these companies. The cultures of these companies are so strong that each self-selects the team members who will become successful. If someone fits the culture, they're in. If they don't fit the culture, they're out *fast*."[412]

The interesting part is that in these cultures, most of the pressure that causes people to leave these companies is from peer pressure, not actions of management. According to Dan DiMicco, the CEO of Nucor, "When you measure and pay for productivity and have people on teams, most of the personnel issues are resolved quickly. Other team members don't want slouches that negatively affect their weekly paycheck. If we have fifteen people on a team and made a couple of errors in hiring and end up with two bad apples, chances are good that within ninety days they'll be gone."[413] In one extreme case at Nucor, the team members chased one person right out of the plant with an angle iron.[414]

In the process of being very selective about whom they hire, these companies develop an "eliteness" and a common bond about their company and culture. Many of them proudly announce that only the best, the select few are offered jobs. They make statements like "We interview over one hundred people for every one we hire." They describe their companies and the culture with words like special, moral, great and "the best." "Only the best are offered a job at our company." By creating this sense of eliteness, the employees feel like they belong to something that is special and superior. The employees of these companies take pride in being part of an organization that is "the best." One example of this is P&G. "P&G people feel proud to be part of an organization that describes itself as 'special,' 'great,' 'excellent,' 'moral,' self-disciplined,' full of 'the best people,' 'an institution,' and 'unique among the world's business organizations."[415] P&G has "long-standing practices of carefully screening potential new hires, hiring young people for entry-level jobs, rigorously molding them into P&G ways of thought and behavior, spitting out the misfits, and making middle and top slots available only to loyal P&Gers who grew up inside the company."[416]

The prior quote highlights another aspect of these companies. They promote from within. They do not as a rule hire managers from outside the company. In a company with a strong culture, it is vital that the management, who are the carriers of the culture, be sourced from within in order to maintain the integrity of the culture. Only those who have demonstrated their loyalty and fit for the culture can be trusted with the future of the culture. By promoting from within, the management and employees all share a common bond, which is the company purpose, values and culture. These elements unite all of the employees in a common cause and a common language.

John Smale, the CEO of P&G, described it this way: "Procter & Gamble people all over the world share a common bond. In spite of cultural and individual differences, we speak the same language. When I meet with Procter & Gamble people – whether they are in sales in Boston, Product Development at the Ivorydale Technical Center, or the Management Committee in Rome – I feel I am talking to the same kind of people. People I know. People I trust. Procter & Gamble people."[417]

Because these companies have such strong company cultures that ingrain the company values, it is the culture, peer pressure, the company purpose and driver measurements that negate the need for management oversight. In this environment where the management system is a trust-based system, with Level-5 leadership, the need for management oversight is basically eliminated. Jim Collins observed this during his research for the book, *Good to Great*. He says that these companies "paid scant attention to managing change, motivating people, or creating alignment. Under the right conditions, the problems of commitment, alignment, motivation and change largely melt away."[418] Those "right conditions" as Mr. Collins calls them, are the type of culture that is created when the information-age purpose-driven business model is implemented in a company. An example of the need for oversight "melting away" is the Nordstrom employee handbook, which is a single five-by-eight-inch card. On the card it says:

Nordstrom Rules:
Rule #1: **Use your good**
judgment in all situations.
There will be no additional rules.[419]

When a company's leadership knows the company purpose and values, lives by that purpose and values, then *trusts* the employees and treats them with respect and like adults, the result is an environment where there is no real need for management oversight. In this environment, an employee handbook like Nordstrom's can exist and work very well. Sociologist Emile Durkheim made the following observation: "When mores [cultural values] are sufficient, laws are unnecessary; when mores are insufficient, laws are unenforceable."[420] Remember, trust is the lubricant that minimizes friction and increases speed within the organization.

In summary, these companies simply out-execute their competition. They do this by creating very strong company-unique cultures, which ingrain the company's purpose and values into the culture, and as a group, their cultures have the following common characteristics:

- Culture of Trust
- Culture of Integrity
- Culture of Respect
- Culture of Transparency
- Culture of Loyalty
- Culture of Constant Improvement
- Culture of Being the Best
- Culture of Performance and Superior Execution
- Culture of Serving the Customer

And finally, the management of these companies has been able to utilize the concept of intelligent control instead of unintelligent control. The concept of intelligent control is not new. Lao Tzu, writing in the *Tao Teh King* 2,600 years ago, explained it this way:

> Intelligent control appears as uncontrol or freedom.
> And for that reason it is genuinely intelligent control.
> Unintelligent control appears as external domination.
> And for that reason it is really unintelligent control.
> Intelligent control exerts influence without appearing to do so.
> Unintelligent control tries to influence by making a show of force.[421]

Using the industrial-age profit-driven business model can be characterized as using unintelligent control, while using the information-age purpose-driven business model can be characterized as using intelligent control.

Chapter 15
It's all about people and purpose

"It's amazing to me, how the obvious escapes us."

– Dean E. Tucker

In the end, the success or failure of any company is really all about people and how the company does or does not create an environment that allows and encourages the people to become productive, successful and fulfilled. Every constituency of a company consists of people. Customers, managers, employees, suppliers, business partners and stockholders are all people. On one level, everyone knows that all of these constituencies consist of people. However, companies operating under the industrial-age profit-driven business model seem to forget that point. They operate as if, for example, vendors are not really people, and therefore do not need to be treated with the respect that any person off of the street would be given, and that employees are not really people either. They are just another expense line item to be controlled like any other expense line item. They look and act like people, but they really aren't people, or they wouldn't be treated the way they are in some companies today. Therein is a fundamental difference between a profit-driven company and a purpose-driven company. The purpose-driven company treats all constituencies with the respect that they would afford any person off of the street or better. The profit-driven company does not accord their constituencies the same level of respect and courtesy.

All people share some common basic human needs. People want to:

- Be accepted for who they are and feel a sense of belonging
- Have their self worth recognized and affirmed

- On some level be appreciated as human beings and for what they do
- Find meaning in their work and life

Be accepted for who they are and feel a sense of belonging

In Maslow's hierarchy of needs, after the need for basic survival, safety and security have been satisfied, the next need that humans seek to satisfy is belonging. David Pitonyak, PhD, the author of *The Importance of Belonging,* said, "People are hotwired to belong to groups and communities that acknowledge their existence, accept them, provide security and companionship and help them define their identity. That's why people belong to fan clubs; go to churches; wear sports memorabilia; and join associations, political parties, and even street gangs. People's need for an identity is so great they'll do almost anything to feel like they belong." Also, in an analysis of more than 150 studies on wealth and happiness done by two professors for the journal, *Psychological Science in the Public Interest*, the study concluded that "happiness doesn't come from wealth or money but instead from social relationships, enjoyable work, a sense that life has meaning, and belonging to groups."[422]

In a profit-driven company, where the employees are next to the bottom of the priority list, just above the environment, there is little or no sense of belonging. The job is just a job, or as some call it, a McJob. The job has no meaning or purpose to it. In these companies, management shows little or no loyalty to the employees and has a history of laying off employees at the drop of a hat to make the quarterly profit objectives. The management and the employees are pursing different objectives. The management is attempting to minimize the company's labor cost and the employees either individually or collectively through a union are trying to maximize their income. In this environment, there is little or no sense of unity, belonging or common purpose. It is every person for himself.

But for the people who work for purpose-driven companies, the company provides a sense of belonging and a sense of identity that they are looking for. The noble, uplifting company purpose that is shared by both management and the employees provides the foundation for a company culture that addresses the needs of people. It is the shared purpose, values and vision of the purpose-driven companies that provide the social relationships, belonging, recognition and meaningful work that the employees (people) are looking for. The purpose-driven companies with the stated purpose and values, which are then ingrained in the company culture, naturally select people who share a passion for the company purpose and also share the same common values. It is in this environment of a community of people who share common values that the employees find the social relationships that give them satisfaction. This is particularly attractive to Generation X because they are looking for a surrogate family in both their work and social lives. When the employees have a passion for the company purpose, and share the company values, the employees think of themselves not as an employee, but as an "IBMer," "Nordie," or P&Ger. The purpose-driven companies are very selective in their hiring practices, often interviewing over a hundred applicants for each one hired, which reinforces the employees' sense of being accepted, being valued as a person and belonging to a special, unique and select group or community of people. By having a policy of no layoffs and providing above-average compensation, the purpose-driven companies also provide the security that people are looking for. People are much more productive when they do not have to continuously worry about losing their jobs and what management may do to them in the future.

Have their self-worth recognized and affirmed

The purpose-driven companies publicly recognize and affirm the value they place on the employees in a number of ways. First, on the priority list of constituencies, the purpose-driven companies have the employees positioned at second from the top, just behind the customer, instead of next to the bottom like the profit-driven companies have. Purpose-driven companies demonstrate the value they place on the employees by trusting them to carry out important tasks with no supervision, empowering them, sharing all company information with them, sharing the profits with them, treating them as equals, giving them a vote in important company matters, and treating them as responsible adult human beings with the human dignity that they deserve. The egalitarian nature of the leadership in purpose-driven companies goes beyond just empowering the employees to make decisions, trusting them and respecting them. These companies and leaders treat the employees as "partners" rather than employees. For example, Starbucks implemented a stock-option plan for all employees beginning in 1991, even before they became a publicly held company. In the first year of the plan, each employee received stock options equal to 12 percent of their annual base salary. Since then, the stock options have been raised to 14 percent of the annual base salary. Howard Schultz, the CEO of Starbucks, said, "From that day on, we stopped using the word 'employee.' We now call all our people 'partners,' because everyone is eligible for stock options as soon as he or she has been with Starbucks for six months. Even part-timers who work as little as twenty hours a week qualify."[423] Whole Foods Market also provides their employees with stock options. According to their web site, and their data source, Profits with Principles, in 2005, the top executives in the average business received 75% of all stock options and 25% went to the category of "other." However, at Whole Foods, 7% of the stock options went to the top 16 executives and *93% of the stock options went to the employees.* What better way to affirm the self-worth and contribution of all the employees than to grant them stock options just like the top executives receive?

On some level to be appreciated as human beings and for what they do

Purpose-driven companies show their appreciation and caring for their employees in many different ways. They share the profits with them such as the 23% at Semco and 10% at Nucor. In addition to the profit-sharing, Nucor established a scholarship fund that pays for every child of every employee (excluding officers). The program was announced in 1975 and at that time paid $1,000 per year for four years for each child. Just after the program was announced, Ken Iverson, the CEO at Nucor, said, "An employee approached Marv

Pullman, our general manager in Darlington, South Carolina, at the time. 'You mean to tell me Nucor will give me a thousand dollars a year for four years for each of my kids?' the employee asked. Marv assured him it was true. 'I have eleven children,' the man said. 'That's forty-four thousand dollars! There's no way you're going to drive me away.'" By 1996, the scholarship program had been improved and paid $2,200 on an annual basis for each child.[424] Notice that at Nucor, EVERY child received assistance for college! At most companies that give any college assistance, it is done on a limited, competitive basis.

Jeffery Swartz, the CEO at Timberland, believes that "executives fool themselves if they fail to acknowledge that the people they manage have important needs outside work." Mr. Swartz personally checks the security logs to see if employees are consistently coming in on weekends. When he spots a trend, he figures that there must be a problem, perhaps a lack of equipment or understaffing as an example. When he learned that an employee was stretching the workday into the wee hours for a demanding client in Europe, he urged her to talk to her counterpart to set cross-time-zone hours that would make life easier for her. He reasoned that if things went on like they were, she would become overwhelmed and leave. He says, "Nothing is more wasteful than to burn up people."[425] Mr. Swartz is clearly a Level-5 Leader. Another Level-5 Leader, Jack Stack of SRC, had this to say, "I didn't want my work to come at the expense of my family, or at the expense of my principles and beliefs. I wanted to lead a balanced life. I was looking for a life of achievement, fulfillment, opportunities, challenge, competition, and fun, and I wanted to work in a place where I would find those things."[426] Jack went on to say, "I really don't want people to work more than forty hours a week. That's enough. People should have balance in their lives. When you're lying on your deathbed, you never look back and wish you'd spent more time at the office."[427] It is leaders like Jeffery Swartz and Jack Stack that are key to the creation of purpose-driven companies with a strong company culture that produces high levels of productivity.

Another example is IKEA. IKEA shows their appreciation and caring for their employees by the flexibility and support they show in their dealings with the employees. "Pernille Spiers-Lopez, president if IKEA North America, tries to keep regular hours and not take work home. She avoids business travel on weekends, and expects her employees to do the same. By various means IKEA demonstrates its commitment to its employees and nurtures them through slumps. The company expects all supervisors and managers to serve as mentors and to match their stores' needs with those of employees. To accomplish this, they offer flexible work schedules, job sharing, and compressed workweeks. IKEA conducts regular employee surveys to gauge morale and identify issues that it needs to address."[428] "IKEA genuinely cares for its employees and wants them to be able to work without shortchanging what is important in their personal lives, such as families. This can be seen in its benefits package and by the amount of attention to employee 'quality-of-life' issues."[429]

The examples of the purpose-driven companies Nucor and IKEA are in direct contrast to the example of profit-driven Home Depot under Mr. Bob Nardelli. In IKEA's case, the president tries not to take work home and to not travel on weekends, and expects the employees to do the same. In the case of profit-driven Home Depot, their CEO Mr. Nardelli, "is no believer in work-life balance; he treats Saturdays and Sundays as ordinary working days and often expects those around him to do the same."[430]

The prior few examples of the differences between human resource practices at a profit-driven company with a Level-4 Executive compared to a purpose-driven company with a Level-5 Leader demonstrate the magnitude of the difference between the two types of companies. The purpose-driven companies operating from the ecosystem paradigm also utilize the same type of approach in dealing with other constituencies that they use in dealing with their employees. These companies seek a mutually beneficial, cooperative relationship with all of their constituencies. The profit-driven companies, however, operate in a win/lose mode and attempt to dominate every transaction with every constituency. A question many people may ask is the following one: Which approach produces the best business results? Chapter four demonstrated the fact that the stock of purpose-driven companies clearly outperforms the stock of profit-driven companies by anywhere from three to six times in a multi-year period. However, there is another group of companies that are highlighted in the book, *Firms of Endearment: How World-Class Companies Profit from Passion and Purpose*, by Raj Sisodia, Jag Sheth, and David B. Wolfe, which focuses on those companies that are purpose-driven and are also leading the way in utilizing the ecosystem paradigm aspect of the information-age business model. The book was published by Wharton School Publishing, and the authors selected 28 companies (FOEs) to be included in the book: companies such as IKEA, Google, Starbucks, Whole Foods, Southwest Airlines, Costco and Johnson & Johnson. In their analysis of financial performance, they compared their 28 companies to the S&P 500 as well as the companies highlighted in Jim Collins' book, *Good to Great*. That data is shown in figure 15.1.

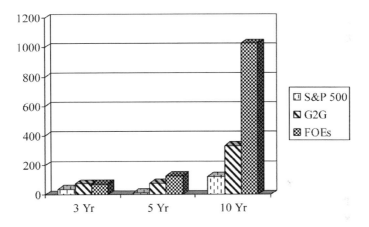

Fig. 15.1.[431] FOEs Stock Performance

Figure 15.1 shows that the stock of the *Firms of Endearment* (FOEs) companies were able to outperform the S&P companies by a factor of 8 times and the *Good to Great* companies by a factor of 3 times in a ten-year period. The primary reason for this higher level of performance by the FOEs is that they, as a group, have implemented more elements of the new, information-age, purpose-driven business model and in particular, they have progressed further in the implementation of the ecosystem paradigm with respect to all of their constituencies. The ecosystem paradigm views the company as being in an interdependent relationship with all of its constituencies, which includes the environment. Within this paradigm, the rules are that in order for one element of the ecosystem to be healthy (the company), that all of the elements of the ecosystem must be healthy (suppliers, stockholders, employees, etc.). Therefore, under this paradigm, it is in the best interest of all of the constituencies to work together for the common good of all.

One of the better examples of a company that operates in line with the ecosystem paradigm is Whole Foods Market. On the Whole Foods' web site (www.wholefoodsmarket.com) under "company" and "The Whole Philosophy," Whole Foods Market has posted the company values and also, their Declaration of Interdependence. The Whole Foods Market core values are:

- Selling the Highest Quality Natural and Organic Products Available
- Satisfying and Delighting Our Customers
- Supporting Team Member Excellence and Happiness
- Creating Wealth Through Profits and Growth
- Caring about Our Communities and Our Environment[432]

On the Whole Foods web site is the most recent version of their Declaration of Interdependence, which according to the web site was written by sixty employees of Whole Foods Market. It expands on the company's core values and is very enlightening. The Declaration of Interdependence was created originally in 1985 and was updated in 1988, 1992 and 1997. It is worth going to the web site and reading the most current version. Following is the last section of the Declaration of Interdependence, which is titled, "Final Thoughts":

> *"Our Vision Statement reflects the hopes and intentions of many people. We do not believe it always accurately portrays the way things currently are at Whole Foods Market so much as the way we would like things to be. It is our dissatisfaction with the current*

reality, when compared with what is possible, that spurs us toward excellence and toward creating a better person, company, and world. When Whole Foods Market fails to measure up to its stated Vision, as it inevitably will at times, we should not despair. Rather let us take up the challenge together to bring our reality closer to our vision. The future we will experience tomorrow is created one step at a time today."

Here we can see an excellent example of the tension that exists in purpose-driven companies between their current position and their goal, which is defined by their purpose and vision. Notice the words "our dissatisfaction with the current reality, when compared with what is possible"; that dissatisfaction is the source of the drive that purpose-driven companies demonstrate and that is missing in profit-driven companies. Also on the web site is a posting under John Mackey's Blog (John is the CEO) that discusses executive compensation at Whole Foods. It states that the board of Whole Foods has recently voted to raise the cap on executive compensation from 14 to 19 times the average employee pay. This was done in response to other companies attempting to lure away the top executives of Whole Foods. Whole Foods (as well as all of the other companies highlighted in *Firms of Endearment*) is clearly a purpose-driven company.

Find meaning in their work and life

When the leadership of a company identifies and communicates a company purpose that is noble and that serves a higher purpose, and when the company values all of its constituencies, the company then creates a reason for the employees to be passionate about the company and its purpose, and it creates a reason for customers to feel good about buying the company's products or services. The stated purpose of companies such as Merck (to preserve and improve human life) or Cargill (to improve the standard of living around the world) or Disney (to make people happy, especially children)[433] provides meaning and purpose for those who join with these companies in the pursuit of the company purpose, and it also makes customers feel good about doing business with them. Konosuke Matsushita, the founder of the Japanese electronics giant that bears his name, when speaking about the purpose of his company said, "The mission [purpose, my addition] of a manufacturer should be to overcome poverty, to relieve society as a whole from misery and bring it wealth."[434] Matsushita does not only stand for quality products, it stands for something higher. It stands for overcoming poverty, relieving society from misery and providing society with wealth, and those are things that employees can become passionate about. When employees can share this type of purpose, participate in its execution, be valued, appreciated, and recognized financially for their contribution, then they will pour their hearts and everything they have into it. That is the power of a noble company purpose.

It is purpose statements such as these examples that provide the meaning and purpose to a person's work life that people are looking for. When a company has a stated purpose that the employee can support and feel good about pursuing, then their employment with the company is no longer just a 'McJob," it is or can be their life's work. Who could not feel good about making people happy, especially the children, or relieving society of misery or improving human life? The purpose of these companies appeals to the very core of every human being and fulfills their need to have meaning in their life. To fully understand why these purpose-driven companies are able to outperform their profit-driven peer companies by multiples rather than percentages, it is necessary to understand the degree to which purpose, which provides meaning, is a motivational and driving factor in a person's life. Insight into this linkage can be found in the book, *Man's Search For Meaning,* by Viktor E. Frankl. Dr. Frankl was a psychiatrist by training who survived three years in the Nazi concentration camps of World War II. In his book, Dr. Frankl makes the following observations:

1. "It is a peculiarity of man that he can only live by looking into the future."[435]

Every individual must have some "thing" in their future that gives them a reason to endure the everyday trials and tribulations of life. Without some "thing" in the future worth living for, people will soon die.

2. "The greatest task for any person is to find meaning in his or her life."[436]

Many people are unable to find a meaning or purpose to their life, and when this happens, they often express the lack of meaning through aggression, addiction, depression and even suicide. Another expression of a lack of meaning or purpose is boredom on the job.

3. "Striving to find meaning in one's life is the primary motivational force in man."[437]

A survey done by John Hopkins University of 7,948 students in forty-eight colleges asked the students "what they considered 'very important' to them now; 16 percent of the students checked 'making a lot of money'; 78 percent said their first goal was 'finding a purpose and meaning to my life.'"[438]

4. "Man is able to live and even die for the sake of his ideals and values."[439]

A public opinion poll found the following, "Eighty-nine percent of the people polled admitted that man needs 'Something' for the sake of which to live. Moreover, 61 percent conceded that there was something, or someone, in their own lives for whose sake they were even ready to die for."[440]

The above observations by Dr. Frankl provide insight into how important a company purpose and values can be to the employees of a company. At an individual level, the company purpose and values fulfill some very basic needs that every person has, and that every person needs to fulfill in order to maintain their mental health. Earlier, the tension that exists between today and the fulfilling of the company purpose was discussed. Dr. Frankl also discussed this tension at the individual level. He said, "Mental health is based on a certain degree of tension, the tension between what one has already achieved and what one still ought to accomplish."[441] Then he went on to say, "Such a tension is inherent in the human being and therefore is indispensable to mental well-being. We should not, then, be hesitant about challenging man with a potential meaning for him to fulfill."[442] And finally, Dr. Frankl said, "What man actually needs is the striving and struggling for a worthwhile goal, a freely chosen task."[443] With the insight of Dr. Frankl's observations, it is much easier to understand how the company purpose and values can elicit the levels of dedication, loyalty, passion, energy and drive that the employees of purpose-driven companies show. This is what Jack Stack at SRC was trying to communicate when he said, *"People can accomplish almost anything if they have a common purpose, a higher goal, and they all know what it is, and they're going after it together. They can survive the darkest hours, beat the longest odds, scale the greatest heights."*

Dr. Frankl also explained why and how Level-5 Executives are able to facilitate such high performance levels from the employees that they manage. Dr. Frankl observed that "Love is the only way to grasp another human being in the innermost core of his personality. No one can become fully aware of the very essence of another human being unless he loves him." Then he went on to say, "By his love he is enabled to see the essential traits and features in the beloved person; and even more, he sees that which is potential in him, which is not yet actualized but yet ought to be actualized. Furthermore, by his love, the loving person enables the beloved person to actualize these potentialities."[444] The Level-5 Executive, through his modest and humble personality and the values of equality and respect for the individual, is able to see the potential in others and strives to make those potentials a reality through trust and empowerment. The Level-4 Effective Leader, on the other hand, is blinded by his ego, the hunger for power, ego satisfaction and the pursuit of personal profits so much that the he is unable to see, much less enable the same potentialities.

The inclusion of Dr. Frankl's observations here is not intended to turn this book into a book on psychology, but it is important to understand the human and psychological linkage between the information-age purpose-driven business model and how it relates the very basic needs of all employees for belonging, human dignity, purpose and meaning in their life. The fact that college students rated finding meaning in their life as very important in their life at a rate five times greater than making a lot of money, combined with the fact that 61 percent of survey respondents said that something or someone in their life was worth dying for, helps explain why a stated company purpose and values are such a strong driving force. The linkage between the needs of the individual to find purpose and meaning in their life and the company purpose and values in concert with Level-5 leadership when combined with employee equity in the company, is the secret to the high levels of productivity, innovation, creativity, and financial performance that the purpose-driven companies have demonstrated time after time.

Closing

By adding the 28 FOE companies and the elite 43 companies together, we now have a total of 71 companies that clearly demonstrate, beyond any question, that by being purpose-driven, any company can achieve the following:

1. Produce higher returns for the stockholders by an average factor of six times.
2. Achieve much higher levels of customer satisfaction and loyalty.
3. Have happier, more satisfied and loyal employees.
4. Make larger contributions to the community and improving the environment.
5. Operate with very high ethical standards.
6. Deliver outstanding levels of productivity and financial performance.

Howard Schultz of Starbucks expresses his feelings on this subject this way: "I'm convinced, more than ever, that we can both do well and do good. We can be extremely profitable and competitive, with a highly regarded brand, and also be respected for treating our people well. In the end, it's not only possible to do both, but you can't really do one without the other. We have to lead with our hearts. In business, as in life, we each should have an internal compass that guides our decisions, an instinctive understanding of what matters most in this world. For me, it's not profits, or sales, or number of stores, but the passion, commitment, and enthusiasm of a dedicated group of people. It's not about the money, it's about pursuing a dream others think you can't achieve, and finding a way to give something back, to the employees, to the customers, to the community."[445] Howard goes on to say of pursing the company purpose and vision, "If it has a noble purpose, the rewards are far greater. Success should not be measured in dollars: It's about how you conduct the journey, and how big your heart is at the end of it."[446]

The days of companies operating under the profit-driven business model, and being successful in the long run, are coming to an end. "Capitalist fundamentalists fixated on the bottom line need to come to terms with the reality that the idea of building and protecting shareholder wealth is no longer sustainable as the sole rationale for business."[447] Ricardo Semler states it more directly. He says, "No company can be successful, in the long run anyway, if profits are its principal goal."[448] Companies such as Google, Costco and Whole Foods are leading the way in transitioning business from the old, industrial-age, profit-driven business model to the new, information-age, purpose-driven model. The challenge now, is for the rest of industry to follow their lead.

In Chapter One of this book, it was noted that any company that wants to hire and retain Generations X and Y would at a minimum need to address six work environment issues that these generations have.

Issue 1. Transparency and trust
Issue 2. Work that has a purpose

Issue 3. Clear objectives with the freedom to do the job their way
Issue 4. Low-stress work environment
Issue 5. Work/Life balance
Issue 6. Non-threatening, intimidating, disrespectful, manipulative or coercive management

The combination of the information-age purpose-driven business model, self-directed teams and Level-5 Leadership addresses all of these issues. The purpose-driven business model with its core purpose and values provides the meaning and purpose that Generations X and Y are striving to find, and the driver measurements provide the clear objectives they are looking for. Level-5 Leadership addresses their issues regarding trust, transparency, work/life balance, a low-stress work environment and non-threatening, non-micromanaging, respectful management. In addition to finding solutions to the issues of hiring and retaining Generations X and Y, companies must find a way to dramatically increase productivity to compensate for a shrinking workforce as the Baby Boomers retire. The solution to the productivity issue is also provided by the combination of the information-age purpose-driven business model and Level-5 Leadership. This was shown in dramatic fashion by companies such as Nucor, IKEA, SRC Holdings and World Savings. The increases in productivity that will be required to compensate for a shrinking workforce are easily within the reach of business. However, to achieve those increases in productivity will require that management transition from the industrial-age management model to the information-age management model. Not all managers will be able to make this transition, and Mr. Nardelli is probably one of them. Unfortunately, many management teams may wait until they are facing bankruptcy before they decide that it is time to make a change, and then it may be too late.

With the coming labor shortage and the challenges in hiring and retaining the network-connected Generations X and Y, those companies who do not make the transition from the industrial-age profit-driven management paradigm to the information-age purpose-driven management paradigm will have a very difficult future, and may eventually disappear. Having read this book, you now understand that there is an alternative to this dim future. By making the transition from the industrial-age profit-driven business model to the information-age purpose-driven business model, businesses can have a bright future and at the same time, enrich all of its constituencies. It doesn't matter what industry or current business state that a company may be in. SRC is a classic example. Any company can turn their business fortunes around just as SRC did, if they have a noble purpose that is beyond profit, and the leadership to pursue it. Business can provide meaningful, rewarding work in a trusting, respecting, appreciating, caring environment for the employees. Business can engage in mutually beneficial relationships with all of its constituencies while improving the condition of all of the constituencies as well as itself. Business can achieve the necessary increases in productivity to offset a decreasing workforce. The seventy-one companies spotlighted in this book have proven that point beyond any shadow of a doubt. The ability of a company to achieve the kind of success that these companies have demonstrated has very little to do with a company's industry, product, or circumstance. Any company that chooses to move out of the industrial-age profit-driven management paradigm and into the information-age purpose-driven paradigm can achieve similar success for itself, while improving the status all of its constituencies. Achieving business success is not a matter of circumstance, it is a matter of choice. Any and every company can choose to transform itself into a high–performing, information-age, purpose-driven company. To survive and be successful in the future, companies must make the one, singular monumental choice that can change everything about the company and its future. **The company must choose to become a purpose–driven company rather than remain a profit–driven company!** Dr. Frankl expressed the choice facing management today in these terms: "Man is ultimately self-determining. What he becomes — within the limits of endowment and environment — he has made out of himself."[449] Dr. Frankl also said, "Man is capable of changing the world for the better if possible, and of changing himself for the better if necessary."[450] Companies and their leadership must now choose to either remain a profit–driven organization that exists primarily for the benefit of the executive team and the stockholders, or to become a purpose–driven company that exists for the benefit of everyone: the customers, employees, managers, business partners, the community, the environment AND the stockholders. This choice, *and it is a choice that every company can make,* will affect everyone in the company and should be made by everyone in the company. So, the question is, what are YOU going to do about it? Are you going to sit on the sidelines and wait for someone else to lead the transition, or are you going to be one of the people leading the transition? The choice is up to you. Best wishes!

Endnotes

[1] Friedman, Thomas L. *The World is Flat*, p. 163.

[2] Ibid., p. 39.

[3] Ibid., p. 128.

[4] Covey, Stephen R. *The 8th Habit: From Effectiveness to Greatness*, p. 3.

[5] Ibid., p. 3.

[6] "Managerial pool shortfalls...fewer people, more jobs" Article, Demographics are Destiny, hot jobs, cool communities, October 18, 2002. Author, Rebecca Ryan

[7] Zemke, Ron, Claire Raines, and Bob Filipczak. *Generations at Work*, Introduction, p. 3.

[8] Ibid, p. 3.

[9] Ibid, p. 31.

[10] Ibid, p. 30.

[11] Ibid, p. 31.

[12] Ibid, p. 47.

[13] Ibid, p. 35.

[14] Ibid, p. 48.

[15] Ibid, p. 30.

[16] Ibid, p. 41.

[17] Ibid, pp. 38-39.

[18] Ibid, p. 46.

[19] Ibid, p. 65.

[20] Ibid, p. 69.

[21] Ibid, p. 70.

[22] Ibid, p. 64.

[23] Ibid, p. 65.

[24] Ibid, p. 67.

[25] Ibid, p. 67.

[26] Ibid, p. 68.

[27] Ibid, p. 83.

[28] Ibid, p. 76.

[29] Ibid, p. 81.
[30] Ibid, p. 79.
[31] Ibid, p. 79.
[32] Ibid, p. 95.
[33] Ibid, p. 95.
[34] Ibid, p. 125.
[35] Ibid, p. 98.
[36] Ibid, p. 98.
[37] Muetzel, Michael R. *They're Not Aloof…Just Generation X*, pp. 31-52.
[38] Zemke, Ron, Claire Raines, and Bob Filipczak *Generations at Work*, p. 99.
[39] Ibid, p. 99.
[40] Ibid, p. 100.
[41] Ibid, p. 49.
[42] Ibid, p. 100.
[43] Ibid, p. 114.
[44] Ibid, p. 101.
[45] Ibid, p. 101.
[46] Ibid, p. 100.
[47] Ibid, p. 101.
[48] Ibid, p. 111.
[49] "In the 1980s GM, IBM, AT&T, US West and other cut" Article, "Employee Loyalty Died at the Dinner Table" Author, Rebecca Ryan July 31, 2002 Entrepreneur Magazine.
[50] Zemke, Ron, Claire Raines, and Bob Filipczak *Generations at Work*, p. 101.
[51] Ibid, p. 102.
[52] Ibid, p. 104.
[53] Ibid, p. 112.
[54] Ibid, p. 113.
[55] Muetzel, Michael R. *They're Not Aloof…Just Generation X*, p. 64.
[56] Ibid, p. 43.
[57] Martin, Carolyn A., Ph.D. and Bruce Tulgan, *Managing Generation Y*, p. 4
[58] Ibid, pp. 4-28.

[59] Zemke, Ron, Claire Raines, and Bob Filipczak. *Generations at Work*, p. 129.

[60] Ibid, p. 132.

[61] Ibid, p. 144.

[62] Ibid, p. 130.

[63] Martin, Carolyn A., Ph.D. and Bruce Tulgan, *Managing Generation Y*, p. 63.

[64] Ibid, p. 6.

[65] Ibid, p. 25.

[66] Ibid, p. 7.

[67] Ibid, p. 101.

[68] Ibid, p. 44.

[69] Ibid, p. 41.

[70] Ibid, p. 45.

[71] Ibid, p. 37.

[72] Ibid, p. 60.

[73] Ibid, p. 56.

[74] Ibid, p. 60.

[75] Ibid, p. 26.

[76] Ibid, p. 27.

[77] Ibid, p. 13.

[78] Stack, Jack with Bo Burlingham *A Stake in the Outcome* p. 12.

[79] Chandler, Alfred. *The Visible Hand of Management*, p. 195.

[80] Ibid, p. 463.

[81] Friedman, Thomas L. *The World is Flat*, p. 161.

[82] Ibid., p. 163–4.

[83] Ibid., p. 153.

[84] Ibid., p. 152.

[85] Ibid., p. 169–170.

[86] Ibid., p. 171–172.

[87] Ibid., p. 172.

[88] Ibid., p. 46.

[89] Ibid., p. 46.

[90] Covey, Stephen M. R. with Rebecca R. Merrill, *The Speed of Trust*, p. 99.

[91] Stewart, Thomas. *Intellectual Capital: The New Wealth of Organizations*. New York: Doubleday Books, 1997.

[92] Collins, Jim. *Good to Great*, p. 6.

[93] Ibid, p. 3.

[94] Ibid, p. 96.

[95] Collins, Jim. *Good to Great*, pp. 12—13.

[96] Jennings, Jason. *Think Big, Act Small*, p. 212.

[97] Ibid, p. 21.

[98] Ibid, p. 49.

[99] Ibid, p. 12.

[100] Ibid, p. 13.

[101] Ibid, p. xv-xvi.

[102] Jennings, Jason. *Less is More*, p. XVII.

[103] Iverson, Ken. *Plain Talk*, p. 79.

[104] Jennings, Jason. *Less is More*, p. 7.

[105] Ibid, p. 63.

[106] Ibid, p. xix.

[107] Ibid, p. 6–7.

[108] Ibid, p. 14.

[109] Ibid, p. 13.

[110] Ibid, p. 14.

[111] Ibid, p. 26.

[112] Ibid, p. 111.

[113] Ibid, p. 112.

[114] Collins, Jim. *Built to Last*, p. 1.

[115] Ibid, p. 2.

[116] Ibid, p. 3.

[117] Ibid, p. 2.

[118] Ibid, p. 3.

[119] Ibid, p. 4.

[120] Ibid, p. 48.

[121] Ibid, p. 8.

[122] Ibid, p. 32.

[123] Ibid, p. 32.

[124] Ibid, p. 33.

[125] Ibid, p. 33.

[126] Ibid, p. 22.

[127] Ibid, p. 225.

[128] Collins, Jim. *Good to Great*, p. 20.

[129] Charles Handy, "What's a Business For?" *Harvard Business Review*, Volume 80 (December 2002), pp. 3–8.

[130] Sisodia, Raj, et al. *Firms of Endearment,* p. 134.

[131] William L. Shanklin, "Offensive Strategies for Defense Companies – Surviving Defense Spending Cutbacks," *Business Horizons*, July–August 1995.

[132] Collins, Jim. *Good to Great*, p. 26.

[133] Institute for Policy Studies – United for a Fair Economy 2006

[134] David Lysy, Farrah Hassen, Cheryl Smith "Executive Excess 2002 CEOs Cook the Books, Skewer the Rest of Us," *Institute for Policy Studies/United for a Fair Economy*, p. 1.

[135] The Corporate Library's 2006 CEO Pay Survey, *The Corporate Library*, September 29, 2006.

[136] MSNBC.COM, Home Depot's CEO Pay Fiasco – *Newsweek,* Allan Sloan, Jan 4, 2007.

[137] David Lysy, Farrah Hassen, Cheryl Smith "Executive Excess 2002 CEOs Cook the Books, Skewer the Rest of Us," *Institute for Policy Studies/United for a Fair Economy,* p. 5

[138] Collins, Jim. *Good to Great*, p. 28.

[139] Ibid, p. 28.

[140] Ibid, p. 29.

[141] Ibid, p. 26–27.

[142] Ibid, p. 26.

[143] Ibid, p. 10.

[144] Ibid, p. 36–37.

[145] Stack, Jack with Bo Burlingham *A Stake in the Outcome,* p. 116.

[146] Chandler, Alfred. *The Visible Hand of Management*, p. 17.

[147] Ibid, p. 224.

[148] Ibid, p. 230.

[149] Ibid, p. 232.

[150] Ibid, p. 275.

[151] Tribus, Myron. *Deming's Redefinition of Management*. MIT, p. 2.

[152] Champy, James. *Reengineering Management*, p. 12.

[153] Ibid, p. 12.

[154] Ibid, p. 96.

[155] Salsbury. *Boston & Albany*, pp. 186–187.

[156] Chandler, Alfred. *The Visible Hand of Management*, p. 97.

157 Ibid, p. 97.

158 Ibid, p. 90.

159 Ibid, p. 91.

160 Tribus, Myron. *The Quality Imperative in the New Economic Era.* MIT, August 1985, p. 12.

161 Tribus, Myron, and Yoshikazu Tsuda. "The Quality Imperative in The New Economic Era." MIT Video Courses, p. 12.

162 Stack, Jack with Bo Burlingham, *The Great Game of Business,* p. 6.

163 Covey, Stephen M. R. with Rebecca R. Merrill *The Speed of Trust*, p. 11.

164 Ibid, p. 11

165 Ibid, p. 139

166 Ibid, p. 13

167 *Quality Progress Magazine.* October 1998, p. 95.

168 Chandler, Alfred. *The Visible Hand of Management*, p. 381.

169 Ibid, p. 102.

170 Ibid, p. 268.

171 Stack, Jack with Bo Burlingham, *The Great Game of Business,* p. 188.

172 Ibid, p. 148.

173 Joiner, Brian L. and Peter R. Scholtes. "The Quality Manager's New Job." *Quality Progress.* October 1986, p. 53.

174 Ibid, p. 53.

175 Tribus, Myron. *Deming's Redefinition of Management.* MIT, p 9.

176 Collins, Jim. *Built to Last*, pp. 43—45.

177 Tribus, Myron. *Creating the Quality Service Company.* MIT, p. 9.

178 *Quality Progress*, April 1985, p. 40.

179 Ibid, p. 41.

180 Ibid, p. 40.

181 Ibid, p. 42.

182 Ibid, p. 43.

183 Ibid, p. 40.

184 Covey, Stephen R. *The 8th Habit: From Effectiveness to Greatness*, p. 259.

185 Semler, Ricardo. *Maverick,* p. 4.

186 Ibid., p. 59.

[187] Ibid., p. 4.
[188] Ibid., pp. 5–6.
[189] Ibid., pp. 75–76.
[190] Ibid., p. 76.
[191] Ibid., p. 79.
[192] Ibid., pp. 96–97.
[193] Ibid., p. 4.
[194] Ibid., p. 97.
[195] Ibid., p. 97.
[196] Ibid., p. 136.
[197] Ibid., p. 166.
[198] Ibid., p. 88.
[199] Ibid., p. 131.
[200] Ibid., p. 131.
[201] Ibid., pp. 170-171.
[202] Ibid., p. 7.
[203] Ibid., pp. 2–3.
[204] Ibid., p. 289.
[205] Ibid., p. 202.
[206] Ibid., p. 266.
[207] Ibid., p. 284.
[208] Ibid., p. 261.
[209] Collins, Jim. *Good to Great,* p. 21.
[210] Ibid, p. 3.
[211] Ibid, p. 22.
[212] Jennings, Jason. *Less is More,* p. 111.
[213] Collins, Jim *Good to Great* p. 20.
[214] Covey, Stephen M. R. with Rebecca R. Merrill. *The Speed of Trust,* p. 64.
[215] Collins, Jim. *Good to Great,* pp. 27–28.
[216] Ibid, p. 23.
[217] Ibid, pp. 23-25.
[218] Ibid, pp. 17-21.
[219] Ibid, p. 193.
[220] Ibid, p. 193.
[221] Ibid, p. 34.
[222] Ibid, p. 33.

[223] Ibid, p. 34.

[224] Collins, Jim. *Built to Last,* p. 22.

[225] Ibid, p. 25.

[226] Collins, Jim. *Good to Great,* p. 26.

[227] Ibid, p. 26.

[228] Mobley, Lou, and Kate McKeown. *Beyond IBM,* p. 85.

[229] Tribus, Myron. *Deming's Redefinition of Management.* MIT, p. 2.

[230] Collins, Jim. *Good to Great,* p. 196.

[231] Collins, Jim. *Built to Last,* p. 225.

[232] Stack, Jack with Bo Burlingham. *A Stake in the Outcome,* p. 21.

[233] Watson, Thomas Jr. *A Business and its Beliefs,.* pp. 5-6.

[234] Collins, Jim *Built to Last,* p. 74.

[235] Covey, Stephen M. R. with Rebecca R. Merrill *The Speed of Trust,* p. 70.

[236] Stack, Jack with Bo Burlingham. *The Great Game of Business,* p. 226.

[237] Ibid, p. 71.

[238] Ibid, p. 71.

[239] Covey, Stephen R. *The 8th Habit,* p. 70.

[240] Collins, Jim. *Built to Last,* pp. 24, 49-50.

[241] Ibid, p. 237.

[242] Ibid, p. 98.

[243] Stack, Jack with Bo Burlingham *A Stake in the Outcome,* . 26.

[244] Mobley, Lou, and Kate McKeown. *Beyond IBM,* p. 85.

[245] Collins, Jim. *Built to Last,* p. 236.

[246] Ibid, p. 203.

[247] Ibid, p. 204.

[248] Zemke, Ron, Claire Raines, and Bob Filipczak. *Generations at Work,* p. 173.

[249] Ibid, p. 173-174.

[250] Ibid, p. 173.

[251] Ibid, p. 173.

[252] Stack, Jack with Bo Burlingham *A Stake in the Outcome,* p. 152.

[253] Covey, Stephen R. *The 8th Habit: From Effectiveness to Greatness,* p. 278.

[254] Tribus, Myron. *Deming's Redefinition of Management.* MIT, p. 10.

255 Tribus, Myron. *Reducing Deming's 14 Points to Practice*. MIT, June 1984, p. 8.

256 Collins, Jim. *Built to Last*, p. 117.

257 Jennings, Jason. *Think Big Act Small*, p. 141.

258 Friedman, Thomas L. *The World is Flat*, p. 142.

259 Ibid, p. 142.

260 Ibid, p. 143.

261 Ibid, p. 144.

262 Ibid, p. 201.

263 Stack, Jack with Bo Burlingham. *A Stake in the Outcome*, p. 239.

264 Stack, Jack with Bo Burlingham. *The Great Game of Business*, p. 13.

265 Ibid, p. 18.

266 Case, John. *Open-Book Management*, p. 176.

267 Ibid, p. 176.

268 Ibid, p. 176.

269 Stack, Jack with Bo Burlingham. *The Great Game of Business*, p. 73.

270 Case, John. *Open-Book Management*, p. 136.

271 Ibid, p. 144.

272 Stack, Jack with Bo Burlingham. *The Great Game of Business*, p. 93.

273 Moore, David S. *Statistics Concepts and Controversies*, p. 186.

274 Deming, W. Edwards. *Out of the Crisis*, p. 386.

275 Stack, Jack with Bo Burlingham *A Stake in the Outcome*, p. 5.

276 Ibid, p. 14.

277 Ibid, p. 4.

278 Ibid, p. 15.

279 Ibid, pp. 11-12.

280 Collins, Jim. *Built to Last*, p. 225.

281 Sisodia, Raj, et al. *Firms of Endearment*, p. 267.

282 Schultz, Howard. *Pour Your Heart Into It*, p. 138.

283 Collins, Jim. *Built to Last*, p. 56.

284 Ibid, p. 76.

285 "Renovating Home Depot," op. cit.

286 Sisodia, Raj, et al. *Firms of Endearment*, pp. 208–210.

287 Collins, Jim. *Built to Last*, p. 114.

288 Ibid, pp. 82—83.

289 Ibid, p. 85.

290 Schultz, Howard. *Pour Your Heart Into It,* p. 6.

291 Ibid, p. 131.

292 Collins, Jim. *Built to Last,* p. 48.

293 Ibid, p. 201.

294 Ibid, p. 207.

295 Ibid, pp. 208–209.

296 Ibid, p. 209.

297 Ibid, p. 207.

298 Ibid, pp. 74—75.

299 Collins, Jim. *Built to Last,* p. 243.

300 Jennings, Jason. *Less is More,* pp. 17—18.

301 Ibid, pp. 67—68.

302 Ibid, p. 65.

303 Jennings, Jason. *Less is More,* pp. 102–106, 216—217.

304 Jennings, Jason. *Think Big, Act Small,* p. 79.

305 Iverson, Ken. *Plain Talk,* p. 55.

306 Sisodia, Raj, et al. *Firms of Endearment,* p. 117.

307 Ibid, p. 117.

308 Iverson, Ken. *Plain Talk,* p. 13.

309 Ibid, p. 14.

310 Ibid, p. 23.

311 Ibid, p. 59.

312 Ibid, p. 131.

313 Jennings, Jason. *Think Big, Act Small,* p. 170.

314 Schultz, Howard. *Pour Your Heart Into It.* p. 128.

315 Ibid, p. 127.

316 Jennings, Jason. *Less is More,* pp. 104—106.

317 Iverson, Ken. *Plain Talk,* p. 178.

318 Jennings, Jason . *Think Big, Act Small,* p. 15.

319 Ibid, p. 13.

320 Ibid, pp. 16—17.

321 Ibid, p. 13.

322 Jennings, Jason. *Less is More,* p. 34.

323 Sisodia, Raj, et al. *Firms of Endearment,* p. 134.

324 Jennings, Jason. *Less is More,* p. 123.

[325] Iverson, Ken. *Plain Talk*, pp. 17–20.

[326] *Business Week*, March 26, 2007, p. 75.

[327] Sisodia, Raj, et al. *Firms of Endearment*, p. 133.

[328] Collins, Jim. *Built to Last*, pp. 192—193.

[329] Covey, Stephen M. R. with Rebecca R. Merrill. *The Speed of Trust*, p. 6.

[330] Jennings, Jason. *Less is More*, p. 26.

[331] Collins, Jim. *Built to Last*. p. 214.

[332] Jennings, Jason. *Less is More*. p. 40.

[333] Ibid, p. 40.

[334] Covey, Stephen M. R. with Rebecca R. Merrill. *The Speed of Trust*, p. 29.

[335] Jennings, Jason. *Less is More*, pp. 13—14.

[336] Ibid, p. 201.

[337] Ibid, pp. 14–15.

[338] Iverson, Ken. *Plain Talk*, p. 67.

[339] Ibid, p. 96.

[340] Sisodia, Raj, et al. *Firms of Endearment*, pp. 57—58.

[341] Jennings, Jason. *Less is More*, p. 40.

[342] Covey, Stephen M. R. with Rebecca R. Merrill. *The Speed of Trust*, p. 40.

[343] Ibid, p. 18.

[344] Sisodia, Raj, et al. *Firms of Endearment*, p. 219.

[345] Covey, Stephen M. R. with Rebecca R. Merrill. *The Speed of Trust*, p. 21.

[346] Zemke, Ron, Claire Raines, and Bob Filipczak. *Generations at Work*, p. 117.

[347] Ibid, p. 121.

[348] Ibid, p. 122.

[349] Ibid, p. 14.

[350] Ibid, p. 13.

[351] Jennings, Jason. *Think Big, Act Small*, p. 105.

[352] Ibid, p. 146.

[353] Ibid, p. 162—163.

[354] Jennings, Jason. *Less is More*, p. 49.

[355] Sisodia, Raj, et al. *Firms of Endearment*, p. 243.

[356] Covey, Stephen M. R. with Rebecca R Merrill. *The Speed of Trust*, p. 81.

[357] Sisodia, Raj, et al. *Firms of Endearment*, p. 245.

[358] Ibid, p. 9.

[359] Ibid, p. 33.

[360] Ibid, p. 122.

[361] Ibid, p. 260.

[362] Collins, Jim. *Built to Last*, p. 186.

[363] Covey, Stephen M. R. with Rebecca R. Merrill. *The Speed of Trust*, p. 252.

[364] Collins, Jim. *Built to Last*, p. 188.

[365] Google Web Site.

[366] Sisodia, Raj, et al. *Firms of Endearment*, p. 249.

[367] Ibid, p. 249.

[368] Ibid, p. 249.

[369] Jennings, Jason. *Less is More*, p. xix.

[370] Ibid, p. 15.

[371] Ibid, p. 7.

[372] Ibid, p. 61.

[373] Iverson, Ken. *Plain Talk*, p. 79.

[374] Jennings, Jason. *Less is More*, p. 152.

[375] Iverson, Ken. *Plain Talk*, p. 80.

[376] Ibid, p. 84.

[377] Collins, Jim. *Built to Last*, pp. 152—153.

[378] Covey, Stephen M. R. with Rebecca R. Merrill. *The Speed of Trust*, p. 182.

[379] Ibid, p. 117.

[380] Ibid, p. 182.

[381] Ibid, p. 183.

[382] Iverson, Ken. *Plain Talk*, p. 149.

[383] Sisodia, Raj, et al. *Firms of Endearment*, p. 203.

[384] Collins, Jim. *Good to Great*, p. 51.

[385] Jennings, Jason. *Less is More*, p. 87.

[386] Ibid, p. 88.

[387] Ibid, p. 11.

[388] Jennings, Jason. *Think Big, Act Small*, p. 170.

[389] Ibid., p. 143.

[390] Iverson, Ken. *Plain Talk,* p. 23.

[391] Ibid, p. 83.

[392] Ibid, p. 70.

[393] Ibid, p. 71.

[394] Jennings, Jason. *Less is More,* pp. 83—84.

[395] Ibid, p. 83.

[396] Ibid, p. 82.

[397], Raj, et al. *Firms of Endearment,* p. 34.

[398] Iverson, Ken, *Plain Talk,* p. 106.

[399] Ibid, p. 5.

[400] Jennings, Jason. *Less is More,* p. 165.

[401] Jennings, Jason. *Think Big, Act Small,* p. 120.

[402] Ibid., p. 119.

[403] Iverson, Ken. *Plain Talk,* p. 118.

[404] Jennings, Jason. *Think Big, Act Small,* p. 65.

[405] Semler, Ricardo. *Maverick,* p. 140.

[406] Jennings, Jason. *Less is More,* p. 202.

[407] Sisodia, Raj, et al. *Firms of Endearment,* p. 200.

[408] Collins, Jim. *Built to Last,* p. 121.

[409] Jennings, Jason. *Less is More,* p. 161.

[410] Collins, Jim. *Built to Last,* p. 119.

[411] Ibid, p. 131.

[412] Jennings, Jason. *Think Big, Act Small,* p. 22.

[413] Jennings, Jason. *Less is More,* p. 54.

[414] Collins, Jim. *Good to Great,* p. 51.

[415] Collins, Jim. *Built to Last,* p. 134.

[416] Ibid, pp. 131–132.

[417] Ibid, p. 134.

[418] Collins, Jim. *Good to Great,* p. 11.

[419] Collins, Jim, *Built to Last,* p. 117.

[420] Covey, Stephen M. R. with Rebecca R. Merrill. *The Speed of Truth,* p. 254.

[421] Kelly, Kevin. *Out of Control,* p. 126.

[422] Jennings, Jason. *Think Big, Act Small,* pp. 161–162.

[423] Schultz, Howard. *Pour Your Heart Into It,* pp. 134–135.

[424] Iverson, Ken. *Plain Talk,* pp. 119–120.

[425] Sisodia, Raj, et al. *Firms of Endearment,* p. 225-226.

[426] Stack, Jack with Bo Burlingham. *A Stake in the Outcome,* p. 26.

[427] Stack, Jack with Bo Burlingham. *The Great Game of Business,* p. 53.

[428] Sisodia, Raj, et al. *Firms of Endearment,* p. 80.

[429] Ibid, p. 226.

[430] Ibid, p. 209.

[431] Ibid, p. 138.

[432] Whole Foods Market Web Site, http://www.wholefoodsmarket.com/.

[433] Collins, Jim. *Built to Last,* p. 225.

[434] Sisodia, Raj, et al. *Firms of Endearment,* p. 204.

[435] Frankl, Viktor. *Man's Search For Meaning,* p. 73.

[436] Ibid, p. X.

[437] Ibid, p. 99.

[438] Ibid, p. 100.

[439] Ibid, p. 99.

[440] Ibid, p. 99.

[441] Ibid, p. 104.

[442] Ibid, p. 105.

[443] Ibid, p. 105.

[444] Ibid, pp. 111–112.

[445] Schultz, Howard. *Put Your Heart Into It,* p. 332.

[446] Ibid, p. 337.

[447] Sisodia, Raj, et al. *Firms of Endearment,* p. 256.

[448] Semler, Ricardo. *Maverick,* p. 284.

[449] Frankl, Viktor. *Man's Search For Meaning,* p. 134.

[450] Ibid, p. 131.

Index

Intel 6, 52
International Harvester 72, 73,
198, 292
Internet 5, 6, 19, 34, 38, 51, 53,
54, 55, 57, 304
Israel Military Industries 113,
114, 115
Itanium 6
Iverson, Ken 73, 187, 188, 191,
282, 286, 288, 289, 293, 306,
307, 308, 312, 326, 344, 350,
351, 352, 353

J

Jay, Antony 158, 167
Jennings, Jason 68, 71, 187, 199,
286, 287, 289, 291, 294, 299,
310, 313, 319, 344, 347, 349,
350, 351, 352, 353
Johnson & Johnson 75, 290, 329
John Hopkins University 333
Jordan's Furniture 305

K

Kamprad, Ingvar 279, 307
Kelleher, Herb 280
Kenwood 75
Kimberly-Clark 66, 189, 190
Kmart 271
Koch, Charles 280
Koch Industries 69, 70, 280
Kroger 66

L

Lancaster, Pat 279, 294
Lantech 71, 294
Leonard, Stew 213, 214

Level 4 80, 87, 90, 92, 94, 106,
127, 191, 193, 194, 312
Level 5 80, 94, 186, 188, 190,
194, 281, 286, 287
Lowe's 271
Lucent 54

M

Mackey, John 331
Manco 234
Marriott 75, 302, 318
Marriott, J. Willard 302
Martin, Carolyn 37, 342, 343
Mary Kay 17, 197
Matsushita 332
Matsushita, Konosuke 332
McClellan, George B. 117
McDonnell Douglas 75
McKeown, Kate 195, 348
McKnight, William 78, 302, 307
Medline 69, 316
Melville 75
Merck 75, 205, 206, 273, 277,
302, 331
Merck, George II 273
Merck, George W. 205
Mid-States Technical 234
Mills, Charlie 316
Mobley, Lou 195, 348
Mockler, Coleman 188
Montgomery Ward 97
Morita, Akio 203
Motorola 75, 318

N

Nardelli, Robert 89
Nassef, Dave 310

Made in the USA
Columbia, SC
08 January 2020